PR

A GOD OF

A uniquely critical, honest, readable and wide-ranging introduction to Jewish and Christian Theology.
—*Bernard S. Jackson, Alliance Professor of Modern Jewish Studies Emeritus, University of Manchester*

Traditional theology all too often presents assertions and even preconceived doctrines instead of pursuing and posing questions. Here is an author who questions basic assumptions of Hebrew Bible interpretation and also his own childhood convictions. After painstaking research in Ancient Near Eastern history and Biblical exegesis, Daniel Kohanski now presents his own conclusions on religion, God, Torah. His work certainly is a stimulating contribution to vital discussions in Biblical studies and the science of religious history.
—*Erhard S. Gerstenberger, Prof. em. in Old Testament, Marburg University*

This volume offers an original take on the Christian tradition and on how it has built on and interrelated with Judaism. The various chapters interconnect vital aspects of Christianity in a way that offers a most fruitful analysis of both traditions.
—*Dag Øistein Endsjø, Professor in the Study of Religion, University of Oslo, author of* Greek Resurrection Beliefs *and* Sex and Religion

Daniel Kohanski's *A God of Our Invention* is solidly researched history that traces the development of the major concepts in Judaism and Christianity and their impact on human civilization. Secular but not irreligious, erudite but not heavy, this book is notable for its balanced judgments and lucid presentation. A useful starting point for anyone seeking to understand the origins of the Abrahamic faiths and the roots of Western thought, culture, and politics.

—*Richard Robbins, Professor emeritus in Russian History, University of New Mexico*

In *A God of Our Invention*, Daniel Kohanski reveals the results of a long quest to understand the roots of religion and to connect them to the human condition. In tracing the development of religion from our Neolithic ancestors through the first Christians and its impact on society from the Roman empire to the present, he is systematic, objective, and impartial. He is also courageous, writing it at a time when religious differences have become as polarizing and divisive as at any other time in history. Ultimately, the answers to his questions are open-ended and private for each of us. Accordingly, each of us will take away something different. I am a theoretical physicist and, due to personal circumstances, steeped in all three great Western religions. With Kohanski's explanations, I understand how each of these religions was influenced by the religions that came before. I regard *A God of Our Invention* as a fascinating must-read.

—*Bulent Atalay, Ph.D., author of* Math and the Mona Lisa

A GOD OF OUR INVENTION

HOW RELIGION SHAPED THE WESTERN WORLD

DANIEL KOHANSKI

APOCRYPHILE
PRESS

APOCRYPHILE PRESS / PO Box 255, Hannacroix, NY 12087

Please join our mailing list at
www.apocryphilepress.com/free
We'll keep you up to date on all our new releases,
and we'll also invite you to download a FREE BOOK.
Visit us today!

For Jean, always.

CONTENTS

"I beseech you in the bowels of Christ,
think it possible you may be mistaken."
—OLIVER CROMWELL

"Si Dieu n'existait pas, il faudrait l'inventer."
("If God did not exist, it would be necessary to invent him.")
—VOLTAIRE

INTRODUCTION

Voltaire once quipped that "if God did not exist, it would be necessary to invent him." Whether there actually is a God—an all-powerful Being who created the universe—is ultimately a matter of faith, not of reason, and as such not a question that can ever be definitively answered. The question that I do propose to answer is whether we invented the idea of God that currently holds sway in the western world. I contend that this is exactly what happened. The God that we in the western world have lived with for millennia is a construct made by human beings and by human beings alone. This is what I intend to demonstrate in the first part of the book.

As best we can determine, our current idea of God began to take shape several thousand years ago in the Ancient Near East. The peoples of this region worshipped a number of different gods at different times and places. But one of the things their religions generally had in common was a belief that the gods interfered in human affairs. It was therefore important for people to obey the gods as well as worship them.

The ancient Israelites were originally polytheists like all the other Semitic groups, but they gradually reduced their gods to a single one, Yahweh. Sometime after that, they started to argue that Yahweh was more than just *their* god; he was everyone's god. He was the god of the universe, the only god who had ever been or would ever be. Around the same time, they also began to explore ideas of personal immortality. That led to the belief that after they died they would be judged for what they had done in life—especially on how well they had obeyed Yahweh's laws and whether they had worshipped only Yahweh.

The Israelites—from this point on, the Jews—demanded this obedience and worship only from their fellow Jews. But the first Christians, who were all Jews, decided that these rules—some of them, anyway—applied to everybody. They insisted that all people everywhere needed to worship and obey the God Yahweh and only Yahweh. Christians also preached that everyone was a sinner from birth, and damned to hell for all eternity—unless they accepted the idea that Jesus, their leader, had sacrificed himself to save everyone from sin. On this foundation, they built what is now the most popular religion in the world.

This popularity, and other factors such as the centuries of European colonization, allowed Christianity to exert enormous influence over the whole world. In the second part of this book, I will examine just a few of the areas where Christianity's beliefs have had an existential and often damaging impact on the world. First up is Jewish-Christian relations. This is critical not just in itself, but because the way Christians dealt with the Jews is replicated in the way they dealt with other issues. Of those many other issues, I will focus on four: sex, war, death, and the expectation of the end of the world.

This is in a sense a two-way look at history. The first way is "vertical." It looks at history chronologically, from the ancient Mesopotamian ideas of gods in the third millennium BCE to the Christian idea of God in the first century of the Common Era. The second way is "horizontal," meaning that it looks at one topic at a time, each time starting at more or less the same chronological point of origin and extending into the present day.[1] Lastly, I acknowledge that there is a place for religion in our modern secular and pluralistic world—so long as religion is kept from political power.

Before we go on, though, I need to add one note of caution: nothing that I've written here is final. One of the most frustrating and at the same time fascinating aspects of history is that it doesn't give final answers. There is always more to learn, always some new piece of evidence uncovered, always some new theory that explains the evidence better. In the course of this research, I've changed my mind on a lot of things I thought I knew, and I will be surprised if I never adjust my thinking again. In the meantime, what I'm giving you in this book is my best effort to date to understand what happened and why it happened.

WHY I WROTE THIS BOOK

I was raised as a Jew in the Conservative tradition. I studied the history, the prayers, the sacred texts. I have taken part in the study of the Talmud—the collection of laws and discussions of the rabbis in the first centuries of the Common Era. All this time, I have been bothered by the conflicts between the Bible and recorded history, by the discrepancies between the characters in the sacred texts and the way people really behave, by the internal contradictions. The best way I know to resolve these kinds of questions is to write a book about them. There is nothing like writing for publication to force one to do the research, to organize one's thoughts, to get everything as accurate as one can.

Several years of research have led me to an understanding that God does not exist. To quote Stephen Hawking, the greatest physicist since Einstein, "It's my view that the simplest explanation is that there is no God. No one created the universe and no one directs our fate."[2] At a minimum, Newton, Laplace, Einstein, and the rest of the scientific pantheon have conclusively demonstrated that the creation of the universe and the Earth did *not* happen as Genesis describes it. Beyond that, there is no way we can reasonably be expected to believe that a universe of more than two trillion galaxies (and counting), each one with hundreds of billions of stars and possibly trillions of planets, was all created for the benefit of some protoplasm inhabiting the third planet of an average star on an outer limb of one of those galaxies (in other words, us).

But religion, particularly revealed religion, isn't reasonable and doesn't rely on reason. It relies on faith. A Jewish fundamentalist once tried to convince me that the dinosaur bones were created "old" because of some law of physics that we don't yet understand. Others insist that God had planted those fossils as a test of our faith. Noah's flood becomes a reason to discount carbon dating because the flood waters altered the ratio of carbon-12 to carbon-14. (It doesn't work that way.)

There is no arguing with such a position, and I have learned not to try. Therefore, this is not a book about whether or not there is a God, although it started out as one. Instead, I felt it more useful to examine two issues that arose in the course of my studies: how we developed our idea of God, and how that idea has impacted the world. That is what this book is about.

HOW I WROTE THIS BOOK

One can examine religion as a theologian or as a historian, but trying to have it both ways is difficult at best. Theologians can fall back on faith when they run into difficulties. The rabbis of the Talmud had a word, *teyku,* that they used when they had a conflict or a contradiction that they couldn't solve with any of the tools at their disposal.[3] It's understood to be an acronym for "when Elijah the prophet comes to announce the arrival of the messiah, he will solve all these problems and difficulties." (Hebrew is a very compact language.) In other words: we know we're right, we just can't figure out how. The rabbis had faith that there was a solution to every dilemma that would preserve the sanctity and unity of the sacred texts, even if they just couldn't see it.

Historians, however, don't have to take *teyku* for an answer. They can accept a solution based on a finding that the texts, however sacred they are said to be, actually are incomplete, have been altered or corrupted, or simply got it wrong. They are allowed to doubt whether the text is true. Historians must be skeptical of any claim to truth (especially absolute truth), must be willing to question it, reexamine it, discount it, or even discard it if it's found to be fatally flawed.

Doubt is therefore my first rule when reading the sources and the scholars. The second rule is Occam's Razor: the simplest explanation that covers all the known evidence is most likely the correct one. A corollary to this rule is that it doesn't matter whether I *like* the explanation. If it makes sense, I have to accept it unless I can come up with one that makes better sense. There are people who object to historical criticism of the Bible on the grounds that if the Bible's claims about God and his judgments are false, then evil will run rampant in the world. This is a logical fallacy known as the *argument from consequences*: the conclusion must be wrong because of the consequences if it's right. No. If you don't like the conclusion, that is incentive to find proof that it is wrong. But it isn't proof.

A third rule is especially significant to religion: Hume's Maxim. This says that extraordinary claims require extraordinary evidence. If you claim that some supernatural force caused an event, and there is a natural explanation for it that makes sense, you should accept the natural explanation.[4] For example, in the Biblical book of Joshua it says that Joshua made the sun and the moon stand still. From our perspective, we see the sun and moon making their way across the sky, but in reality it is the earth's spin that makes them appear to move. If the story in the book of Joshua is accurate, then Joshua actually made the earth stand still. He would have had to freeze in its tracks a solid planet that rotates at about a thousand miles an hour at the equator. And he would have to do it without triggering any earthquakes and other disasters, since according to the book nothing like that happened. But let's look at the story in a different way. In the seventh century BCE, when the book of Joshua probably had something close to its current form, the kingdom of Judah was a vassal state of the Assyrian empire, and the sun and moon were major Assyrian gods. Now the story makes sense: the author of Joshua wasn't reporting an actual event; he was using a metaphor to say that the God of Israel was more powerful than the gods of Assyria.

This leads me to another rule historians have to follow: historical events must be evaluated according to their own *time* and their own *space*. Whatever we may think of slavery now, for instance, we have to examine it from the perspective of the standards and beliefs of that time. We can certainly use present-day standards in judging whether we should behave as our forebears did, but that is a different question that I will address separately. Similarly, we must examine events in the space—the context— of what was going on around them. A couple of chapters from now, I will be discussing how the author of Daniel and the authors of the New Testament lifted passages from the prophets out of context and claimed that those earlier writers really meant what they, the new writers, wanted them to mean. That may (or may not) be acceptable theology, but it's bad history.

JUST HOW RELIABLE ARE THE SOURCES?

This is a historian's question, one that has to be asked of every source text or archeological find. It's a question that carries heavy emotional baggage when applied to sources like the Bible, which hundreds of millions of people hold to be sacred, sometimes even calling it the literal word of God. But when they claim that the Bible is reporting history, then it becomes subject to the tests of history.

There are Biblical minimalists who view every verse in the Bible as a myth unless it is confirmed by several outside sources —and even then they look for ways to discount it. They are, in their own way, as absolutist as the Biblical maximalists for whom every word of whatever translation of the Bible they use is literally true.[5] The scholars I rely on shy well away from either extreme. For them, as for me, if one part of the Bible is verified or contradicted, that does not necessarily validate or invalidate other parts of the Bible.

So, how reliable are the parts of the Bible? Well, that depends. To start with, the Bible comes in two (or three) divisions. The first division is called by Jews the Hebrew Scriptures or the *Tanakh* and by Christians the Old Testament. I'll be calling it "Scripture" in this book. Exactly what it contains depends on whether you're reading the Jewish version, the Catholic version, the Protestant or the Orthodox Christian versions. Again, I will be using the Jewish version—not just for sentimental reasons, but because all the Christian versions agree that all the books in the Jewish version of Scripture are part of their Old Testament. There are some additional books from Jewish writers that were included in the first translation of Jewish sacred texts into Greek (the Septuagint), but which were left out of the final edition of the Jewish canon. Catholics and Orthodox include them in their edition of the Old Testament (with a few differences). Protestants starting with Martin Luther separate those books into a third section, called the Apocrypha. Fortunately, almost all Christians nowadays agree on the contents of the New Testament, the other major division of the Christian Bible. On top of all that, there are other manuscripts in the "Biblical" style from the period of perhaps 200 BCE to around 500 CE, which were influential at one time but were never part of any of the canons. I'll be referring to a few of them from time to time. Then there are the Dead Sea or Qumran Scrolls, a set of manuscripts hidden away around 67 CE, at the start of the Jews' war with the Romans, and only rediscovered starting in 1947. Some of these are copies of Scripture texts and other texts then considered sacred, while others are documents written by the people who collected and hid the scrolls.

On top of all *that*, we don't have the original texts or anything like them. What we have are copies of copies of copies. All the books of Scripture have been edited over time, and many of them show "seams" where multiple manuscripts were collated and redacted into one. These seams are particularly noticeable in the first five books (Genesis, Exodus, Leviticus, Numbers, and Deuteronomy), known as the Torah, the Pentateuch, or the Five Books of Moses. As Robert Alter observes in his masterful translation of Scripture, "creating a purposeful collage of sources was demonstrably a standard literary procedure in ancient Israel."[6] The Scripture we use today was compiled by scholars known as the Masoretes in Tiberias between the sixth and tenth centuries CE, and there are some discrepancies between the Masoretic text and the manuscripts found at Qumran and other places.[7] The oldest known New Testament documents are from the second century, and there is a whole field of scholarship devoted to analyzing the various versions and how they came to vary. A similar collection of scholars has been arguing over Scriptural seams for two centuries now.[8]

You can see why I have trouble taking Biblical literalists seriously.

In general, and with many caveats, I find the so-called "historical books" of Samuel,[9] Kings, and the prophets such as Jeremiah and Isaiah (and also Judges, to a lesser degree) to be reasonably reliable for the most part, unless what they are reporting fails the test of Hume's Maxim, is internally inconsistent, or is contradicted by other evidence. We also have to bear in mind that they are not objective history, but were written for partisan purposes. For example, the book of Kings was written and edited by court historians of the kingdom of Judah, who had almost nothing good to say about Israel, the rival kingdom to the north. Similar cautions apply to Paul's letters and to the gospels. As we get into the various texts, Biblical and otherwise, I'll go into more detail about how reliable they are generally judged to be and why.

SOME NOTES ON TERMINOLOGY

Dates. In current scholarship the common practice is to use BCE, meaning Before the Common Era, and CE for years in the Common Era, rather than BC (Before Christ) and AD (*Anno Domini*, the Year of Our Lord). 1 CE corresponds to AD 1, which was supposed to be the year Jesus was born according to the monk Dionysius Exiguus in the 6th century. By the twelfth century, AD (now CE) was used as the standard year designation in much of western Europe, and over time became the most common world standard.

"Israelites" and "Jews." There appears to be no agreement on when to use which of these terms to describe the people whose lives are recorded in Scripture and who were the ancestors of the Jews of today. When I use "Israelites" (and sometimes "ancient Israelites"), this covers the period from the earliest days (c. 1400 BCE) up to around 500 BCE. After that, I will call them "Jews" to keep things simple and to avoid getting into the weeds of scholarly arguments.[10] Let's just accept that it's inadequate but necessary and move on.

The names of God. Yahweh, one of the gods of the ancient Israelites, is written Yod–Heh–Waw–Heh (or Yod–Heh–Vav–

Heh). Ancient Hebrew was written without vowel signs and some pronunciations have been lost. Scholars today generally accept "Yahweh" as the way it was most likely pronounced. In English Bibles, it is usually rendered as "Lord" or "LORD." I use "Yahweh" to refer to the primary and eventually only god of the Jews when he was in competition with other gods. "God" with a capital 'G' is a reference to the Jewish, Christian, and occasionally Muslim, concept of god. (I don't use "Allah," as that is just the Arabic word for "God," and is no more a distinct "God of the Muslims" than "Dieu" is a special "God of the French.") I will also use masculine pronouns for this god, purely as a matter of convenience; a being that doesn't exist doesn't have a gender anyway.

"Canaan," "Israel," "Judah," "Judaea," "Palestine," "Israel." The land between the Jordan River and the eastern shore of the Mediterranean Sea, where much of the action takes place, has many names. Its earliest known name was probably Canaan. The people of Scripture divided it into two kingdoms, Israel (the larger) to the north and Judah to the south. From the start of the Persian Empire (c. 330 BCE) through the first Roman years (63 BCE–135 CE), I use the Roman name Judaea for convenience. (The Babylonians and Persians called it Yahud or Yehud, but that name is little known today.) Following several Jewish revolts, the last one in 132–135 CE, the Romans changed the name to Palestine. Starting in 1948, much of the land is once again called Israel—though, as with everything else about that part of the world, the name is controversial.

"Jesus Movement." The earliest followers of Jesus were all Jews and saw themselves as Jews. I'm using "Jesus Movement" as some scholars do to make this point clear. Only toward the end of the first century did believers in Jesus start to call themselves "Christians." I'll cover this in more detail in Chapter 3.

Church. When capitalized, this means organized Christianity in the early centuries, then the hierarchical church under the popes based in Rome. After 1054, and especially after the Protestant Reformation starting in 1517, it specifically means the Roman Catholic Church speaking as a unity.

TRANSLITERATIONS AND TRANSLATIONS

Hebrew transliterations are done so as to most closely approximate the sound of the word in English, rather than being faithful to the Hebrew orthography. Transliterations from Greek follow the scholar I am quoting at that point. Translations from Scripture use the recently completed monumental work by Robert Alter, with a few exceptions where I provide my own translation, primarily for stylistic reasons. New Testament citations are from the New Revised Standard Version, HarperCollins Study Edition, designated NRSV(HC). My Greek is pretty much non-existent, so I have relied on the NRSV(HC) notes and some scholarly references to explain some Greek words. A particularly useful research tool for Hebrew (and Aramaic) and Greek words in the Bible is Strong's online concordance (biblehub.com).

USE OF ENDNOTES

I'm writing this book for the general audience, the "intelligent lay reader," as one scholar once said to me. I have tried to avoid the sorts of arguments that are meat and drink to academics. Still, for those of you who do want to know more about them, I've provided extensive references in the endnotes to scholars whom I have found to support my positions, as well as to some who take contrary or opposing positions. As I will have frequent occasion to remark in those notes, I am the one responsible for my analyses and conclusions, and any errors or misunderstandings of the works I cite are my responsibility alone.

With those caveats and guidelines established, let's get started.

PART ONE
THE INVENTION
OF GOD

The goal of this section is to explore the texts of the Hebrew Scripture and the New Testament, together with other sources from the Ancient Near East, using the analyses and evaluations of critical scholarship to determine, as best I can, how the Jewish and Christian ideas of God and about God developed in the 1500 years or so between the first appearance of the ancient Israelites in Canaan through the end of the first century of the Common Era.

This is a historical examination, not a theological one. My interest is in what we can learn as a matter of history, not what precepts can be gleaned from a revealed text. From a historian's perspective, the texts that make up today's Bible are documents that were written over nearly a thousand years in the case of Scripture, and almost a century for the New Testament. They had many different authors, some with very different ideas about God, and especially in the case of Scripture, many different editors, not all of whom had the same understanding of the texts they were working on.

As this is a historical evaluation, historian's rules apply. This means making my best effort at an objective analysis of the evidence, without regard for whether it fits some predetermined narrative or for what the consequences of the analysis could be. It also means that the evidence must be evaluated in the context of the time in which it is located. Then we have to ask what the internal and external correlations, conflicts, and contradictions are, and whether they can be resolved. I also rely on Hume's Maxim, which states that if there is a natural explanation for a supernatural claim, you must accept the natural explanation, and on Occam's Razor, that the simplest explanation that covers all the known evidence is the best one. I can sum up these rules with a maxim I learned in the Foreign Service: Does the story make sense? Which version makes the most sense?

With that in mind, let's look at three questions. First, what was the nature of religion in the Ancient Near East in general, and in particular among the Israelites, prior to the destruction of the First Temple in 586 BCE? Second, how did the Israelite idea of God evolve in the aftermath of that destruction, and what further ideas did the Israelites develop in the period of the Second Temple (515 BCE to 70 CE)? Third, how did the early disciples of Jesus adapt these ideas when developing their own idea of God?

CHAPTER ONE

GODS OF THE ISRAELITES

I deas about God and the laws of God are among the most powerful and influential in the history of the western world. But the evidence is clear and convincing that these were not handed down from Mount Sinai, as it were. They were invented by some of the oldest civilizations in the world, whose beliefs about gods and whose ideas about society gradually evolved into the familiar western religions of today.

In this chapter I want to explore the beginnings of that evolution by pursuing two lines of argument. First is that the early Israelites were polytheists much as their Canaanite neighbors and other Semitic kin were. As Israelite leadership shifted from elders to kings around the eleventh century BCE, one cult asserted that its god, Yahweh, was the only god Israel should worship, and wanted the kings to enforce this. The Yahwist cult often had great influence, but finally achieved its goal only during the Babylonian exile (586–538 BCE). By Persian times (538–330 BCE), prophets were declaring that the Israelite god Yahweh was God for everyone, the only god in all the universe.

My second argument is that what we now call Biblical law is really a compendium of laws, customs, and traditions of the

Ancient Near East that gradually evolved into commandments given by Yahweh to Moses while the Israelites wandered around Sinai. This evolution happened, I suggest, in large part because the Israelite leadership in exile needed a way to enforce their cultic laws in the absence of a king.

THE ANCIENT NEAR EAST

What we now call the Ancient Near East dates back to 3400 BCE or thereabouts and ends sometime around the start of the Common Era, depending on whom you ask. It includes the territory from Persia (modern Iran) to Egypt, as well as Anatolia in what is now central Turkey. The earliest centers of civilization were in Mesopotamia, the land between the Tigris and Euphrates rivers in modern Iraq, and along the Nile on the edge of Africa. Mesopotamia was home to a succession of empires, starting with the Sumerians in the fourth millennium BCE. Later empires were mostly Semitic, defined as such by the languages they spoke—Hebrew and Arabic are Semitic languages—and by shared cultures and customs. These empires included the Akkadian, the Assyrian, and the Babylonian (twice). Then there were the Hurrians and the Hittites, two non-Semitic nations who built empires in what is now northern Iraq and central Turkey. Throughout all this time there was Egypt, whose empire centered on the Nile and extended at times into Canaan.

By 1479 BCE, Thutmose III (the sixth pharaoh of Egypt's eighteenth dynasty) was "in firm control of the land of Canaan," and Egyptian soldiers were thereafter garrisoned around the region for over three centuries, in part to block the Hittite empire from invading Egypt.[1] Semitic peoples such as the Ugarits and various Canaanites had to learn to live with those garrisons. The same was true of the original Israelites; archeological evidence strongly suggests that they were in Canaan from the 13th century BCE or earlier.[2] The Merenptah (or Merneptah) stele, which dates well into the period of Egyptian occupation (1209 or 1207 BCE) is an especially useful piece of evidence. Pharaoh Merenptah boasted on this carved stele that he had defeated a number of tribes and towns in Canaan, including Israel. In his survey of the current scholarship, archeologist Michael Hasel concludes that the Merenptah stele allows us to establish that, by the late thirteenth century BCE, an ethnic entity called Israel was already known to be living in Canaan, possibly but not definitively in the central hill country.[3] Israeli archeologist Avraham Faust thinks it possible that at some point, probably after Merenptah's time, a small group—"a few thousands, or even hundreds"—fled Egypt and settled among the Israelites. He speculates that, during the period when the Israelites were becoming a coherent people, these escapees' story "became part of the common history of all the Israelites"—that is, the Exodus.[4]

GODS OF THE ANCIENT NEAR EAST

The beliefs and rituals of the Israelites were heavily influenced by the other peoples of the Ancient Near East. To start with, the idea of God, or the gods, interfering in human affairs was especially prevalent among the Sumerians, the Hittites, and the Semites generally. According to a Sumerian myth, versions of which are over four thousand years old, the high god Ellil (or Enlil) decided to destroy all humanity with a flood because the people were being noisy and not letting him get any sleep.[5] This backfired when the gods began to starve because there were no more sacrificial offerings. However, another god, Enki, had earlier told one man, Attrahasis, and his family to build an ark and escape the flood. When Attrahasis (also known as Utnapishtim) afterwards offered a sacrifice, the gods immediately gathered around it.[6] The gods then persuaded Ellil to relent, and he allowed humans to repopulate the earth—though he also decreed that one–third of all pregnancies would end in miscarriages as a form of birth control.[7] The Israelites would eventually use Attrahasis / Utnapishtim as the model for Noah.[8]

In a similar vein, around 1300 BCE the Hittite king Mursili II prayed to the sun goddess and the other gods to stop a ravaging plague by appealing to their own self-interest—there would be "no one [left who] prepares for you the offering bread and the libation anymore."[9] For the Hittites, all life depended on the good will of the gods, especially the Storm God, the most exalted of the Hittite gods, the "preserver of order in the cosmos," who brought the gentle rain for the crops—but also the thunder and lightning and natural disasters when he was angry.[10]

The various gods of the Semites involved themselves in human behavior even more than their Sumerian and Hittite counterparts did. Human beings had to do whatever the gods commanded if they wanted to avoid floods, famines, and defeat in war. Mesopotamian scholar Jean Bottéro called this the "Semitic 'mentality,'" a cultural heritage which includes a belief that the gods constantly intervene in human affairs.[11]

Unlike much of the Ancient Near East, the Egyptians didn't think their gods were all that interested in them. The Egyptians were required to "satisfy the gods" with sacrifices, festivals, and rituals, and the king was expected to establish "ma'at," the concept of order and abundance. But the gods had little if any interest in justice as such, and unlike the Hittite and Mesopotamian gods they didn't reward and punish the king's behavior with victories or disasters in this world. The king "represents divine justice among the living," but there was a strict separation between justice and the cult of the gods.[12] Egyptologist Donald Redford has done an extensive analysis of Egypt and the Israelites and finds that there is almost nothing in the way of evidence of Egyptian influence on Israelite beliefs.[13] To the contrary, as Christopher Rollston describes it in his study of Israelite monotheism, "early Israelite religion arose within the ancient Semitic world, spoke and wrote in Semitic, and initially accepted the common Semitic belief that there was a pantheon of deities."[14]

EARLY ISRAELITE RELIGION

Probably the earliest god in the Israelite pantheon was El, an early Canaanite god. The very name "Israel" can be translated as "he who strives with (the god) El," though it might equally mean "El (God) will strive" or "El will prevail."[15] Yahweh—who would eventually become the only god the Israelites worshipped —may have originally been a god of the Edomites in the southern reaches of Canaan. Sometime early on, El became identified with Yahweh. Baal, another god whom many of the early Israelites worshipped, became a competitor to Yahweh instead. Even so, some of the attributes of Baal may well have become associated with Yahweh over time. Michael Stahl, a scholar of early Judaism, puts it this way: "the deep resonances between many aspects of YHWH's character and profile in the Hebrew Bible and those of El and Baal...strongly suggests [sic] a historical relationship between them"—though the Israelites added some "unique YHWHistic traits and features."[16]

One has to bear in mind that the books of Judges, Samuel, Kings, and the prophets were written and later redacted and edited by committed Yahwists who believed that Yahweh had made a covenant with the children of Israel. It is instructive, then, that they were willing to include so many stories of the Israelites breaking that covenant by worshipping gods other than Yahweh. Even more striking is that the pattern that emerges in Scripture is not, as the theology would have it, one of Israel backsliding away from an agreement with God Almighty. Instead, the ancient Israelites behaved exactly like all the other peoples of the Ancient Near East: They had a number of gods and goddesses and prayed to whichever one they favored or was likely to help them in their current troubles. They would call on Yahweh for help in battle, but ask Baal (and sometimes Yahweh) when they needed rain. "Along with El," argues Stahl, "the Hebrew Bible's conceptualization of YHWH appears to have been deeply influenced by the Syrian Semitic weather-god Baal-Haddu."[17]

Around the eleventh century BCE, probably because of the need for unity in the face of continual warfare with the Philistines along the Mediterranean coast, the Israelites pressed Samuel, a Yahwist priest and a universally respected leader, to find them a king. (This would have been long after the Egyptian withdrawal from Canaan.) Samuel first chose Saul, and later, when he was dissatisfied with Saul's rule, anointed David, perhaps secretly, to rule after Saul. We are told that Saul, David, and David's son Solomon ruled all the tribes of Israel. Even if that was so, the "united monarchy" didn't last past Solomon's death, when, according to Scripture, the Israelites split into two separate kingdoms.[18] Judah, the southern kingdom, remained under the rule of David's descendants, while the northern kingdom, Israel, endured a series of dynasties. The book of Kings portrays the northern kingdom as continually doing "evil in the eyes of the Lord"—meaning that they worshipped some other god or gods besides Yahweh. In reporting the Assyrian annihilation of Israel, the writer of Kings devoted most of a chapter to listing the reasons for its destruction. Without exception, they were all failures to prevent the worship of any other god than Yahweh.[19] This is only to be expected when we remember that those who wrote and edited the book of Kings were Yahwists from the southern kingdom of Judah and would have been particularly keen to disparage their rivals to the north.

The capital of the southern kingdom, Jerusalem, was also home to Yahweh's Temple, which Scripture says was built by

King Solomon. The Temple was the holiest place in the Yahwist cult and the headquarters of the Yahwist priesthood, which continually pressed the kings to rid the land of its competitors, especially the cult of Baal. They had only intermittent success. Hezekiah, who reigned from the late eighth to early seventh century BCE, broke up the altars of the local gods. His son Manasseh not only put them back, but he also set up altars to other gods in the Temple itself.[20] In 622 BCE, Manasseh's grandson, Josiah, embarked on a campaign to wipe out any trace of other gods in his kingdom. He threw the "vessels made for Baal and Asherah" out of the Temple and burned them. He smashed altars to Ashtoreth, Khemosh, and Milcom that had stood on the hills around Jerusalem since Solomon's day.[21]

Josiah's reforms mark a high point in the Yahwist cult's domination of Judah, but they didn't last. Pharaoh Neco killed Josiah in battle in 609 BCE and put Josiah's son, Jehoahaz, in his place. Three months later, Neco deposed that king and replaced him with Jehoiakim, who reigned for eleven years. He too "did evil in the eyes of Yahweh, just as all his fathers had done," according to the Yahwist author of Kings.[22] The non-polemical version is that, "down to the Babylonian captivity, Israelite religion tolerated some cults within the larger framework of the national cult of Yahweh."[23]

THE ISRAELITE RELIGION IN EXILE

The period of the Babylonian captivity or exile (586–538 BCE) is when the "historical books" of Judges, Samuel, and Kings were most likely edited into something close to their present-day form. According to these books, for centuries the Israelites were warned that bad things would happen to them if they worshipped any god other than Yahweh. They would suffer floods, plagues, famines, and losses at war if they failed their cultic responsibility. In the book of Judges, Yahweh frequently let neighboring nations defeat the Israelites in battle: the Moabites, the Midianites, the Philistines, the Ammonites. Each time this happened, it was because "the Israelites once again did evil in the eyes of the Lord and served the Baalim and the Ashtaroth and the gods of Aram."[24]

But sometimes nothing happened. Once, when "all Israel went whoring after" an artifact of gold that Gideon had made, nonetheless "the land was quiet forty years."[25] At other times, disasters happened for no discernable reason. Yahweh was said to have promised rain and good harvests in return for worship of him alone, and warned the Israelites that they would starve if they strayed from him. But the prophet Elisha had to perform a miracle in order to keep people alive during a famine in King Joram's time, even though Joram had removed his father's pillars to Baal and even though Yahweh had just granted Joram victory in war against the odds.[26]

Even if we assume that these are accurate recordings of events, we still have to admit they made little lasting impression on many Israelites, to the long-running frustration of the Yahwist prophets. Then came the destruction of Jerusalem and the Temple. The loss of the kingdom of Judah and the exile of its leaders to Babylon were a huge national disaster—but also an opportunity for the Yahwists to consolidate Israelite loyalty to Yahweh alone. Both the prophet Jeremiah and the author of Kings insisted that Yahweh had destroyed Judah because he was still furious over Manasseh's idolatry sixty years before.[27] The prophet Ezekiel denounced Israel's continuing "unfaithfulness" to Yahweh in the early years of the exile. "You...spread your legs for every passerby and multiplied your whorings. And you played the whore with the Egyptians, your big-membered neighbors, and multiplied your whorings to vex Me."[28]

In reality, the Babylonian captivity had been the consequence of Judah's rebellions against the Babylonians, who had displaced the Assyrians as masters of Mesopotamia. Judah lay in the pathway between Babylonia and Egypt and was from time to time vassal to each. In 597 BCE, the Babylonian emperor, Nebuchadnezzar, besieged Jerusalem and marched much of the elite of the city, including some of the Yahwist priests, off to exile in Babylon. He also installed a new king, Zedekiah, as his vassal. In 586 (some say 587), Zedekiah tried to switch his allegiance to Egypt (against Jeremiah's advice), and this time Nebuchadnezzar had had enough. He burned Jerusalem and the Temple of Yahweh to the ground, killed Zedekiah's sons in front of him before putting out his eyes, then sent him and the rest of Jerusalem's elite into exile.[29]

The Yahwists' argument that Yahweh had exiled the Israelites for their sins was a justification after the fact, but it was effective nonetheless. By the time the Persians conquered the Babylonians fifty years later, the Israelites—at least those in Babylon—had by and large ceased to worship any god but Yahweh. Second Isaiah, writing as the exile was ending, was the first prophet to make almost no complaint at all about Israel's roving eye. "Comfort, O comfort My people, says your God" were his opening words.[30]

Second Isaiah—the name scholars give to the unknown author who is credited with writing chapters 40–55 of the book of Isaiah shortly after 540 BCE—went beyond acknowledging that the Israelites had lost interest in worshipping any gods other than Yahweh. He proclaimed that Yahweh was not just the only god for Israel, but the one and only universal God.[31] Yahweh of the Ten Commandments had said, "You shall have no other gods beside Me"—implying that other gods do exist, but they are not for you, O Israel. In Psalm 82, "God takes His stand in the divine assembly, in the midst of the gods He renders judgment," while in Psalm 97, "all gods bow down to Him."[32] Second Isaiah did grant the existence of other supernatural beings—but said they were not gods at all. They were under Yahweh's control and followed Yahweh's orders. In recounting how he made the world, Yahweh boasted: "I commanded all the hosts of heaven."[33] Isaiah also rejected the idea that these other beings are holy or divine. "I am the first and I am the last, and apart from Me there are no gods," says Yahweh to Isaiah.[34] They are not worthy of worship by anyone, and one day all the nations of the world will acknowledge this. Writing around twenty years later, the prophet Zechariah was even more specific about the future: One day there will be a great battle by "all the nations against Jerusalem...and the Lord shall sally forth and do battle with those nations." Then "the Lord shall be king over all the earth. On that day the Lord shall be one and His name one."[35]

This shift, which laid the foundation for what would eventually become monotheism,[36] was necessary because the prophets had to solve an existential problem: Even if Yahweh was really that furious with the Israelites for worshipping other gods, why had he allowed the Babylonians to burn down his Temple? The Babylonians worshipped Marduk; didn't this mean that Marduk was stronger than Yahweh?

Two historians of the period, Thomas Römer and Christos Karagiannis, each make the same cogent argument: this destruction happened, according to the prophets, not because of Yahweh's weakness but because of his strength. Yahweh hadn't "allowed" Marduk's Babylonians to destroy Jerusalem; he had *ordered* them to do it. "In the eyes of this prophetic school," Karagiannis explains, "the Exile was not an evidence of Yahweh's defeat but an expression of his just indignation against Israel's sin." Yahweh had "given all these lands into the hands of Nebuchadnezzar My servant, King of Babylonia," said Jeremiah, writing around the time of the destruction. In Römer's analysis, the burning of Yahweh's Temple "clearly signifies that Yahweh's power is not limited to his own people; he is the master even of the enemies of Judah."[37] Isaiah didn't exactly deny that the Babylonian gods existed; he just denied that they were gods. If only by implication, Marduk and Bel and the rest were part of the heavenly host under Yahweh's command. Thus, for Isaiah "the rhetoric of divinity is no longer applied to the members of the host of heaven... Yet the host remain a heavenly reality."[38]

Similarly, when Cyrus the Persian conquered Babylon in 538 BCE and allowed the exiled Israelites to return to Jerusalem, he was following standard "Persian policy...to conciliate its conquered peoples by encouraging them to worship their local deities."[39] But the way Second Isaiah saw it, Cyrus let the Israelites return to Judah because God had decided Israel had suffered enough for its sins. The prophet even hailed the Persian emperor as God's messiah, his anointed one.[40] To the prophets, powerful rulers who did not believe in or even know about Yahweh acted not of their own volition but on the orders of Yahweh, the god of Israel, who was the God of all: *he* had willed their actions.

There is little in the prophetic texts prior to Second Isaiah that even hint that Yahweh was the one and only divinity. He was normally referred to as "the Lord of armies" (or "Lord of hosts") or as "Lord God of Israel." In the ninth century BCE, when the prophet Elijah was contending with the servant of another god, Baal, he called out to Yahweh: "This day let it be known that You are God in Israel"—that is, in opposition to that other god, not as the god of all.[41] There are a couple of places in the book of Kings where Yahweh was said to be the only god: the thanks of an Aramean general who had been healed of a skin disease, and a prayer by King Hezekiah of Judah. In the eighth century, Amos warned Israel's neighbors that they too could face Yahweh's wrath, and the first Isaiah famously hoped that "in future days" all nations would come and worship "Jacob's God."[42] But only at the end of the exile was the exclusivist message explicitly and publicly spelled out: Yahweh is the One and Only God who rules everything on earth and in the heavens.

And it would be well into the Roman occupation of Judaea before Jews fully believed in it.[43]

SOURCES OF ISRAELITE LAW

The development of how the Israelites came to accept Yahweh as their only god, and how and why they declared this god to be God for all, leads to my next question: How and why did they decide to make Yahweh the source and authority of all laws, laws that were actually derived from ancient customs, from judicial rulings, and from the decrees of the kings?

We should start by asking where these laws may have originally come from. Rulings governing sexual relations are a good example of how closely Israelite laws resemble older laws of the Ancient Near East. In his analysis of Hittite life and society, Trevor Bryce gives the example of a law requiring that one of a deceased man's relatives must marry his widow in order to provide for her, a near parallel to the requirement in Deuteronomy that a man must marry his brother's widow if her late husband had left her no children.[44] Hittite law also allowed a man to marry his wife's sister, but only after his first wife had died—exactly as in the Torah.[45] David Stewart wrote a study comparing Hittite and Biblical laws governing permitted and forbidden sexual contacts, noting numerous similarities as well as some significant differences—the Hittites permitted a greater range of behaviors, or in some cases provided for "legal and ritual loopholes."[46] In addition to the Hittites, "a comparison of the list of forbidden unions in Leviticus to those found in other Mesopotamian law codes demonstrates just how similar the holiness codes could be to those earlier laws."[47]

The Assyrian *Code of the Assura*, written around 1075 BCE, requires that "if a woman in a quarrel injure the testicle of a man, one of her fingers they shall cut off." Deuteronomy has a similar and even harsher rule: "If two men are fighting, and the wife of one rescues her husband from his opponent by putting out her hand and grabbing his genitals, you shall cut off her hand."[48] Deuteronomy absolves a woman raped in the hills, where no one could hear her if she screamed, but not if it happened in a town where people would be in earshot. This is a near–identical copy of an older Hittite law: "If a man seizes a woman in the mountains (and rapes her), it is the man's offense, but if he seizes her in her house, it is the woman's offense; the woman shall die."[49] These are only a few of the parallels between Torah clauses and the earlier laws of Hammurabi, the Hittites, and the Assyrians.[50]

One such parallel that has attracted much scholarly attention is the law of compensation for an ox that has killed another ox. In the Laws of Eshnunna, dating back to the twentieth century BCE, there is a ruling that the price of the live ox and the carcass of the dead ox are to be divided between both owners. Except for one small change, the same law in Exodus "could almost be a translation of its predecessor," observes legal historian Bernard Jackson.[51]

There is also evidence that Ancient Near Eastern customs influenced Israelite cultic practices. Moshe Weinfeld lays out the points of similarity between the Israelite Day of Atonement and the Babylonian *akītu* atonement and purification rituals, including washing in water, dressing in linen, censing the temple, banishing the scapegoat, and reciting the confession. (The *akītu* festival was a New Year's celebration dating back to Sumerian times, and was variously held in autumn or spring, or sometimes both.)[52] Indeed, a number of Yahwist rituals were much the same as other priestly rituals practiced throughout the region. For example, the purification ritual in Leviticus for someone cured of skin disease is essentially identical to the Hittite and Hurrian ceremonies. The Biblical purification ceremony used a "living bird...and the cedar wood and the crimson stuff," just as the Hittites and the Hurrians did. There is a similar ceremony in Ugaritic texts as well.[53]

It was customary in the Ancient Near East for kings to announce laws by saying that the gods, out of concern for the well-being of the people, had ordered them to do so. The best-known law text of the era, the Code of Hammurabi (c. 1750 BCE), opened with this announcement by the king: "[the gods] Anu and Bel called by name me, Hammurabi, the exalted prince, who feared God, to bring about the rule of righteousness in the land, to destroy the wicked and the evil-doers; so that the strong should not harm the weak; so that I should rule over the black-headed people like [the Mesopotamian sun god] Shamash, and enlighten the land, to further the well-being of mankind." Brian Doak, a historian of the Ancient Near East, explains that "if the gods are perceived as demanding social justice, the king as the gods' representative on earth must also establish justice."[54]

We know that the Israelites were familiar with the Mesopotamian laws because scribes all over the Ancient Near East, Israel and Judah included, learned them as part of their training. The Code of Hammurabi in particular was copied and studied as part of the standard scribal curriculum, and there are archaeological findings of such scribal exercises at Hazor and Khirbet Qeiyafa not far from Jerusalem.[55] Possible transmission paths from other ancient law codes to the laws of Moses may well be more indirect.[56] But the many close similarities and occasional outright parallels strongly suggest connections that the redactors of the Torah would one day draw upon.

THE LAW OF THE ISRAELITE KINGS

The next question to ask is this: how were these laws implemented in the days of the Israelite kings? Outside of the Torah itself and the book of Joshua, there is almost no mention of Moses. There are also few references to "Torah," and where the word does appear, it is more apt to mean "teaching" in general rather than a specific reference to the Five Books of Moses.[57] Clearly, the Israelites knew about and drew upon the laws of Hammurabi and other legal and cultural traditions, and almost certainly drew inspiration from them. Still, it doesn't seem that these codes carried much weight with the authorities prior to the Babylonian exile. Scholarship has mostly concluded that the law codes, whether of Hammurabi or of Exodus, were likely not binding on judges in ancient Israel and Judah. The king (not Yahweh or Moses) was the source of most of the law, as was the case throughout the Ancient Near East.[58]

For example: just before his fatal battle, King Saul went in disguise to the witch of Endor to consult the ghost of Samuel. When the witch objected, saying the king had made it a capital crime to summon a spirit, Saul reassured her that no harm would come to her. The Torah had condemned necromancy as a sin to be punished by stoning—but the author of Samuel was evidently unaware of this, as he not only credited Saul with making the law himself, but also gave him the authority to waive any punishment.[59]

Then there is the famous story of David and Bathsheba. King David spotted Bathsheba sunning herself on a roof below the palace while her husband, Uriah, was away at war. David had her brought to his chambers and had sex with her. Bathsheba later discovered she was pregnant and told the king. David then summoned Bathsheba's husband, Uriah, to Jerusalem and urged him to go sleep with his wife. But Uriah refused to do so while his fellow soldiers were still fighting at the front. In desperation, David sent Uriah back to the war with secret orders to place him in the thick of battle so that he would be killed. As soon as Bathsheba became a widow, David took her as his latest wife.

Of the Ten Commandments said to have been handed down at Sinai, David had broken three: he coveted his neighbor's wife, he committed adultery with her, and he committed murder, even if by proxy. But when the prophet Nathan went to David's court to condemn the king's actions, he didn't even mention the commandments. He accused David of "despis[ing] the word of the Lord," but did so in connection with his status as king—that is, why had David done this after all that Yahweh had done for him? The prophet also promised the king that someone else would soon lie with his wives as he had lain with Uriah's wife.[60] Repaying adultery with more adultery is no part of the Torah code.

There are a few other instances in Judges, Samuel, and Kings of a king or judge passing judgment on what today we would call a civil or criminal case, but I have found only a single reference to a specific passage of the Torah. The author of the book of Kings commended King Amaziah of Judah for sparing the sons of the assassins who had killed his father, quoting a passage from Deuteronomy: "Fathers shall not be put to death over sons, and sons shall not be put to death over fathers, but each man shall be put to death for his own offense."[61] (The Hebrew texts in Kings and Deuteronomy are almost but not quite identical.) But as Alter's comment on this verse points out, this reads like a later interpolation by an editor. It is more likely that Amaziah had made a political calculation that executing those sons would alienate the court faction to which they belonged.[62] In sum, "the historical record appears to show that it was only slowly that the idea grew that judges were actually supposed to apply *torah*, and even then one has to wait, probably to the postexilic period, for any indication that the judges were expected to refer to an authoritative written source."[63] In the days of the kingdoms of Israel and Judah, Yahweh did not write their laws.

HOW YAHWEH BECAME THE AUTHOR OF THE LAW

One peculiar aspect of the history of the Israelites is their relationship to their kings: they were optional, not essential, in
Israelite thinking.[64] The earliest Israelite leaders had been
priests, village elders, and tribal judges; kings came late to the
scene. Unlike in much of the Ancient Near East, the Israelite
priesthood was, for the most part, separate from the monarchy.
The early split into two kingdoms also suggests that the people
were ambivalent about how a king should rule.

Israeli historian Nili Wazana identifies three passages in
Scripture that she labels "anti-monarchial": in Judges, when
Gideon turns down an offer to become a king; in Samuel, where
the prophet warns the people what a king will do to them; and
in Deuteronomy, which makes the king into little more than a
figurehead.[65] That passage in Deuteronomy is particularly
instructive. The book of Kings reports that during the reign of
Manasseh's grandson Josiah (c. 622 BCE), the high priest
discovered "a book of the teaching" during some Temple repairs
and had it brought before the king.[66] The book, which was probably an early version of what is now Deuteronomy, included a
verse requiring the king to sit before the priests while they read
the law to him. "Even a cursory analysis of the law of the king
[in Deuteronomy] reveals that some expected royal responsibilities are missing."[67] The story told in the book of Kings implies
that Josiah listened to these words, but his actions show that he
thereafter ignored them, a conundrum that has been the subject
of recent scholarship.[68] Eckart Otto argues that much of
Deuteronomy was written in Josiah's time both as an effort to
counter Assyrian influence and in order to provide support for
Josiah's program of cult reform and centralization—but not in
support of the king himself. "Part of this idealistic programme
of the book of Deuteronomy was the idea of a people that
derived its identity from the temple and not the king."[69] In all

events it is further evidence of the ambivalence the Israelites felt about the idea of a king.

That ambivalence continued during the exile and even after. Nebuchadnezzar had deposed and blinded the last king of Judah and now ruled Judah (Yehud) directly, having given up on trusting Israelite vassal kings. Still, the Israelites exiled to Babylon were allowed the same freedoms as other imperial subjects, including the right to worship their own gods. Of course, they would have had to obey the civil and criminal laws of the empire, but they could also follow their own cultic laws, including worship of Yahweh alone, dietary restrictions, priestly purity, and so on.

But the lack of a king of their own meant that they lacked the authority to enforce those cultic laws. The leaders of the exile community must have also worried that the Israelites would start to forget their history and their heritage, and most worrisome, forget Yahweh. The Yahwist cult already had a tradition prior to the exile that Yahweh had authored all law, and now they built on that tradition.[70] They took their scrolls, their oral traditions, history remembered and legends borrowed, their belief in Yahweh, and edited and redacted them all into something resembling the version of the Five Books of Moses that we have today.[71] This explains the similarities discussed earlier between the Torah laws and the other law codes of the Ancient Near East: the Israelites had borrowed from and adapted them all along and saw no reason to exclude them now.

Still, the primary interest of the leaders of the Babylonian exile community was to establish once and for all the exclusive worship of Yahweh as the only god for the Israelites. To stress this, they codified the cultic rituals, the purity regulations, the position of the priesthood, and the special status of the children of Israel as all commanded by Yahweh himself. This is evident in the division of Torah laws. Two-thirds of them, by my count, deal with cultic concerns, and only one-third are secular laws—

civil and criminal laws, laws of inheritance, and similar matters.[72]

The redactors of the Torah used the opportunity created by the loss of the monarchy to make Yahweh, acting on his own authority, the source of the law. This ran counter to the standard practice of the Ancient Near East, where the king was the source of the law, acting on the authority of the gods. But the Israelites had never been entirely comfortable with their kings. Besides, where one king made a law, the next king could change it. Deuteronomy warned that the king must "swerve not from what is commanded right or left." (Elsewhere in Deuteronomy, there is a general warning against anyone changing any law.) This type of warning was common throughout the Ancient Near East[73]—and was commonly ignored. The exiles didn't want any chance of that happening.

In addition, by cutting out the royal middleman, as it were, the Yahwist priests hoped to solidify the supremacy of the priesthood over any future king. "Along with the idea of exalting the status of Moses and especially his role as lawgiver, there was the strategy of diminishing or distancing David as a role model."[74] Since Persian days, the Davidic dynasty's only role has been to continue to exist, so that someday a messiah might come from that line. Until that distant day, "law would be seen as, and at, the heart of biblical religion, the law revealed through Moses at Mount Sinai."[75] Yahweh—God—was now Israel's only king. His priests would enforce Yahweh's laws and rule Israel in his name.

ONE GOD, ONE LAW

The two threads that I have laid out here—that Yahweh is The One and Only God, and that he is the actual author of all the laws of the Israelites—were woven together on a loom a thousand years long. In brief, the ancient Israelites gradually came up with the idea of a universal god using bits and pieces of local deities. Then they claimed this god was the source of the laws, traditions, and customs the Israelites had absorbed from their neighbors or developed over time. Accidents of history, priestly desire for power, prophetic indignation, and the campaigns of nearby empires all contributed to the evolution of a theology that has since come to undergird western religion:

- Yahweh is the one and only one God who has ever existed.
- Everything that happens to us, good and bad, happens by the will of Yahweh.
- The priests are the interpreters of the will of Yahweh.
- Yahweh has decreed laws that cannot be changed.
- Foremost among these laws is that worship of any being other than Yahweh is forbidden.
- Disobedience to Yahweh's laws will bring down famine, floods, plague, and destruction.
- Only the Jews have to obey all of Yahweh's laws now. But someday, all nations will acknowledge Yahweh as God and obey him.

Jews believed (and many still believe) that the universal acceptance of the God Yahweh is something that will happen of itself, in some vague distant time to come. "When the messiah comes" has been used since Talmudic times to mean some far-off future day. Christians, however, undertook to bring about that universal belief as soon as possible: by persuasion, by missionization, by pressure, and often by force of arms. They also insisted that everyone is already bound to obey the laws of God (as the Christians interpret them).

The rest of Part 1 explains how Christianity came to take that position. Part 2 examines some of that position's consequences.

CHAPTER TWO

IMMORTALITY AND THE JEWS

B elief in one universal God who gave laws for all to obey was only the first of the ideas that Jews would develop and that Christians would later adapt and spread around the world. Jewish thinking was shifting from the idea of communal responsibility for sin to a more individual one. That in turn gave rise to a belief in personal immortality and judgment after death, perhaps the most consequential concept after that of a single, universal God. Other new ideas included an apocalyptic end of the world as we know it, a messiah who will rescue the Jews from their oppressors, and a new way of using prophecy.

(I will be using "Jews" from now on to mean the people who were descended from the Israelites and who worshipped Yahweh as their only god. I will also use "Judaea," the Greek and Roman name for the territory that more or less used to be the kingdoms of Israel and Judah. For most of the Second Temple period, almost all of the people who lived in Judaea were Jews, but there were always more Jews living outside Judaea—in the "diaspora" —than within.)

THE SECOND TEMPLE PERIOD

In 538 BCE, Cyrus and the Persians conquered the Babylonian empire. The Persians then allowed the Jews to return to Jerusalem and later gave them funds to rebuild the Temple. The half–millennium between this temple's dedication around 515 BCE and the Roman destruction of Jerusalem in 70 CE is therefore known as the Second Temple period. The new temple was originally a pale copy of the one said to have been built by Solomon. The magnificent structure we think of as the Second Temple was the product of a monumental expansion by King Herod, finished just before the Common Era began and destroyed during the Great Revolt against the Romans seventy years later.

We don't know all that much about what the Jews in Judaea were doing during the early years of the Second Temple period. Relatively few Jews in exile had accepted Cyrus's offer to return to Jerusalem, a small mountain village in the backwaters of the empire.[1] Babylon remained the center of Jewish intellectual life, where work continued on redacting the books that would become the Torah. At some point between 515 and 430 BCE (most likely around 435, according to one scholar), the prophet Malachi complained that the priests in Jerusalem were offering poor quality sacrifices at the Temple, that "Judah has betrayed [Yahweh]...and coupled with the daughter of an alien god," that the people were committing adultery, practicing sorcery, cheating laborers of their hire, and mistreating the widow, the orphan, and the stranger.[2] Sometime after Malachi's complaint, Ezra and Nehemiah each came from Persia with a mandate to urge, even force, the Judaean Jews to follow God's laws. Recent scholarship has questioned the dates and details of their work.[3] In all events, there is little that we know for certain about the happenings in Judaea from then until the end of the third century BCE.

There were great events occurring in the world during those days, though they barely affected the Judaean backwater. In 334 BCE, Alexander the Great invaded the Persian empire, and by 329 he had conquered it all, Judaea included, although there is no record of any fighting there. The first century CE historian Josephus claimed that Alexander had visited Jerusalem,[4] but there is no evidence for it, and it was almost certainly an invented story. Alexander "was too busy conquering the world to bother with an insignificant inland people living around a small temple."[5]

Alexander died in 323 BCE, and his empire immediately broke apart. The various pieces were eventually claimed by his generals, most importantly Ptolemy in Egypt and Seleucus in Syria. As with Israel and Judah in earlier times, Judaea now found itself placed between two empires. The Ptolemies ruled the province, with occasional Seleucid interruptions, until around 200 BCE, when the Seleucids made Judaea a permanent part of their empire.

Neither empire made religious demands on their subjects. Jews continued to observe the sacrificial rites under the leadership of the high priest in Jerusalem. They circumcised their sons, avoided forbidden foods, and followed the customs of their ancestors. Still, like all the people of Alexander's former empire, Jews did have to cope with the influence of Hellenism. This was the mix of Greek culture, ideas, philosophy, literature, gods and myths, and language which Alexander and his successors spread around the Mediterranean basin and the former Persian empire, and which remained the main cultural influence there for several hundred years afterwards. Various other cultures in the region contributed to the mixture that was Hellenism, but the Greek element was by all measures predominant. Among the Jews, Hellenism had an impact on literature, architecture, speculative thought, the use of the gymnasium. Even so, Jews were able to separate cult from culture, and may even have pioneered the distinction.[6] With one highly significant exception, Hellenistic emperors did not interfere with the beliefs of their Jewish subjects.

That exception was the Seleucid emperor Antiochus IV, whose reign began in 175 BCE. Historians are still not entirely certain why Antiochus tried to force the Jews in Judaea to abandon the worship of Yahweh.[7] One factor might be that by this time the high priest was the primary secular authority in Judaea in addition to being the spiritual leader. This meant that the emperor got to decide who would be high priest, as long as he came from one of the hereditary priestly families. Antiochus IV chose (or was bribed by) Joshua, who Hellenized his name to Jason. Three years later, Jason's rival Menelaus offered the emperor a bigger bribe and became high priest instead.[8] When Jerusalem revolted against Menelaus's tyranny and corruption in 168 BCE, Antiochus used that as an excuse to pillage the city.[9] A year or so later, he decided to force his Greek religion on the Jews in Judaea (though not on Jews elsewhere in his empire). He installed a statue of a Greek god (probably Zeus) in the Temple, outlawed Jewish ritual practices, particularly circumcision, dietary laws, and the Sabbath, and ordered other deliberate violations of Jewish law and custom.[10]

In Judaea, the Jews' initial response to these actions can perhaps best be described as stunned. A near-contemporary report claims that "many even from Israel gladly adopted [Antiochus's] religion; they sacrificed to idols and profaned the sabbath."[11] "Many" is perhaps an exaggeration, though there were some Jews of that time whom modern scholarship does label "extreme hellenizers."[12] Other Jews tried to maintain their ancient customs in secret. Then sometime in 167 or 166 BCE, a Seleucid officer ordered Mattathias, a hereditary priest who lived in the hill country, to make a public sacrifice to Zeus. Mattathias refused, fled into the hills with his family, and started a guerilla war against the Seleucids and the Jews who went along with them. "They...struck down sinners in their anger and renegades in their wrath."[13] His son Judah, who became their general, was called Judah the Maccabee (which most likely means "the hammer"), so his rebellion is known as the Maccabean Revolt. In late 164 BCE the Maccabees led by Judah succeeded in retaking the Temple Mount and cleansing its altar. The minor festival of Hannukah commemorates this victory.

After that, a truce of sorts was established between the Maccabees and the Seleucids. It probably helped that Antiochus died while campaigning in Persia around the time of Judah's victory. The Seleucids let their persecutions lapse, which led to less Jewish resistance to Hellenistic ideas. The Maccabees became less interested in fighting and more interested in negotiation. Eventually Judah's brothers Jonathan and Simon achieved a measure of autonomy for Judaea, and around 142 BCE the Seleucids acknowledged Simon as the high priest.

Simon and his sons then established the Hasmonean dynasty, named after an ancestor, Hasmon or Hashmonai. As high priests, they were rulers of what had become a quasi–independent state, and around 104 BCE they began to call themselves kings as well. Their growing independence was supported by the rising power of Rome, which wanted to keep the Seleucids in check. But the Hasmoneans had territorial ambitions of their own that were starting to worry the Romans.[14] When two Hasmonean brothers each claimed the kingdom in 63 BCE and each appealed to Rome for support, General Pompey took advantage of their civil war to seize Judaea on Rome's behalf. He even forced his way into the sacred Temple precincts to make it clear that Rome was now in charge.

Many Jews had disapproved of the Hasmoneans calling themselves kings when they were not of the House of David, but at least they were fellow Jews. Any gratitude Rome had earned by getting rid of them vanished when General Pompey strode into the Holy of Holies—now Jews hated the Romans.[15]

The Romans, who couldn't have cared less what the Jews thought of them, thereafter selected various Hasmoneans as puppet rulers and high priests. In 37 BCE the Roman emperor Augustus appointed his friend Herod as king of Judaea—though not as high priest because he was not a hereditary priest, much less a Hasmonean; he had only married one. Herod was an ambitious ruler, whose building program included turning the Temple in Jerusalem into one of the architectural wonders of the Roman world. But his autocratic and arbitrary rule, not to mention his habit of killing members of his own family, left the place such a mess after he died in 4 BCE that within the next decade the Romans decided they had to rule much of it directly through prefects and procurators appointed by Rome.

RESPONSIBILITY FOR SIN

In the days of the First Temple, the Yahwist sect's idea of sin seems to have been generally religious in nature and national in scope. While the elders, the judges, and the kings dealt with issues of individual wrongdoing—murder, theft, fraud, land grabs, adultery—the priesthood preached that worshiping Yahweh and only Yahweh was the responsibility of the people as a whole. If enough of them committed the sin of idolatry, the whole nation would suffer drought, famine, flood, plague, defeat in war—all brought on, wrote the authors of Judges, Samuel, and Kings, by Yahweh in his anger at Israelite unfaithfulness to him. It fell to the prophets to warn that Yahweh was equally angry with the people over their mistreatment of widows and orphans and for exploiting the poor. The entire nation, they threatened, would suffer for it if they didn't deal with these injustices.

Yet the Babylonian destruction of Jerusalem in 586 BCE was so extreme that it gave even prophets pause. Early on in the exile, Jeremiah and Ezekiel each announced that Yahweh had decreed that from now on everyone was responsible for their own sins. Reversing a popular proverb, they declared that children's teeth would no longer be on edge because their fathers had eaten sour grapes.[16] Early in the exile, Ezekiel compiled a list of secular sins ranging from fraud and adultery to refusing to feed the hungry and clothe the naked, to go along with the cultic sins of idolatry. Those who were righteous and avoided these sins would live a full life, while the wicked, unless they repented, would die early. "Each according to his ways will I judge you, O house of Israel."[17] Even if the nation as a whole was guilty, the righteous would still be spared.[18]

Yet far too often the righteous suffered and died while the wicked prospered and lived long lives. The book of Job, possibly written in the Persian years,[19] offered an answer of sorts: mortal creations have no right to question their creator. This was clearly less than satisfactory for many Jews, who continued to explore other ways to deal with this conundrum. By the time of the Maccabean revolt, some were saying that God would render judgment on the righteous and the wicked alike after they had died.

IMMORTALITY AND THE AFTERLIFE

In order for the righteous and the wicked to face judgment after death, they have to survive the death of the body. We know of such beliefs in Egypt's distant past, though at first only the pharaoh was thought to live on after death. If he had done well, he would enjoy a pleasant afterlife among the gods. If not, the crocodile god would eat his heart and he would die forever in the "second death." Over time, the afterlife became accessible to the nobility and then to Egyptians generally. This "democratization" of death changed the criteria for admission—now everyone could earn an afterlife by living a good and knowing life. Egyptologist Jan Assmann calls this the "moralizing" of the afterlife, and argues that it was "a necessary consequence of the extension of the royal idea of the afterlife to lower social classes."[20]

The similarities between Egypt's moralized afterlife and Christian ideas about judgment after death will play a large role later on in inducing Egyptians to accept Christianity.[21] But the Egyptian afterlife had little if any influence on other cultures in the Ancient Near East. For them, writes Assmann, "the realm of the dead was nothing more than a shadowy realm far from meaning and from the divine." Immortality was found instead in "the succession of generations" or "the recollection of posterity." Assmann finds this different view of immortality in Greece, in Mesopotamia, and in ancient Israel.[22]

In early Mesopotamia, "no one was made to last forever,"[23] not even kings. This was emphatically made clear in that classic Mesopotamian tale, the *Epic of Gilgamesh*. King Gilgamesh, devastated by the death of his friend Enkidu, went on a quest for a way to restore him to life. He learned that he would not find the eternal life he sought because the gods had reserved it for themselves alone.[24] Even so, wrote Jean Bottéro, the notion of absolute non-existence was "far too unimaginable" to those ancient peoples. The Akkadian "City of the Dead was sensed to be lugubrious, crushing, and haunted only by sluggish, melancholy, and floating inhabitants, far from any light or happiness"[25]—but it was still an existence of sorts.

The early Israelite equivalent of the Akkadian City of the Dead was Sheol. In the books of Kings, Psalms, Job, and Ecclesiastes, Sheol was where everyone went when they died.[26] One of the Psalms called it the "land of oblivion." Scripture sometimes softened the descent to Sheol by using euphemisms—"he slept with his ancestors" or "he was gathered unto his people"—but Sheol was still the universal destination. King David on his deathbed told his son Solomon that he was "going on the way of all the earth."[27] More often than not, Scripture just says "he died." Rabbi Neil Gillman observes that "the Bible knows of a peaceful death that follows upon a rich and accomplished life-time, though this in no way dilutes the reality or the finality of death."[28] Even in the Persian period (sixth to fourth centuries BCE), the ideal life would be long and happy—but it still would end at death. The author of the last chapters of Isaiah, writing in this time, promised that much: "No more will there be an infant who lives only a few days nor an old man who does not live a full life" of a hundred years or more.[29]

In the Hebrew Scripture there were two mentions of a kind of community immortality. One was by the prophet Ezekiel, writing early in the exile. God commanded him to speak to a valley of dry bones—a metaphor for the Israelites in exile—and to tell the wind to blow upon these bones so that they will live. Similarly, Isaiah prophesied that "your dead shall live, their corpses rise." In both instances, context makes clear that the prophets were calling for a revival of the nation, not of indi-viduals.[30]

Starting around 200 BCE, we see texts that assume the immortality of the individual. It is possible, though still unde-termined, that these texts benefited from exposure to Persian Zoroastrian beliefs.[31] There is more evidence for Hellenistic influence. Here is just one example: Around 400 BCE, the Greek philosopher Plato described his idea of immortality: "He who lived well during his appointed time was to return and dwell in his native star, and there would have a blessed and congenial existence." Two centuries later, Plato's "astral immortality" would be closely reflected in the book of Daniel: "And the discerning shall shine like the splendor of the sky, and those who guide the many to be righteous, like the stars, forever and ever."[32]

Daniel's is the only explicit declaration of individual immor-tality in the entire Hebrew Scripture, and shows that a shift had indeed taken place in Jewish ideas about judgment after death. The book of Daniel, though set early in the Persian empire period, was actually completed during the Maccabean revolt.[33] The author was aware that the revolt had started, but not that it had succeeded—in fact, he "implicitly rejects the Hasmodean [sic] family's open military resistance, arguing that the invaders will meet their doom by divine intervention, not human action."[34] So he offered a prophecy designed to reassure the faithful: the archangel Michael will soon arrive to rescue the Jews. Even those righteous who die before Michael can get there will be rescued—God will resurrect them and grant them eternal life, while punishing those who cooperated with the enemy.[35]

The author of Daniel was specific about who would face this judgment. Selected individuals—"many of the sleepers in the deep dust"—will awaken to face a destiny determined by how they had responded in life to the existential crisis facing the nation. But he was vague about the details. He didn't explain how or when this resurrection will occur, nor what he meant by the "everlasting contempt" awaiting the evildoers—whether it was eternal torment or a final oblivion. And would this judgment take place right after death, or upon the resurrection? Daniel's author was likely writing for an audience that was familiar with these questions from other writings of the time, and probably left these details as an exercise for the reader, as it were.

Among those other writings was *The First Apocalypse of Enoch*, some parts of which may date back before Daniel. *First Enoch* was popular for a long time: the New Testament quotes from it, almost all of the book has been found among the Qumran scrolls, and it is still part of the canon of the Ethiopian Church.[36] The book "opens with an announcement of the final, coming punishment, the destruction of the wicked ones, and the resurrection of the righteous ones to an endless and sinless eternal life."[37] It taunts sinners—"whither will you flee on the day of judgment"—and warns that those who "have died now in prosperity and wealth" will go down to Sheol where "they shall experience evil and great tribulation—in darkness, nets, and burning flame." The objects of the book's wrath are "the kings, the governors, the high officials, and the landlords" who have oppressed the righteous. Even if they should die full of years and wealth, "vengeance shall be executed on them—oppressors of his children and his elect ones. It shall become quite a scene for [his] righteous and elect ones. They shall rejoice...because the wrath of the Lord of the Spirits shall rest upon them."[38]

The *Wisdom of Solomon*, another popular book from this time, expresses a similar sentiment. The wicked who say, "let us oppress the righteous poor man; let us not spare the widow or regard the gray hairs of the aged," will find themselves on the day of judgment trembling before God, while "the righteous will stand with great confidence in the presence of those who have oppressed them."[39]

Daniel's author was mainly interested in reassuring the faithful at a moment of existential crisis for the nation. *First Enoch* and *Wisdom* had a different agenda: the promise of posthumous revenge for righteous individuals who had suffered at the hands of the wicked. But they all offered the same solace: whatever happens here on earth, God will put it right in heaven. Second Temple period scholar Shaye Cohen comments that this "doctrine of reward and punishment in the hereafter was a much more elegant solution" than Ezekiel's.[40] It had another advantage: it could neither be confirmed nor refuted by evidence. One had to accept it as a matter of faith.

Acceptance was far from universal. When the priest Mattathias died (of old age) during the Maccabean revolt, he was said to have been "gathered to his ancestors" just as his ancestors in Torah times had been.[41] Two books from the third century BCE, Ecclesiastes (which made it into Hebrew Scripture) and Sirach (which is only in Christian Bibles), both state in so many words that death is the end.[42] The Sadducees, the party of aristocrats and priests who controlled Jerusalem in late

Second Temple times, also rejected the doctrine of life after death, believing that "souls die with the bodies."[43]

Other texts of the Second Temple period predict that only the righteous will be resurrected, while the wicked will stay dead forever. In the *Second Book of the Maccabees*, a woman and her seven sons who were martyred for refusing to eat swine flesh all expected God to "raise us up to an everlasting renewal of life, because we have died for his laws." Not only that, their tortured bodies would be restored to perfect condition. The evil king Antiochus, however, would not live on in the hereafter, not even to face punishment. "But for you there will be no resurrection to life!" said one of the sons to the king.[44] A century later, the *Psalms of Solomon* proclaimed that "the destruction of the sinner is forever."[45] On the other hand, the *Fourth Book of the Maccabees*, possibly written in the first century CE, was sure that judgment for both the wicked and the righteous will occur as soon as they die, and it will be an eternal reward or punishment. As in *Second Maccabees*, the seven brothers were tortured and killed for their faith. But in this version, they and "their victorious mother" are already "gathered together into the chorus of their fathers, and have received pure and immortal souls from God." Meanwhile, "the tyrant Antiochus was both punished on earth and is being chastised after his death" as promised by the youngest brother: "justice has laid up for you intense and eternal fire and tortures, and these throughout all time will never let you go."[46] A few centuries into the Common Era, the rabbis of the Talmud would finally settle on a doctrine of *t'ḥiyat maytim*—revival of (almost) all the dead. They would be so defensive about this doctrine that they decreed that anyone who denied it was found in the Torah would be denied his share in the world to come.[47]

THE END OF THE WORLD

The existential crisis confronting the Jews in Judaea in Maccabean times had other consequences beyond encouraging the idea of judgment after death. Jews were in such despair that they felt the end of the world—the apocalypse—was upon them.

"Apocalypse" comes from a Greek word meaning "to reveal" or "to uncover," and originally meant a revelation, either angelic or directly divine, and which was always obscure and therefore required an angelic interpretation. There are a few examples earlier in Scripture, such as in Zechariah, but Daniel's revelation used this technique to predict the end of the world as it then existed. When Daniel had his visions, and needed an angel's help to explain them, the angel Gabriel told him: "Understand, O human, that the vision is for the end-time."[48] Because of Daniel (and also because of the book of Revelation), "apocalypse" now means a dramatic and almost always violent end of the current world as foretold by a mystical divine revelation, which will culminate in establishing the rule of God forever.

There had been previous prophetic expectations about the establishment of God's kingdom, but these were always placed in some vague future "after days." The author of Daniel prophesied a specific number of days until the great event—several different specific numbers, in fact.[49] Again, this is because he was writing at the moment when the existential crisis was at its height. He wanted to offer his readers hope of imminent rescue —which God would accomplish by establishing his kingdom on earth.

Daniel's was only one of the numerous apocalyptic prophecies of the late Second Temple era, though it's not clear how many Jews in Judaea or the Diaspora believed in any of them. The Hasmonean kings and their propagandists "deliberately introduced apocalyptic elements" in an effort to "persuad[e] Jews attracted to apocalyptic circles to remain loyal subjects."[50]

Later apocalyptic texts were specifically aimed at Rome, promising Jews that God would soon do away with the wicked Romans and their unendurable rule. The Essenes, a small isolationist sect present throughout the late Second Temple period, were particularly fond of these apocalypses. It is generally agreed that the Qumran community, near the Dead Sea, was part of the Essene sect.[51] They collected the Dead Sea or Qumran Scrolls, hiding them in caves before the Romans destroyed the Qumran community in the Great Revolt of 66–73 CE. The Essenes were convinced that they were even then living in the last days, when Rome's harsh rule over the Jews would be overthrown in a violent confrontation with the armies of God.[52] The *War Scroll* or *War Rule* predicted a forty–year war against the "Kittim" (generally understood to mean the Romans when used in this context), though it was really a theological war between the forces of light and darkness which would mark the end of days.[53] Many apocalyptic texts described future battles between the righteous and the wicked, and how God at some point would step in to save the day and issue final judgment on everyone. One of the texts from the first century CE is *Fourth Ezra*, whose author used the eagle—the symbol of the Roman legions —as yet another euphemism for the hated Romans. "And as for the lion that you saw...roaring and speaking to the eagle and reproving him for his unrighteousness...this is the Messiah whom the Most High has kept until the end of days... [A]nd when he has reproved them, he will destroy them."[54]

A MESSIAH TO THE RESCUE

"Messiah" is the English equivalent of the Hebrew *mashiach* or the Greek *christos*. In those languages, it originally meant nothing more than "anointed"—part of the ceremony when a new king, or sometimes a new high priest, was installed in office. On at least one occasion, a non–Jew was hailed as a messiah: Second Isaiah said that God had called the Emperor Cyrus of Persia "his anointed one" (*m'shichoh*) because he had released the Jews from exile.[55]

Antiochus IV had been bad enough. In some ways, the Romans were even worse. They were ruthless in suppressing any political dissent, they frequently ignored Jewish religious sensitivities, and their governors were mostly venal and often incompetent. Some Jews began to think that their only hope of survival was for God to send someone to lead them out of this misery and restore the kingdom of David. This would mean a new type of messiah: "either a general or a judge or both [who] serves as God's agent to punish the wicked and reward the righteous."[56]

As with the apocalypse, it's hard to say how popular belief in such a messiah was. Among those who did expect one, there was no agreement on what this messiah was expected to do. Should he lead the Jews into battle? Should he get rid of the Romans himself, as the *Psalms of Solomon* may have demanded?[57] How many messiahs would there be, anyway? The Qumran scrolls sometimes speak of two, or occasionally three, messiahs: a kingly messiah from the House of David and a priestly one from the family of Aaron, and perhaps a prophet messiah who would precede them.[58]

All these variations had one point in common: *the messiah would somehow make life better for the Jews.* There were a number of persons during these tumultuous times who claimed to be, or who were hailed as, the messiah, who promised to do this, but all of them failed.[59]

A NEW TYPE OF PROPHECY

The book of Daniel introduced other new ideas as well. Three of them will be highly significant in the New Testament: a shift in the nature of prophecy to something that might be called "absolute prophecy"; the use of a technique called "prophecy after the event"; and taking the messages of past prophets out of their original context so as to make them fit a new situation.

Absolute prophecy. In the life of the ancient Israelites as documented in the Hebrew Scripture, individual prophets arose from time to time who had influence, and sometimes power, not because of who they were but because of what they had to say. They believed they were delivering messages to the people on Yahweh's instructions. These messages were highly consequential: unless you stop your idolatry, unless you stop oppressing the widow and the stranger, you will suffer Yahweh's wrath. To use modern terminology, prophets spoke "truth to power." They also offered messages of comfort to Israelites in exile and reassurances that Yahweh remembered them.

Other than a few vague descriptions of an idyllic life "in the after days," prophecies of future events were presented as the consequences of past and present actions. David committed adultery with Bathsheba and then had her husband killed so he could marry her. The prophet Nathan told him that, as a consequence, the child David had conceived with her would die. The kings of Judah went after other gods and served them; therefore the "Lord of Armies" would send the king of Babylonia to destroy them, warned Jeremiah. Fifty years later, Second Isaiah promised that Jerusalem would now be restored because "she has taken from the Lord's hand double for all her offenses." The Edomites were going to suffer, Obadiah predicted, for having taken part in "the outrage against [their] brother Jacob" when the Babylonians destroyed Jerusalem.[60] But absolute prophecy, a specific prediction that was not a consequence of whatever someone had done or failed to do, and that will not change regardless of how anyone acts, was something prophets rarely did—until Daniel.[61]

Daniel's prophecies were absolute statements of future fact. The evil king *will* die near Jerusalem and alone. The archangel

Michael *will* come. The righteous *will* escape. Many of the dead *will* rise. The righteous have only to wait and trust in God. But this was just the end of the vision that the archangel Gabriel revealed to Daniel. Gabriel told him about other events that would take place before Michael comes to the rescue. Alexander *will* conquer Persia. His empire *will* be broken into four parts. Egypt and Syria *will* fight each other. Antiochus *will* force the Jews to abandon the holy covenant.[62]

This shift from the earlier Scriptural idea of prophecy as admonition to one of prophecy as pure prediction is likely the result of Hellenistic influence, since this is how the Greek world traditionally viewed prophecies—oracles, as they called them. Bible scholar Robert Miller argues that "the earliest Jewish statement of the Greek-inspired notion of prophecy-as-fate is found in the Book of Tobit," [63] an apocryphal text most likely written in the third century BCE, a hundred years or so before Daniel. By Daniel's time, Miller writes, its author "assumes that his Jewish audience is familiar and comfortable with its hellenized concept of prophecy."[64] In the first century CE, the authors of the New Testament will make extensive use of absolute prophecy, or prophecy as fate.

Prophecy after the event. In order to present this absolute prophecy as a true angelic revelation, the author of Daniel set his protagonist back in the days of the Babylonian and Persian empires over three hundred years before, meaning that Daniel could have known none of these events by any natural means. And since Daniel's readers would know that all the predictions about Alexander and Antiochus had come true, they should accept that the predictions about Michael and resurrection were about to come to pass as well. This is a technique that modern critical scholarship calls "prophecy after the event,"[65] whose use has been traced at least as far back as Akkadian times. Daniel's author may even have been aware of the "Akkadian Apocalypses" of the seventh and sixth centuries BCE which used this same technique and "have parallels with the book of Daniel."[66]

Prophecy out of context. The author of Daniel also took past prophecies out of their original context and reinterpreted them so as to make them relevant to the current crisis. Two examples are of particular importance: Jeremiah's seventy years and Isaiah's suffering servant.

As part of his warning to the king of Judah, Jeremiah predicted that "all this land shall become a ruin and a desolation, and these nations shall serve the king of Babylonia seventy years," after which God will punish the Babylonians and turn their land into "an everlasting desolation."[67] (This might be the only example of an "absolute prophecy" prior to Hellenistic times, though Jeremiah probably followed the typical Scriptural practice of using "seventy years" to mean a very long time.) As it happens, the Persians conquered Babylonia in 539 BCE, only forty-seven years after Nebuchadnezzar tore down Jerusalem's walls and destroyed the Temple in 586. Nor did the Persians destroy Babylon as the prophet had predicted; Cyrus's conquest was a peaceful one.[68] Daniel's author, however, used "the word of the Lord to Jeremiah" as a prediction of Antiochus's destruction rather than Babylon's. He also took seventy to be an exact number and then, speaking as Gabriel, reinterpreted it as "seven weeks of years" and made other calculations to show that after some exact number of years, the Jews would be rescued from Antiochus.[69]

A second passage from the prophets that the author of Daniel reused was Isaiah's famous "suffering servant." Isaiah's first words to the exile community in Babylon were "Comfort, O comfort My people," and the "Songs of the Suffering Servant" continue that theme.[70] Isaiah describes "My servant" who is "despised and shunned by people, a man of sorrows and visited by illness...wounded for our crimes, crushed for our transgressions," who was given a disgraceful burial "for no outrage had he done." Yet "would he lay down a guilt offering, he would see his seed, have length of days." Isaiah used the past tense to describe the servant's suffering and a (conditional) future tense for the servant's reward for his endurance.[71]

It's unclear whether Isaiah meant the servant to be a single person serving as an example, or the nation as a whole. Some scholars think the servant might even have been Isaiah himself and that the "song" was a eulogy for him delivered by a disciple.[72] Either way, the text used the singular form of the verb. When the author of Daniel reused Isaiah's words, however, he put them in the plural form: "Those who guide the many to be righteous." In Hebrew, this is almost word for word Isaiah's "My servant shall put the righteous in the right for many."[73] Isaiah was a popular book in Second Temple times, and I suggest that Daniel's author expected his readers would identify with Isaiah's suffering servant who had suffered even unto death but who had been restored to glory.

Though Daniel's predicted apocalypse never came to pass, the book remained popular with divergent sects in Judaea. Its use of absolute prophecy, often "validated" by "prophecy after the event," and its reinterpretation of prophecy remained potent in Second Temple times: Josephus credited Daniel with predicting the Roman destruction of Judaea.[74] Even today, Daniel's use of numerology continues to provide grist for many an apocalyptic mill, while his tactic of taking Jeremiah's seventy years out of context and his reuse of Isaiah's "servant" will be developed even further in the New Testament.

SAINTIZATION

"Saintization" is a word of my own coinage. It derives from sanitization, in the sense of sanitizing a person's life story—but to the degree that he becomes a saint, a caricature of a human being. This is what the author of Daniel did to his protagonist.

Daniel was "preeminent among the overseers and the satraps, for there was exceptional spirit in him... He was faithful, and no fault or corruption was found in him."[75] Daniel and his friends were "little more than exemplary figures of piety, without nuance or psychology" writes the translator Robert Alter. Elias Bickerman describes this technique as "idealizing the hero, a tendency paralleled in Greek romance." It is also evident in the writings of the Stoics, says Uusimäki, a scholar of Hellenic Judaism. The Stoic wise person "naturally does well anything he undertakes...[and] due to possessing truth, he is unfailingly able to act correctly in any life situation."[76]

The late Chief Rabbi of England, Jonathan Sacks, wrote that there is a "unique mixture of light and shade in all the characters of the Hebrew Bible" which is there "to teach us that even the best are not perfect and even the worst are not devoid of merits."[77] Daniel is the exception.

Saintization of other Scriptural persons appears in other texts of the period. When Abraham (still Abram at the time) had to go down to Egypt because of a famine, he was supposed to trust that God would protect him and his wife Sarah (Sarai). Instead, as told in the book of Genesis, he asked his wife to say she was his sister because he was afraid that otherwise the Egyptians would kill him in order to possess her. It was left to Pharaoh, of all people, to chastise Abram for his deception. But in *Jubilees*, an alternate version of Genesis/Exodus written around the same time as Daniel, Abram behaved flawlessly, like a saint. "And [God] tested him again with his wife, when she was taken... And in everything in which he tested him, he found him faithful." The character of Joseph underwent a similar saintization in *Jubilees*.[78] Later, in Talmudic times, some rabbis will try to turn David into a saint, twisting the texts to argue that he never sinned with Bathsheba.[79]

We will see saintization at work in the New Testament, especially regarding Jesus. The Jesus on Luke's cross shows no emotion, unlike in Matthew and Mark. He goes to his death as Socrates went to his, calmly, stoically, like a philosopher—or a saint.[80]

SEEDS OF A NEW RELIGION

The half–millennium between the end of the Babylonian exile in 538 BCE and the Roman destruction of Jerusalem in 70 CE was a period when, in response to new situations and under the influence of new ideas, many of the beliefs now sacred to Judaism and Christianity developed. The most important of these was the belief that the soul would survive the death of the body and would be judged for its actions in life. The prospect of judgment after death reassured victims of oppression that justice delayed was not necessarily justice denied. Eventually this would evolve into a belief that life on earth was unimportant compared to life after death.

Other ideas that flourished in the literature and popular imagination included a belief (or hope) that the increasingly intolerable life under the Romans meant the world as it then existed was about to come to an end, and then the Jews would live happily ever after. Similar to this was the wish that God would send a messiah at whose hands the Romans would get their comeuppance. The concept of prophecy also changed during this era with the use of absolute prophecy, prophecy after the event, and past prophecies taken out of context.

All of these ideas were vague on the details or clashed on the details. All of them derived from speculations and claims of personal revelations, so there could be—there would be— endless arguments over them. Some of those arguments will be critical to the formation of Christianity.

CHAPTER THREE

SALVATION FOR THE CHRISTIANS

Christianity, which is today one of the most powerful influences on the world, grew out of the beliefs and needs of a small group of Jews in Galilee. They followed a charismatic leader, Jesus of Nazareth, whom they may have thought was the messiah, who preached that the end of the known world and the establishment of God's kingdom on earth were just about to occur. After the Roman authorities executed Jesus, his followers—who had not expected that to happen—had to resolve several existential questions. First, why did Jesus have to die? Second, could Jesus still be the messiah after he had died? Third, why hadn't God's kingdom arrived as Jesus said it would? These questions and the way the first followers of Jesus resolved them became the foundation of Christianity, and therefore the focus of this chapter. (There was another existential question—why wouldn't the Jews accept Jesus—but that one is so complicated and consequential it needs a chapter of its own.)

Before getting into these questions, though, I need a moment to set the scene. After King Herod died in 4 BCE, the Romans divided his kingdom into several parts. They gave the main part, Judaea, to Herod's son Archelaus, but he was unable to stop the civil unrest that followed his father's death, so in 6 CE the Romans removed him and ruled the province directly through a series of governors, or prefects. Another son of Herod, Herod Antipas, ruled Galilee, north of Judaea. He was more successful than his brother, though in 39 CE the Romans removed him as well.

The other point to bear in mind here is that Jesus and his first followers were all Jews, lived as Jews, and took part in the Jewish disputes of the day. For this reason, I will follow a common scholarly practice of referring to the early followers of Jesus as the "Jesus Movement" to emphasize that it was a sect *within* Judaism. Only toward the end of the first century will the distinctions be so clear that we can start calling it Christianity, a new religion.[1]

WHAT WE *KNOW* ABOUT JESUS

It often surprises people to learn that Jesus, who has long been one of the most recognizable names in history, was an obscure figure in his own lifetime. We have no contemporaneous record of him, and very little for decades afterwards other than writings from his followers. The oldest known mentions of Jesus are the letters of Paul, written starting about two decades after Jesus's death. Paul was not concerned with how Jesus lived, but with why he died. The first known descriptions of Jesus's life come decades later, from the gospels of Mark, Matthew, Luke, and John. It is possible Mark was partly written during the Great Revolt of the Jews against the Romans, which started in 66 and came to an end with the capture of Masada in 73 CE. Matthew and Luke were probably written around 80 or 90 CE, and John a little later.[2] We don't know who wrote them; the texts themselves never say. As far as is known, the first person to authoritatively assign authorship to each gospel was Bishop Irenaeus of

Lyon around 180 CE, using names that by then may have become traditional.[3] The gospel writers, whoever they were, were too young to have been active in Jesus's lifetime, and while Paul and Jesus were contemporaries, by Paul's own admission he never knew Jesus in life.[4]

Another problem is that the gospel writers—the evangelists—were not writing history; they were writing gospels—proclamations of "good news." Each writer was working at a different time and probably for a different audience. Each would use, exaggerate, even invent stories that would further develop his message. While some historical elements were woven into the gospel stories, any attempt to reconstruct the historical life of Jesus from them must include a good deal of speculation.

Scholars of the Bible have long recognized the similarities in the gospels of Mark, Matthew, and Luke, and for this reason these three are often referred to as the Synoptic Gospels, in part to distinguish them from the very different gospel of John. Then there is the book of Acts, which focuses on the years immediately after the crucifixion and on the actions of Paul. This book was almost certainly written by the same person who wrote Luke and is also dated to around 80–90 CE.

There is almost no mention of Jesus, and very little about his followers, in the Roman or Jewish writings of the first 120 years or so of the Common Era. Early in the second century, the Roman historian Tacitus had a brief and unflattering mention of Jesus; Pliny the Younger asked the emperor what to do about these "Christians" who wouldn't worship the state gods; and Suetonius made a passing reference to someone named "Chrestus."[5] The Jewish historian Flavius Josephus wrote a short paragraph on Jesus—the so-called *Testimonium Flavianum*—around 90 CE. It was heavily edited by later Christian copyists and is useful mainly as testimony that Jesus did exist and that his followers were still active. Josephus wasn't even interested in Jesus for his own sake, only in using what happened to him as just one more example of the perfidy of the Roman prefect Pontius Pilate.[6] Josephus also refers to this Jesus in order to identify James the Just as his brother.[7]

There are some things we do know about Jesus. He was almost certainly born in or near the village of Nazareth in Galilee around the time King Herod died, most likely in 4 BCE. At some point he became a follower of John the Baptist, who roamed Galilee early in the first century CE preaching dire warnings of a coming apocalypse. Herod Antipas eventually had the Baptist arrested, perhaps because he was concerned that John might trigger a rebellion (according to Josephus) or because John was making accusations about Antipas's personal life (so says the gospel of Mark).[8] After (or perhaps even before) his mentor's arrest, Jesus went around Galilee repeating the Baptist's message about the coming end of days: "The time is fulfilled, and the kingdom of God is at hand; repent, and believe in the good news."[9] He evidently had a charismatic personality, since by the time he was around 30 years old he had attracted a dedicated following, similar to that of the Baptist and of other itinerant preachers and "holy men" who were roaming all over the region in those years. The size of the crowds who came to listen to him is a matter of dispute, but almost certainly they were nowhere near as large as the gospels claim, or else Antipas might have taken action against Jesus as he had done against John the Baptist.[10]

Sometime between one and three years after he started preaching, in the year 33 (or possibly 30) CE, Jesus and some of his followers traveled from Galilee to Jerusalem in Judaea for the Passover festival, one of the high points of the Jewish religious year. For some reason, Jesus came to the attention of Roman or Jewish authorities there and was arrested. The Roman prefect Pontius Pilate (who governed Judaea from 26 to 37 CE) briefly interrogated Jesus and then condemned him to be executed by crucifixion; the sentence was carried out later that day. Jesus's followers, stunned by this turn of events, scattered and then regrouped to discuss how to deal with their leader's death on a cross.

WHY DID JESUS HAVE TO DIE?

The execution of Jesus by crucifixion, a particularly cruel and degrading punishment, triggered an existential crisis among his followers. It is unlikely that Jesus expected to die that way, as his original message of repentance made no mention of it. It is even more unlikely that his followers expected it. According to the gospels, when Jesus told them what was going to happen to him, they didn't believe him, and when it did happen they fled in terror. In order to properly understand this question, however, we need to look at it not just from the perspective of the Jesus Movement, but also from the perspectives of the Romans and the Jews.

The perspective of the Romans. The primary duties of the governors of the Roman Empire were straightforward: collect the taxes and keep the peace. The empire was mainly interested in results, and officials frequently used extremely brutal methods to get their jobs done. Roman law and practice allowed them to execute anyone, so long as they were not Roman citizens, for acts we today would consider barely worth a fine. (A Roman citizen was entitled to a trial in Rome.) The governors of Judaea frequently used crucifixion to punish bandits and troublemakers, to suppress political aspirations, and to frighten the population into obedience. "They could classify the disturbances as *seditio*, or troublemaking (*se turbulente gessere*), or simply actions against the *quies* (quiet) of Judaea."[11] Now *seditio*, sedition, was a serious offense and Rome was constantly vigilant against any hint of it. But even just disturbing the peace was a quick way to end up on a cross; Rome had little patience and plenty of wood. After the revolts following Herod's death in 4 BCE, Governor

Varus of Syria crucified some two thousand Jews. In the 50s CE, Governor Felix captured the bandit Eleazar and his gang and crucified "a multitude not to be enumerated."[12] During the Roman siege of Jerusalem in 69-70 CE, the legions captured as many as five hundred Jews a day as they tried to escape the city. Since it was too much trouble to keep a guard over them, the soldiers first tortured and then crucified so many of them that, in Josephus's vivid description, "room was wanting for crosses, and crosses wanting for bodies." (He adds that the Romans hoped that the sight would induce the city to yield.)[13] Pilate's pattern of cruelty was not out of line with that of some other Roman officials, but even so, it got to the point where, in 36 CE, Governor Vitellius ordered Pilate recalled to Rome for the murder of some Samaritans.[14]

Still, it is possible that Pilate really did think Jesus was guilty of sedition. The gospels had Pilate ask Jesus: "'Are you the king of the Jews?' He answered him, 'You say so.'"[15] Claiming to be king over Rome's subjects without Rome's permission would certainly amount to sedition. In Mark and Matthew, the other two people crucified with Jesus were identified as *lēstai*, a Greek word which can mean "bandits" or "robbers" but can also mean "insurrectionists." Legal historian Bernard Jackson documents how Roman authorities commonly used "robbers" to characterize people who caused political trouble.[16]

Other possibilities include being a troublemaker or disturbing the peace. This would have been a problem at any time, but it was particularly dangerous during Passover week. The Passover festival celebrates the liberation of the Israelites from the tyranny of Egypt, and Jews in Roman Judaea could very easily see it as an inspiration to free themselves from the tyranny of Rome. The governors of Judaea normally ruled from Caesarea, a seaport on the Mediterranean that Herod had built, but for Passover week they would move to Jerusalem and bring soldiers with them. If we accept the story of Jesus overturning the tables of the moneychangers in the Temple court,[17] that alone would have been reason enough for Pilate to execute him. Or Pilate may simply have been worried that Jesus was a rabble-rouser who might stir up the crowd—which would be disturbing the peace. Whatever the reason, Pilate had no compunctions whatsoever about nailing one more Jew to one more cross.[18]

The perspective of the Jews. This is more difficult to determine, because the only reports we have were written by members of the Jesus Movement who had, as I shall explain in the next chapter, strong motives to blame the Jews for a Roman execution.

We can start with how the Judaean Jews felt about the Romans: they hated them, and they also feared them. The Roman governor appointed the high priest of the Jews and could dismiss him at any time. Rome's control over the high priest extended even to his ritual garments: until around 45 CE, the legions had custody of them, and the high priest had to get permission to wear them each time he needed them for a special occasion.[19] The high priest and his associates would be even more concerned than the Romans to keep the peace. "The priests were held responsible not only by Rome; they felt their responsibility acutely themselves."[20]

According to Josephus, Pilate crucified Jesus "at the instiga-tion of the principal men amongst us."[21] I think it likely that these really are Josephus's words, since a later Christian inter-polator would have accused the Jews as a whole. However, Jose-phus wrote this around 90 CE, when some of the gospels were already circulating, so it is possible he drew on them as his source. Given the way most Jews in Judaea felt about the Romans, it is difficult to imagine any Jewish authority, even a collaborator, giving up any Jew to them, even a troublemaker, unless they felt they had no other choice, which could have been what happened.

The gospels portray the priests and other Jewish leaders as

being jealous of Jesus, even afraid of him, because they were unable to answer his arguments. Such a portrayal is reminiscent of what Plato did in his dialogues, where he set up straw men for Socrates to knock down. This was first-century Judaea: Jews argued constantly (one habit that hasn't changed) about all kinds of theological questions, from when the messiah would arrive and what he would do when he got here to the correct way to sacrifice and how to observe the Sabbath. New Testament scholar Paula Fredriksen describes the Jews of Judaea hurling Scripture verses at each other and calling each other names such as hypocrites and blasphemers. The authors of the gospels, she writes, "present a fairly typical portrait of Jewish interactions both in Jesus' day and in their own." Indeed, in comparison to what the Pharisees and the Sadducees had to say about each other, "what passes between the scribes and Jesus is fairly mild," and what the Essenes at Qumran said about the Jerusalem priests was worse than what the Pharisees are quoted as saying about Jesus.[22] It strains the imagination to think that such energetic disputants would so quickly concede an argument the way the gospels claimed, or be so upset at losing a debate that they would devise a horrible death for the winner.

The gospels also accused the priests of charging Jesus with blasphemy, a capital crime. As I just pointed out, Jewish disputants were not above calling each other blasphemers in the heat of argument, but a formal charge of blasphemy was quite different and had to meet a strict standard set by the Torah: cursing God by name.[23] Claiming to be the messiah, or even the son of God (a title sometimes given to the kings of Judah and even collectively to Israel[24]), is not blasphemy under Torah law, and the Sadducees, who made up most of the priesthood, accepted only Torah law and no later legislation.[25] "Other Jews made this claim [to be the messiah] about themselves and about others both before Jesus and afterward, never with the charge of blasphemy" being leveled against them.[26]

In any event, if Jesus had indeed committed blasphemy, the Jews could have punished him themselves. In the gospel of John, Jews twice tried to stone Jesus when he claimed to be divine (he escaped each time).[27] According to Acts, when Stephen was accused of "blasphemous words against Moses and God" and the high priest offered him a chance to defend himself, Stephen's speech so enraged the crowd that they stoned him to death on the spot.[28] Furthermore, Josephus wrote that the Essenes claimed the authority to execute anyone caught blaspheming not only God but also Moses.[29] It seems the Jews were quite capable of executing blasphemers without Roman help.

The perspective of the Jesus Movement. Here too we have a historical difficulty: there are no known documents by the Jesus Movement from the first twenty years after the crucifixion. All the material in the New Testament was written by the winners of the debates during that crucial time. (We know there were debates because there are occasional mentions of the losers.) Still, we can draw some hints. For instance, in Mark, the oldest of the four canonical gospels, when Jesus told his apostles that he was going to die and rise again, they didn't understand what he was talking about. Nor did they stand by him through his arrest, trial, execution, and burial. It was left to the women to do that, and to make the first claim to having witnessed the resurrection.[30] In this version, at least, it would appear that Jesus's followers didn't expect him to die on them, and had no idea what to do when he did. If Jesus's execution was an ordinary event for the Romans, or a regrettable or irrelevant one for the Jews, it was catastrophic for the Jesus Movement: their leader, the man they had hailed as the messiah, savior of the Jews, had just been unceremoniously crucified.

By the time the apostle Paul wrote his first known letters, two decades after the crucifixion, the Jesus Movement had found a way to explain Jesus's death, though they still acknowledged the difficulties it was causing them. Paul admitted this in his first letter to the Corinthians in 54 CE: "We proclaim Christ crucified, a stumbling block to Jews and foolishness to Gentiles."[31]

When reading Paul's authentic letters,[32] we need to bear in mind that they were almost all written to specific communities to deal with specific issues or problems, and do not lay out any detailed theology. Presumably Paul had done that when he established or visited those communities. In Paul's last known letter, his epistle to the Jesus followers in Rome around 57 or 58 CE, he did explain some of his theological ideas, including how they were derived from Jewish beliefs.

In Romans, Paul admitted that Jesus had indeed died on the cross. But three days later he was resurrected to life—proof, said Paul, that there is eternal life after our deaths. "We know that Christ, being raised from the dead, will never die again; death no longer has dominion over him."[33] The most significant of the ideas Paul presented in Romans, however, was his explanation for why Jesus *had* to die the way he did: it was not merely to prove that life was eternal, but to save man from sin. "God put forward [Jesus] as a sacrifice of atonement by his blood, effective through faith."[34] His crucifixion was meant to be the final sacrifice, the ultimate sin offering.

Sin—disobedience to the laws of God—and atonement for sin were specifically Jewish ideas, so in order to explain to the Gentiles how they too were under the power of sin, Paul laid out his concept of original sin: "sin came into the world through one man [Adam, the first man], and death came through sin, and so death spread to all because all have sinned." Because of that, said Paul, sin, and the need to be saved from sin, were universal. "For we have already charged that all, both Jews and Greeks, are under the power of sin."[35] The way for both Jews and Greeks to escape the damnation of sin was through Jesus and his willing self-sacrifice. If—and only if—we accept that and believe that

Jesus laid down his life for us can we free ourselves from sin and live eternally in paradise.

Whether Jesus actually saw himself in that light is more problematic. Particularly in the Synoptic gospels (Mark, Matthew, and Luke), when Jesus was preaching his message that the kingdom was coming and everyone needed to repent, people would ask him how they could do that. Jesus would tell them that they just had to follow God's commandments. He also demanded that they sell all their possessions—a reasonable demand if the kingdom of God was at hand and money would soon be useless—and that they must "follow me," an ambiguous instruction.[36] "Believe in me" would have been more in line with Paul's theology. The famous parable of the sheep and the goats in Matthew is also instructive. Jesus explained that all people would be separated as a shepherd separates sheep and goats. Those who welcomed the stranger, fed the hungry, clothed the naked, visited the sick and those in prison, were the righteous "sheep" who would go on to eternal life. But those who did not do these things were the "goats" and would be sent to eternal punishment.[37] One's eternal destiny was determined by one's actions; Jesus did not say anything about believing in him.

It's possible to argue that the Synoptics wanted to put more emphasis on Jesus's message about the need to repent and to live a good life than on Jesus being a sacrifice for sin. On the other hand, the gospel of John, the last of the four canonical gospels, was even more explicit than Paul in insisting that one must believe in the crucified Jesus in order to gain salvation. John's Jesus told Martha, "I am the resurrection and the life. Those who believe in me, even though they die, will live, and everyone who lives and believes in me will never die."[38] Earlier, the same gospel quoted John the Baptist saying about Jesus, "Here is the Lamb of God who takes away the sin of the world."[39] John relied on two of the same arguments for Jesus's death that Paul had used: you must believe in Jesus to obtain eternal life and to be saved from sin.

There is also the gospel of Luke, which was probably written about the same time as Matthew, around 80 to 90 CE. Luke chose to deal with the problem of Jesus's death by focusing less on why he died than on how he faced his death. A dean of Yale Divinity School, Greg Sterling, makes a strong case that Luke portrayed Jesus as dying a hero's death in the manner of the Greek philosophers. Luke "carefully reworked the death of Jesus at critical points to remind the hearer/reader of Socrates, the paradigmatic martyr of his society."[40] I suggest that this was Luke's way of dealing with the Greeks who saw worship of Jesus as "foolishness" (to use Paul's term). Jesus had died stoically and heroically, so worshipping him was not foolish at all.

One reason for this shift in description was the movement's increasing focus on converting Gentiles (the New Testament uses "Gentiles" and "Greeks" interchangeably). If Jesus died for everyone's sins, then everyone had to believe in Jesus or they would not be saved from sin. (The problem of what should be done about people who had died before Jesus was born, or who lived and died without ever hearing about him, continues to occupy theologians even today.[41]) In taking this position, Paul and the rest of the Jesus Movement introduced a new theological concept: the universality of a particular belief. They wanted *their* particular beliefs to be everyone's beliefs. They arrived at this point not only as the logical extension of their explanation for the death of Jesus, but from the Second Temple period belief that one day all nations would acknowledge Yahweh of Israel as God of all. But where the rest of the Jews expected it "in the after days," the Jesus Movement wanted it *now*.

COULD A DEAD MAN STILL BE THE MESSIAH?

There is general agreement that Jesus's followers (though possibly not Jesus himself) claimed during his lifetime that he was the messiah that many Jews were hoping for.[42] One reason we know this is that the Jesus Movement went to some lengths to explain how Jesus could still be the messiah even after he had died. As I showed in the previous chapter, Jews in the Second Temple period had a number of different ideas about who the messiah would be and what he would do, but they were in agreement on two points: He would be a leader of Israel who would make life better for the Jews, and he would be alive while he did it. Jesus did not fit this description. Toward the end of the second century CE, Bishop Irenaeus of Lyon would admit this in observing that Jesus "rebuked Peter, who imagined that He was the Christ as the generality of men supposed [that the Christ should be], and was adverse to the idea of His suffering."[43] In other words, Irenaeus is saying that Peter, like most Jews of his time, didn't think the messiah would suffer.

To solve this problem, the Jesus Movement invented a new concept of messiah: he would make life better for the Jews through his suffering, not through militancy. Moreover, the messiah would be identified not by what he had done but by what he was going to do. Luke put it this way: "Was it not necessary that the Messiah should suffer these things and then enter into his glory?"[44] They deliberately compared Jesus to Isaiah's suffering servant. Paul reminded the Corinthians that "I handed on to you as of first importance what I in turn had received: that Christ died for our sins in accordance with the scriptures"—that is, in accordance with Isaiah.[45]

In order to do this, the Jesus Movement relied on a concept of prophecy that didn't exist in Scripture times but which had since been accepted by Jewish writers under Hellenistic influence: "the Greek-inspired notion of prophecy-as-fate."[46] Previously, prophecy was meant to warn, to advise, and on occasion to comfort the people who were listening to what the prophet had to say. But now prophecy was shifting to mean an absolute prediction of something that was *fated* to happen someday in the future. The book of Daniel shows part of this shift. The author of Daniel used Isaiah's "suffering servant" as a prior example of persecution and thus of future comfort, as well as a prediction for Daniel's time. The Jesus Movement read Isaiah purely as prediction, and then took that reading completely out of context by identifying the suffering servant as the Messiah, who was Jesus. Just as the servant had died and been restored to life, so Jesus had died and been restored. In so doing, they transmuted Isaiah's servant from a prophetic reassurance to the people of his time into an absolute prophecy about something completely different. As New Testament scholar Craig Evans acknowledges, "there was no pre-Christian understanding of [Isaiah's] Servant as Messiah, at least nothing has yet come to light to indicate this."[47]

The Jesus Movement pored over other Hebrew texts for verses that they could somehow argue were other absolute predictions of Jesus. Robert Miller argues that New Testament authors and the Church Fathers frequently combined disparate verses, extracted parts of verses, and sometimes even rewrote verses to make practically all of Scripture appear to be prophecies about Jesus.[48] "It is [the scriptures] that testify on my behalf," said John's Jesus to the Jews.[49] The Jesus Movement viewed prophecy as absolute and predictive, unconnected to its original context. The Jesus Movement also saw all of Scripture as predicting that the last days were already upon them, though there is little evidence that most other Jews, apart from the Qumran community, were saying the same.[50]

WHY HASN'T THE KINGDOM COME?

The imminent end of the world as it then existed was a paramount principle of the Jesus Movement. Paul used Jesus's resurrection three days after his death as evidence that the kingdom of God was at hand. "But in fact Christ has been raised from the dead, the first fruits of those who have died."[51] In the oldest text of the New Testament, the First Letter to the Thessalonians (c. 50 CE), Paul told his readers that they shouldn't worry even though some of their number had already died before the kingdom had come. "We who are alive" will witness the resurrection of the dead, and then right after that, those "who are left, will be caught up in the clouds together with them...and so we will be with the Lord forever" any moment now.[52] Several years later, in Romans, his last known epistle, Paul still expressed confidence in the imminent arrival of the kingdom. "For salvation is nearer to us now than when we became believers; the night is far gone, the day is near."[53]

The Synoptics continued this line of argument. In Mark, the oldest of the four canonical gospels, the first words Jesus spoke were that "the kingdom of God is at hand." Later, Jesus told a crowd, "Truly I tell you, there are some standing here who will not taste death until they see that the kingdom of God has come with power." Matthew's Jesus said much the same.[54] However, while Luke's Jesus repeated the promise made in Mark and Matthew, he made it less apocalyptic—"before they see the kingdom of God"—possibly a reference to the immediately following verses where some of the disciples watched as Jesus was greeted by Moses and Elijah. Later in Luke, when people asked Jesus to specify when the kingdom would come, he was even more vague, saying only that it would happen unexpectedly.[55]

In John, the fourth and last canonical gospel (c. 95 CE), the emphasis is entirely on eternal life for the believers, while the kingdom is put off until sometime in the future. "All who see the Son and believe in him may have eternal life; and I will raise them up on the last day" is the message of John's Jesus.[56] John described several appearances of the risen Jesus to his disciples, explaining that "these [signs] are written so that you may come to believe that Jesus is the Messiah, the Son of God, and that through believing you may have life in his name."[57] But he did not say when the "last day" would come.

By the end of the first century CE, it had become clear that the coming of the kingdom was going to be delayed, perhaps indefinitely. "The later the writing, the lower its level of commitment to an imminent Apocalypse," observes Paula Fredriksen. She points in particular to Second Peter, written around the start of the second century. This letter rationalized the delay by explaining that God has a different understanding of time, alluding to a line in the Psalms that a single day in God's view was like a thousand years to us. Even so, warns the author of Second Peter, we must always hold ourselves ready, for "the day of the Lord will come like a thief."[58]

Then there is the book of Revelation. According to recent scholarship, it was not a response to any actual persecution then taking place but a perception of past persecutions and an anticipation of future ones.[59] At the start of the book, the author said he shared with his readers "the persecution and the kingdom and the patient endurance," and he continues in the next chapters with stories of churches being persecuted.[60] Throughout the book, he encouraged his readers to have "patient endurance" and reassured them that Jesus would soon return to bring the kingdom: "See, I am coming soon; my reward is with me, to repay according to everyone's work."[61] The author of Revelation differed from the author of Daniel, however, in not naming a specific date, saying rather that "the time is near" and "the hour of his judgment has come."[62]

Revelation's reuse of immediacy notwithstanding, other

texts such as 2 Peter provided a rationale for explaining away the absence of the kingdom that Jesus had predicted: God's idea of immediacy is not the same as man's.

WAS JESUS BELIEVED TO BE GOD?

I pose this question in a purely historical sense, not a theological one. Whether Jesus was God, whether he was always God or became God, whether he was (sometimes) human and sometimes divine, whether the Son was equal to the Father, what role the Holy Spirit played—these are questions for faith, not for history. All that history will say is that by sometime around the end of the first century, nearly everyone began to label the faith of the followers of Jesus as Christianity, and distinguished it from the Judaism of the Jews. The belief that Jesus was in some way God probably became part of the definition of a Christian around the same time. My concern is limited to how this resolution impacted the relations between Christians, who believed Jesus was (in some way) God, and the rest of the world, which did not.

My reading of the sources and the scholars leads me to think that the Jesus Movement decided early on that Jesus was in some way divine, though they were still unsettled on the details. In the earlier gospels, Jesus spoke of the "Son of Man" and the "son of God" in sometimes ambiguous ways and in the third person, not surprising since these terms have an ambiguous history.[63] By the time of the gospel of John, however, Jesus was not coy at all about calling himself the Son of Man and the Son of God the Father.[64] Whether John was explicitly identifying Jesus as God is still a debatable point.

I don't believe it was inevitable that the Jesus Movement—that Christianity—had to arrive at the claim that Jesus was somehow God. But once they did so, there was no way to accommodate Christianity with Judaism, which held that there was an absolute distinction between the human and the divine. The Gentile world, however, was accustomed to blurring that distinction. Once the early Jesus disciples decided to take their message out into that world, they found it receptive to the idea that a man could be god, or could become god.

On the other hand, the Gentile world was not accustomed to thinking there was only one god; polytheism was the norm. They knew the Jews believed that their god was the only God, and they thought the Jews were foolish to do so. The Jesus Movement set out to convince the Gentile world to accept that Jesus was the only way to find salvation—and at the same time to reject all their other gods as the Jews had done. They had to do all this *now* because at any moment Jesus was going to return and then it would be too late. This was all new to the Gentiles and it took centuries for many of them to accept it. The history of that acceptance and its consequences will occupy the rest of this book.

PART TWO
IMPACT OF AN INVENTED GOD

Like other Semitic groups, the ancient Israelites started out with a number of gods. Over time, they began to think of one of those gods, Yahweh, as the chief of their gods, and finally, after some significant military and religious disasters, as their only god. Later they claimed that Yahweh was not just their only god, but everyone's only god: Yahweh was God. After that, they developed a belief that God would judge everyone after they died for how they had behaved while alive.

The Israelites, now called the Jews, hoped that all the world would come to understand this in future times, after which everyone would worship God the way the Jews did. But then a small group of Jews, led by Jesus of Nazareth until his crucifixion, warned that the world as it then existed was going to end any day now. When that happened, God would issue his final judgment for all eternity. His judgment would be based not just on how people had behaved, but on whether they believed that Jesus died on the cross—and then rose from the dead—in order to save them from sin. The time was growing short, and the followers of Jesus wanted everyone to believe in him right away. "In future times" would be too late.

The first Christians modified the God that had gradually evolved among the Jews into a God of their own invention. But from the beginning, very few Jews have ever accepted Christianity's modifications, and this posed a threat to the Christian mission to the world. To the Christians, Jewish resistance or indifference to their message was as much an existential threat as the crucifixion and Jesus's failure to return. Christians developed a number of ways of coping with the threat the Jews posed, as we'll see in the next chapter. In the chapters after that, I will discuss how these coping mechanisms influenced the way Christians dealt with four selected issues. The first of these is human sexuality, because it is so central to our being and because Christianity had problems with sex early on that it still has not resolved. Second, I will examine the nature of and justification for war in Biblical times, and how it changed as Christianity changed. Third is Christianity's focus on life after death, often at the expense of life on earth. Finally, I will explore in greater detail how Jesus's original message that the world was just about to come to an end continues to this day to dictate the way in which many Christians want to run the world.

CHAPTER FOUR
WHY WON'T THE JEWS BELIEVE IN JESUS?

W hy won't the Jews believe in Jesus, neither back then in his generation, nor in all the generations since then, down to the present day? I posed this as the last of the four questions of the previous chapter, but said then that it deserved a chapter of its own. This way, I can spend more time on how the Jesus Movement's arguments for Jesus were irreconcilable with some basic Jewish ideas. In addition, some of the missionary actions put Jews in danger from Rome, while Jewish indifference or resistance was making it difficult for the missionaries to persuade Gentiles to their cause. The first disciples of Jesus and the Church Fathers who succeeded them solved these problems, but did so in a way that led to two thousand years of Christian-Jewish conflict.

Let me start this chapter as I did the previous one by setting the scene. We begin with Judaic studies professor Yaron Eliav's "conservative" educated guess that there were around 50 to 60 million people living under Roman rule at the start of the Common Era. Of these, maybe half a million to a million were Jews living in Judaea and Galilee, out of perhaps 5 million Jews in the empire as a whole. Géza Vermes, a preeminent Dead Sea Scrolls scholar, writes vaguely of several million Jews.[1]

When Jesus died, he left behind twelve apostles and perhaps seventy disciples ("apostles" and "disciples" are not entirely distinguishable). Though the book of Acts, written close to the end of the first century, claimed that the apostles converted thousands of Jews in the first months after the crucifixion, these numbers are not credible. Philo of Alexandria, Pliny the Elder, and other writers of that time who were following events in Judaea didn't even notice what Acts described as a major event. Writing around the same time as the author of Acts, the Jewish historian Flavius Josephus made a passing mention of a "tribe of Christians" that included both Jews and Gentiles and who were "not extinct at this day." But he didn't consider them numerous enough nor important enough to qualify as a Jewish group or "school" comparable to the Pharisees, Sadducees, or Essenes (each of whom numbered no more than a few thousand).[2]

New Testament scholar David Sim uses "informed speculation governed by the available evidence" to estimate that there were at most 800 followers of Jesus living in Jerusalem in the last years before the Romans destroyed the city. He posits that there were never more than a thousand or so Jewish believers in Jesus throughout the first century, while there were a little over 7,000 Gentile believers around the year 100. "One can only conclude," says Sim, "that the Christian mission to the Jews was a dismal failure."[3] The causes and the consequences of this failure are the subject of this chapter.

IRRECONCILABLE DIFFERENCES

Why did only a fraction of one percent of all Jews in the empire or even in Judaea ever believe in the message of the Jesus Movement? The answer starts with that message itself. The first followers of Jesus were all Jews themselves, saw themselves as

Jews, and argued that Jewish traditions and beliefs inevitably led
to their version of Judaism. However, the way they used those
traditions and beliefs to solve the dilemma of their founder's
crucifixion was too radical for most Jews to accept. I want to
focus on three aspects of that solution that were particularly
troublesome for Jews: belief in the individual resurrection of
Jesus, belief in Jesus as the messiah after he had died, and belief
that Jesus's crucifixion brought salvation. There is also the belief
that Jesus was born of a virgin, which was not necessary to solve
the problem of the crucifixion, but which was equally unaccept-
able to Jews.

Belief in the individual resurrection of Jesus. Many—though by no
means all—Jews in the late Second Temple era believed that they
would be resurrected to life someday. There were many arguments about just how this was supposed to happen, such as
whether they would have their old bodies, new bodies, or no
bodies at all. But they all expected the resurrection of the dead
would happen to all of them together, and at the end of time.
Jesus's disciples announced he had been resurrected in advance
of everyone else as a sign that the end-times were at hand. This
was central to Christian belief, but, as Dag Endsjø explains in
his study of resurrection beliefs, the disciples faced a "dilemma.
There is apparently nowhere in Jewish tradition any clear
example of an individual resurrecting from the dead for thereupon gaining an immortal existence *before* the end of time."[4]
The resurrection of Jesus in his physical body also posed a problem. While there was a great variety of Jewish ideas about resurrection, there was almost nothing in the way of belief in the
resurrection of the flesh.[5] It simply made no sense to almost all
Jews.

Belief in Jesus as the messiah after he had died. The claim that
Jesus *had been and would be* the messiah was also alien to Jewish
thinking. As we saw in the previous chapters, Jews in the
Second Temple period had a number of different ideas about a

messiah, and it's not clear how many believed in a messiah at all. But those who did believe in one expected that he would be a powerful leader—whether as judge, general, priest, or king—who would establish God's kingdom in the Holy Land where Jews would live in peace and prosperity. Particularly in first-century Judaea under the Romans there was also a "common expectation for a violent messiah," though not all those expecting a messiah felt this way.[6]

The various Jewish portraits of a messiah were of a mortal man. The *Psalms of Solomon*, "one of the most detailed messianic expectations in the immediate pre–Christian centuries," envisions the messiah as a descendant of King David, who would establish the kingdom of God, and who would be "without sin, and...with all the ancient virtues." But he was "not a supernatural being."[7] Nor would he share in the Godhood, which belonged to God alone. Jesus had come and gone, the Jews were still oppressed, and the Romans were still ruling what should have been God's kingdom. He didn't fit any of the Jewish ideas of a messiah.

However, Jesus's death by crucifixion in and of itself was *not* a difficulty for the Jews. Paul thought it was. "A stumbling block to Jews," he called it. But it was no such thing. There were an innumerable number of Jewish victims of Roman ruthlessness, and the Jews honored many of them. As Fredriksen explains, "nothing in first-century Judaism (or thereafter) seems to require that a crucified man *ipso facto* be seen as 'cursed by God,' and we have no evidence of Jews ever actually having done so."[8]

Belief that Jesus's crucifixion brought salvation. This was possibly Christianity's most original idea—you must believe that Jesus died for your sins in order to be saved from sin. But it was the idea least likely to attract Jews. Not all Jews of that period even believed in life after death, but those who did also believed that its rewards and punishments would be based on how one behaved, not on what one believed. This was not unreasonable, since there is no evidence that Jews of that time even questioned the belief that God had given to Moses laws to govern their behavior. There were huge disagreements over *how* to obey the laws, and about whether to use the prophets and traditions to help interpret the Torah (the Pharisees said yes, the Sadducees said no). Even Jesus took part in these arguments: his differences with the Pharisees about the Sabbath were not over *whether* to observe it but *how*. "Judaism was defined more by its practices than its beliefs," writes Shaye Cohen, a major scholar of the Second Temple period. He adds that "no one in antiquity thought to promote any single interpretation or set of interpretations as exclusively correct." Paula Fredriksen offers this memorable metaphor: "we [should] imagine the Torah as widely dispersed sheet music: the notes were the notes, but Jews played a lot of improv."[9]

This highlights another reason why Jews found the Jesus Movement's message impossible to accept. Jews argued with each other constantly, often intemperately, and occasionally violently. But it appears that few of them thought their opponents were eternally damned by God for having a different interpretation of things. Yet this was precisely what the Jesus Movement insisted on: Believe our way or you will be damned forever. No wonder Jews ignored them.

Belief that Jesus was born of a virgin. This belief wasn't necessary to solve the crisis of the crucifixion, and it doesn't appear to have been part of the earliest doctrines. Paul preached to the Galatians that "God sent his Son, born of a woman," which was a perfect opening to talk about the virgin birth. But he didn't, so it's unlikely the idea was well-known in his day.[10] In all of the New Testament, only the gospels of Matthew and Luke spoke of Jesus being born of a virgin. The "Gospel of Q," a reconstructed possible early source for Matthew and Luke, also made no mention of a virgin birth.[11] All this suggests that belief in a virgin birth was at best uncommon prior to around 80 CE, when

Matthew wrote that Mary was still a virgin when she gave birth to Jesus. Then he claimed that Isaiah had prophesied this over 700 years before when he said to King Ahaz: "Look, the virgin shall conceive and bear a son."[12] Matthew had declared Mary to be a virgin so that he could claim she had fulfilled the prophecy of Isaiah.

It didn't work, at least not with the Jews. Other ethnicities may have had a concept of virgin birth, but it was foreign to Jewish thinking.[13] It was also a case of prophecy out of context: Isaiah's prophecy hadn't been about the birth itself but about its timing. By the time the child was old enough to know the difference between right and wrong, Isaiah told the king, the two rulers that Ahaz despised would no longer threaten his kingdom —instead, Assyria would. But Matthew had not just misused Isaiah; he had misquoted him.

Matthew had used an early Greek translation of Scripture known as the Septuagint. The Septuagint translation of this verse used the Greek word *parthenos*, which can mean "young woman" but more often means a "virgin woman." Isaiah had used the Hebrew word *'almah*, a chronological term for a young woman of marriageable age who may or may not be a virgin but who has not yet had a child. When writers in Scripture meant "virgin," they used a word that specifically means a virgin: *b'tullah*.[14] Any Jew who knew his Isaiah (and many did; at least eight copies of the book have been found among the Qumran scrolls) would have known Matthew had made a mistake. By the second century the "virgin birth" had become another irreconcilable difference between Jews and Christians.

Matthew was particularly prolific in extracting verses from the Hebrew Scripture to argue that they all were predictions of Jesus, and in arguing that the Jews were perverse in not acknowledging the messages of their own prophets. But as I discussed in the previous chapter, Matthew, as well as other New Testament authors and the Church Fathers, used—"misused" is more accurate—these verses in ways to make them say what they were never intended to say; Isaiah's young woman is only one of many examples. We may charitably acknowledge that such reuse of Scripture was an acceptable technique of the day, one that rabbis of the Talmud would later resort to in arguing for their interpretations of Torah law. But this charity does not extend to the demand that these particular interpretations be accepted as the *only* valid ones, nor that failure to accept them leads to eternal damnation. In any event, neither Jews of that time nor at any time since have been swayed by this argument. As Robert Miller takes several hundred pages to demonstrate, the argument from prophecy "is persuasive only for those who already believe in the [Christian] Bible—that is, for those who don't need to be persuaded."[15]

WHY DOES IT MATTER?

Why did it matter so much to the early Jesus Movement, why does it matter even now, that almost without exception Jews were and still are indifferent to Jesus? There are a number of reasons that have been offered over the years, but I suggest there are three crucial ones. First is that the Jesus Movement claimed its version of Judaism was the only true one, and they wanted—needed—all other Jews to agree with them. Second is that the non-Jews kept asking why they should believe a crucified criminal was their salvation when the Jews, his own people, didn't. Third, it often happens that people are more angered by indifference than by hatred.

The only true Judaism. The last decades of the Second Temple period (c. 100 BCE to 70 CE) were a time of serious religious disputes among those Jews who cared about such things (almost certainly just a small part of the population). These disputes could get quite heated, their partisans would swear at each other and call their opponents blasphemers, and occasionally they erupted in violence. The Jesus Movement went much further: If you didn't accept that their interpretation of Judaism was the one and only valid Judaism, you would go to hell for all eternity.

Permit me to briefly step away from my role as a student of history. I suggest that this attitude betrays a level of insecurity as well as a sense of superiority; indeed, the two often go together. If you believe you know the only true way to escape eternal damnation, you owe it to everyone to tell them so; it's what's best for them. At the same time, there is still that tiny seed of doubt: do I *really* have the right answer? Might they know something I don't? Making a mistake, even an honest one, could cost you for all eternity.

It is a classic human response to this kind of doubt to demonize whatever is causing it. That is exactly what the Jesus Movement did to the Jews. Paul was the first, even if he was not consistent. In First Thessalonians he denounced Jewish stubbornness, but then in Romans he said God had made the Jews stubborn to give the Gentiles more time to be saved. The rest of the New Testament texts, however, were written after the destruction of Jerusalem in 70 CE, which the Jesus Movement saw as a sign from God that they were right and the Jews were wrong. The Jews didn't see it that way at all, and the gospels increasingly demonized the Jews for it.

Objections from the Gentiles. By the time of First Thessalonians, Paul's first known letter, he had evidently been missionizing to the Roman world for a number of years, and outreach to the Gentiles may even have begun before him. Early on, Paul admitted he was having trouble persuading Gentiles to worship someone crucified by Rome; they said it was "foolishness." This may be why, in First Thessalonians, he accused "the Jews" of having killed Jesus. However, he never did so more than that once as far as we know, so perhaps that argument hadn't worked for him.[16]

The evangelists saw it differently. They had evidently decided that if they could blame the Jews for the crucifixion, they could turn Jesus from a crucified criminal into an innocent victim of Jewish malice and manipulation. It would be anything but "foolishness" to believe in him. The gospels increasingly portrayed Pontius Pilate, the remorseless Roman governor, as a helpless pawn in the face of Jewish insistence that Jesus had to die. Mark and Matthew each wrote that Pilate understood that the Jews were jealous of Jesus for being the messiah and the "king of the Jews." Luke had Pilate send Jesus to Herod Antipas for judgment. (Antipas sent him back.) John's Pilate would have released Jesus, but he was afraid of the priests and the crowd—though this was the same Pilate who had once slaughtered a large crowd of Jews for protesting his seizure of Temple funds.[17] This was also the same Pilate who would eventually be recalled to Rome in 36 or 37 CE for the murder of some Samaritans, brutality that went too far even by Roman standards.[18]

Shifting the blame to the Jews solved another problem the movement was having with the Gentiles. Why, the Gentiles wondered, should they believe in Jesus when his own people didn't? Toward the end of the second century, the pagan philosopher Celsus would put it this way: "What God that appeared among men is received with incredulity, and that, too, when appearing to those who expect him? or why, pray, is he not recognized by those who have been long looking for him?"[19] The Christians' answer was that the Jews had indeed recognized Jesus—but they had rejected him. The Jews were so stubborn, said the evangelists and Church Fathers, that even after God had let his own Temple be destroyed—just as Jesus had said would happen—they still refused to admit that they were wrong and Jesus was right.

Hate can be more satisfying than indifference. I suggest that yet another reason for the vilification of the Jews can be found in Elie Wiesel's famous observation that the opposite of love is not hate but indifference. Except for a fraction of a percent, all those Jews who heard the message of Jesus's followers thought it was simply not credible. It just made no sense, and Jews couldn't be bothered with it. Anyway, as long as the Jewish followers of Jesus behaved according to Jewish law and didn't get the Jews in trouble with Rome, they could believe almost anything they liked (and Jews didn't care what the Gentiles believed).

It is a perverse truism that people would rather be hated than ignored. Persecution, whether real or imagined or misunderstood, can be seen as proof that one is right, an attitude that showed up even at the beginning of Christianity. The last of Matthew's beatitudes promised that those "who are persecuted for righteousness' sake" will be rewarded in heaven. The First Letter of Peter reassured its readers that "if you are reviled for the name of Christ, you are blessed."[20] Being hated meant you were doing or saying something meaningful enough, powerful enough, dangerous enough that others, especially the Powers That Be, were afraid of you. Rome was the Power That Was, of course, but the Jesus Movement wanted to recruit in the Roman world. Jews were an easier target. When Gentiles wanted to know why Jesus's own people didn't believe in him, Christians would explain that it was because they were perverse and wrong-headed, even that they were, as John's Jesus called them, children of the devil.

THE PEACE OF THE GODS

There was one situation where Jewish authorities could not afford to remain indifferent to what the Jewish followers of Jesus were doing. This was when Paul and others used the Diaspora synagogues to preach Jesus to the Gentiles.

In order to see why this was such a problem, we have to understand the role of gods in the Roman world. The function of these gods was to ensure the stability of the state, victory in war, peace and tranquility at home. In return, the gods expected the people to pay them homage. "Much of the life of the polis [city] pulsed around public displays of respect to these gods. This was simple prudence: gods superintended the well-being of their cities."[21] This arrangement was known as the *pax deorum*, the peace of the gods.[22]

Rome associated religion with ethnicity: your gods were the gods of your ancestors, and you owed them the same duty your ancestors had. Rome also wanted the gods of the Roman state to be honored as well. This posed a problem for the Jews, for whom sacrifice to any god other than Yahweh was idolatry, the gravest of sins. The Romans thought this idea was peculiar, to say the least. However, they also respected the antiquity of Jewish belief, and granted the Jews an exemption from the requirement to sacrifice to the state gods. At the same time, Jews were cautioned not to show contempt for anyone else's religion.[23]

Jews sometimes went to watch local ceremonies for the gods of the city out of courtesy to their neighbors, or at least to avoid antagonizing them.[24] They also welcomed into their homes and synagogues pagan Gentiles, known as Godfearers, who were attracted to some aspects of Judaism.[25] These Godfearers rarely became full Jews—and thus subject to the Jews' laws against worshiping other gods—and the Jews wouldn't ask them to do so, as that would endanger their exemption.

But Paul and other missionaries did ask. Paul would stand up in a synagogue, knowing there were Gentiles there, and say: "'You Israelites, and others who fear God, listen.'"[26] He would tell everyone there they needed to accept Jesus in order to be saved. But he had an additional message just for the Gentiles: "What pagans sacrifice, they sacrifice to demons and not to God... You cannot drink the cup of the Lord and the cup of demons." (By "demon," Paul meant a lesser divine being not worthy of worship, not an evil creature as we use the word today.)[27] In saying this, Paul was telling these Gentiles not to honor the *pax deorum*. But breaking the *pax deorum* was a "species of treason" against the state.[28] Paul was putting the city at the risk of angering their gods. When he did this inside the synagogue, he also put the Jews at risk as well.[29] And he was violating the agreement not to show contempt for another's religion.

Both Jewish and Roman authorities took action. When Paul complained (or boasted) that the Jews punished him five times with the 39 lashes, and also that he was beaten with the rod—a Roman discipline—three times, it was almost certainly because his behavior was putting the city and the synagogue in danger.[30] Naturally, Paul saw it differently. To him, the Jews "displease God and oppose everyone by hindering us from speaking to the Gentiles so that they may be saved."[31]

EARLY CHRISTIANS, ROMANS, AND JEWS

The Jesus Movement—which, let's remember, is just a modern scholars' term for the first generations of Jesus believers—morphed into Christianity sometime late in the first century. This is when we first see "Christians" in common use. Earlier uses of the term are very rare and may be anachronistic. There are a couple of mentions in the book of Acts and Josephus's *Antiquities*, both of which date to around 90–95 CE, and in 115 CE Tacitus accused Nero of having used Christians as scapegoats for the fire in Rome back in 64.[32]

It was around that same time that Roman emperors first began to be aware of Christians as different from Jews. (Nero might be the exception.) In 96 CE, the Emperor Nerva decreed that the followers of Jesus, even if they were ethnic Jews, would no longer be subject to the *fiscus Judaicus*, the humiliating tax imposed on all Jews in the empire as a penalty for the Judaean revolt against Rome in 66–73 CE.[33] By 112 CE, the emperor

Trajan knew enough about Christians to advise Pliny the Younger, a governor in Asia Minor, on dealing with complaints that Christians would not pay homage to the gods of the state, thus endangering the *pax deorum*. They also refused to buy sacrificial meat (which cut into butchers' income) and were disturbing the populace with their strange ways. Trajan's brief reply said that Pliny was right to execute them if they persisted. However, Trajan also advised Pliny to be careful not to seek Christians out, and not to pay any attention to anonymous accusations.[34]

As is often the case in human affairs, the people on the opposite sides of an action view that same action differently. Roman authorities wanted to keep the locals at peace and the gods satisfied, and many of them just wanted Christians to go away.[35] Christians, on the other hand, were convinced they were being persecuted for their faith. Some even welcomed it—they would suffer as Jesus had suffered and their martyrdom would ensure them a higher place in heaven. Around 212 CE, the early Church Father Tertullian told the Roman proconsul of Africa that Christians would not be deterred by persecution. "Your cruelty is our glory," he proclaimed. "We have no dread of them [persecutions], but on the contrary, even invite their infliction." He described how a Roman governor, Arrius Antoninus, was once confronted by a large crowd of Christians. After he had a few of them executed, the rest demanded that he execute them too. The exasperated Arrius refused, telling them to go hang themselves or jump off a cliff if they wanted to die that badly.[36]

In turns out that Christians, whether they were afraid of martyrdom or welcomed it, rarely suffered it. Martin Goodman concludes that "in practice, most Christians lived quite peacefully for the first three centuries of the Church."[37] Around 247 CE, the Church Father Origen acknowledged this. "For in order to remind others, that by seeing a *few* engaged in a struggle for their religion, they also might be better fitted to despise death, some, on special occasions, and these individuals who [sic] can be easily numbered, have endured death for the sake of Christianity."[38] Shortly after he wrote this, however, there were empire-wide attacks on Christians by the emperors Decius in 249–51 and Valerian in 257–60, although each of them may have had political rather than theological motives, including Christians' refusal to honor the *pax deorum*.[39] Then in 303, Diocletian launched the "Great Persecution," which accounted for perhaps half of all martyrdoms. Diocletian's orders included destroying all churches and confiscating all Christian sacred texts; later orders called for the arrest of all their clergy. Ehrman describes it as "a state–sponsored attempt to wipe out the Christian church."[40] However, enforcement of Diocletian's decrees appears to have ceased around 306 in the western empire, while it continued sporadically in the east until 313.[41] In that year, Emperor Constantine issued his edict of toleration for Christianity and Christians.

CHRISTIANS IN POWER

The earliest Christian congregations were makeshift operations, understandable since they expected that any day now their world would end and God would take over. By the end of the first century, however, it was no longer practical to wait for an ending that showed no signs of happening. Communities became more organized, choosing bishops to govern them. Soon after that, councils of bishops began to meet to settle issues of doctrine, faith, policy, administration, discipline. Christians were no longer just members of churches; now they were the Church.

Constantine's recognition of Christianity did more than put an end to the persecutions. It started the process by which the Church began to acquire secular power, which accelerated after Theodosius declared Christianity the official state religion of the empire in 380. The mere continued existence of the Jews none-theless remained a threat to Christianity, because they *still* refused to admit that they had lost and the Church had won. Church leaders also worried about what they called *Judaization*. Newly converted Christians, not understanding the theological chasm between Christianity and Judaism, might see nothing wrong with making friends with Jews and celebrating festivals with them. Doing this exposed them to Jewish errors and threatened their newfound salvation. It was one of the reasons why, in 325, the Council of Nicaea mandated that Easter be cele-brated on a different date than Passover—to stop this socializ-ing.[42] Many church leaders delivered sermons warning against contact with the Jews, a body of work that has come to be known as *Adversus Judaeos* (Against the Jews; *Kata Ioudaiōn* in Greek), partly because John Chrysostom used it as the title of several of his homilies.

Around 387 CE, Chrysostom, then a presbyter—a category of priest—delivered a series of sermons in Antioch unmatched in the venom and vitriol they unloaded on the Jews. Just in one homily, he called the Jews "wretched and miserable," "dogs," and compared them to "animals...unfit for work...marked for slaughter." He accused the Jews of being greedy, of being thieves and robbers, of abandoning the poor, of making "shady deals." The synagogue was a theater, a brothel, a den of thieves and animals, a dwelling place of demons. In one particularly revealing passage, he declared that "if theirs [i.e., their ways] are hallowed and mighty, ours are false." Chrysostom was preaching all this, he explained, because there were "loyal Christians...accustomed to attend the places where the [Jewish] festivals are held... This wicked practice I now desire to expel from the church."[43] If these phrases sound familiar, that is because we hear them in the later rantings of Martin Luther and the Nazis, among many others.[44] Regardless of Chrysostom's intentions, for centuries his words would be klaxons summoning massacres and pogroms.

A saving grace of sorts came early in the fifth century from Bishop Augustine of Hippo (near modern Tunis), one of the most influential theologians in all of Christian history. He declared that God had exiled the Jews from their land and scattered them around the world both as punishment for having killed Jesus and as eternal witnesses to the triumph of Christianity. Because of this, Christians were to tolerate their presence among them.[45] Scholars call this formulation Augustine's "witness doctrine."

The witness doctrine describes the attitude of the Catholic Church, or at least its official attitude, until recent times. But even in the Middle Ages it showed signs of weakening. In the twelfth century, Bernard of Clairvaux "declared, following the witness theory, that though one must not kill the Jews, it might be permitted to plunder their property and cancel debts owed to them."[46] In 1555, Pope Paul IV, incensed that the "insolent" Jews in the Papal States persisted in remaining Jews and even making a decent living, ordered them to be forced into ghettos, forbade them from associating in any way with Christians, and barred them from every trade except "rag–picking."[47]

If the first Protestants did pay any heed to Augustine's doctrine of tolerating the Jews, that tolerance didn't last long. Early in his career, Martin Luther expected his version of Christianity to win over the Jews who, in his view, had rightly rejected Catholicism. He penned *That Jesus Christ Was Born a Jew* in 1523 with that goal in mind.[48] Twenty years later, however, Luther concluded that the "Jews were [still] refusing to fulfil their appointed destiny in the end-time by converting to Christianity."[49] He published *On the Jews and Their Lies* in 1543, accusing the Jews of being vile and rancorous, of committing every possible depravity. He urged the civil authorities to burn their synagogues, destroy their houses, take away their prayer-books and the Talmud, forbid their rabbis to teach on penalty of death, refuse them safe-conduct on the roads, make them work as farmhands, and, if necessary, expel them.[50] It seems that Luther was no more able than Paul IV would be to deal with the reality that the Jews were just not interested in Jesus.

THE MODERN NATION-STATE AND THE JEWS

From the sixteenth through the eighteenth centuries, Europe underwent a series of religious and philosophical upheavals. The Protestant Reformation, the Renaissance, the wars of religion, the scientific revolution, the French Revolution, and the Enlightenment all served to widen the separation of modern nation-states from the authority of religion. This led to a growing toleration of Jews, if only for practical reasons. It was gradual and inconsistent—"grudging" is how one scholar describes France's grant of emancipation to the Jews in 1791.[51] The nineteenth century also witnessed the growth of anti-Semitism: hatred of Jews on the basis of race rather than (just) religion. In some ways, this made things worse, since Jews could not escape anti-Semitism by converting to Christianity. Also, truly secular states cannot by definition be anti-Jewish, but they can be anti-Semitic. Anti-Semitism led to atrocities from the Dreyfus Affair to the Holocaust, and once again it is on the rise.

From the beginning, Christians have insisted that Jews have to accept Jesus, and even today there are many Christians who haven't been able to let that go. Christians have tried to cope with Jewish indifference by bribery, torture, staged disputes, confinements, degradations, expulsions, massacres, exterminations. There are Protestant evangelicals whose support of the modern state of Israel is based on an apocalyptic fantasy that Jesus's return will be preceded by Israel's establishment—and by its subsequent destruction, to be followed by the conversion of the remaining Jews to Christianity (see chapter 8). In 1965, the Catholic Church at the Second Vatican Council issued *Nostra Aetate*, which officially absolved Jews of continued blame for the crucifixion and rejected all forms of persecution against Jews or anyone. Yet in the same breath it expressed its full confidence that on "that day, known to God alone," everyone, Jews included, would "address the Lord in a single voice"—presumably meaning a Christian voice.[52] A Vatican statement on relations between Christians and Jews issued in 2015 agreed that, "while there is a principled rejection of an institutional Jewish mission, Christians are nonetheless called to bear witness to their faith in Jesus Christ also to Jews, although they should do so in a humble and sensitive manner, acknowledging that Jews are bearers of God's Word, and particularly in view of the great tragedy of the [Holocaust]."[53] Adam Gregerman, a scholar of Christian–Jewish relations, comments that the authors of the 2015 document admit that God's covenant with the Jews is still valid. Even so, Gregerman writes, they argue that Catholics should keep trying to persuade Jews to accept the "new covenant" with Jesus because the old covenant was incomplete and exclusive to the Jews. God had always intended to make a "superior" one which makes Jewish ideas of one god and the hope of a messiah universal. Jews should convert "not because it is necessary ...but because there is something to be gained" from doing so.[54]

I suppose it's a waste of time to say that these continuing efforts to convert Jews are a waste of time. Still, consider that for over a thousand years the Church in Europe had tremendous secular power and used all of it to pressure the Jews into giving up, and yet by and large it didn't work. Jews are simply not interested in Jesus, period. Besides, we live in a pluralistic world now, and the only way to keep peace in that world is to accept that everyone is entitled to find their own way to heaven, hell, reincarnation, or oblivion.

THE IMPACT ON THE WORLD

Let me close this chapter with a few comments on some themes Christians developed in these early formative years in order to cope with difficulties both the Jews and the Romans were making for them. Among the ones that I see as having the most impact on the world are: universalism, intolerance of dissent, a persecution complex, judgment after death, and demonization. These were techniques that Jews had used to varying degrees to help them cope with the indignities and disasters that had befallen them over the centuries, which Christians then appropriated and expanded upon for their own purposes. They will recur throughout the rest of this book.

Universalism. By this I mean the conviction that a specific belief is universal and that it is, or ought to be, held by all humanity. By Second Temple times, Jews hoped that all the world would someday acknowledge the god of Israel as the one universal god. However, they didn't expect it to happen at any particular time. The Jews of the Jesus Movement took this future universalist expectation and insisted that everyone had to believe *right now* that Jesus was the universal savior. More than that, they insisted that the only way for anyone on earth to be saved for heaven was to accept that belief. If you are convinced that one's beliefs on earth determine one's eternal future in the afterlife, and you are also convinced that you know the one and only true belief that will ensure that eternity, you have an obligation to get everyone else to believe as you do. This leads to more than simple proselytizing. It allows, even commands, you to do whatever you can to make everyone see the truth as you see it.

Intolerance of dissent. For Christians, getting everyone to see the truth goes beyond telling them about it. It also requires suppressing all differing ideas about salvation lest they tempt people away from the truth. This involves more than warning against Judaization and wiping out all other religions except Christianity. It also means wiping out all other variations of Christianity. It is not enough to believe in Jesus; one has to believe the *right* way. Even getting the details wrong could get one condemned to hell. The medieval Inquisition sent thousands of believing Christians to the stake for thoughts it deemed heretical. Catholics and Protestants almost destroyed Europe when they went to war over which of them knew the right way to get to heaven.

This intolerance also applies to any challenge to the Word of the omniscient God as written in his Holy Bible. The testimony of the Lord is perfect, and to question that testimony is heresy. The Catholic Church burned Giordano Bruno at the stake in 1600, and confined Galileo to house arrest for life in 1633, for saying that the earth went around the sun, in contradiction to the book of Joshua. For the past century, Protestant fundamentalists in the US have campaigned to ban the teaching of evolution because it contradicts the creation stories in Genesis.

Persecution complex. Jews suffered under Antiochus and the Romans, and the belief that persecution was a test of their faith helped them to endure it. Early Christians rarely experienced persecution to the same degree, but part of the Christian mythology is that early believers were constantly being persecuted for their belief, starting with Jesus himself. Tales of martyrs were enormously popular among early Christians and inspired them in their faith. Today some Christians cry "persecution" when they want to turn a political argument into a religious one. A few years ago, when England was considering whether to allow same-sex marriage, the Catholic Online website posted a warning with the headline "Gay marriage could result in largest persecution of Catholics since Reformation."[55] In trying to cope with the Covid-19 pandemic, various health authorities in 2020 restricted the number of people who could gather in public, including at houses of worship. Many religious groups, including some very conservative ones, complied with the rules,[56] but others invoked the persecution complex. Michael Youssef, a televangelist and the senior pastor of the Church of the Apostles in Atlanta (Georgia), said in an interview that "I think we are only seeing the beginning of the unfair treatment and persecution that lies ahead for the church."[57] When sociologist Robin Veldman was studying evangelical attitudes to global climate change recently, many of her interviewees used "persecution" to describe their feelings about the teaching of evolution, the separation of church and state, even their reaction to a pro-life television commercial. Veldman argues that this feeling of being persecuted, this "sense of embattlement with secular culture," is one of the reasons why many evangelicals are skeptical of climate change.[58]

Judgment after death. Jews in Second Temple times had developed the concept of divine judgment after death as a way of explaining how it was that the righteous suffered in life while evil prospered. Hell exists in Jewish thinking, though it plays only a small, ill-defined role. The Jesus Movement built on the Jews' idea of judgment after death to argue that life on earth is meaningful *only* in determining what will happen to them after death. "Those who love their life lose it, and those who hate their life in this world will keep it for eternal life," said Jesus in the gospel of John.[59] ("Hate," in this context, probably means to be disinterested in, to disregard.[60]) Also, because the risk of missing out on heaven was so great, Christians early on developed an obsessive fascination with hell. The threat of hell was one of the main tools the medieval Catholic Church used to hold on to power, and is still useful to fundamentalists today.

Demonization. This is a defense mechanism against any challenges to the precepts listed above. Those who challenge the universal truth, who hold heretical views, those for whom hell holds neither fear nor fascination, are not just dissenters but are children of the devil. They are not fully human because they do not accept the truth. They are not the equals of the true believers, and they are entitled to neither dignity nor respect. At times, they can even be killed with impunity.

None of these is unique to Christianity except in the details. They are each of them classic human weaknesses. The Jews used them to help them cope with the powerless position they were in throughout much of their history. Christians copied and expanded on them for much the same reason. But then they continued to use them once they were in power. Even more consequential was their insistence that these techniques have been sanctioned by God himself, who is omniscient and omnipotent, who can do no wrong, who must be obeyed on pain of eternal damnation. God has revealed the one and only universal truth and commanded his true believers to make the rest of the world believe it by any means necessary.

Europe at the end of the first millennium was a time and place where Christianity had largely eliminated all competition. Only the Jews were left, humbled witnesses to the Church's eternal triumph. But in the history of the human race, no eternal triumph has ever lasted long. Pressure from the new religion of Islam, exposure to the cultures of the Orient, the stubborn resistance of the Jews, the fracturing of the universal Catholic Church into Orthodox, Protestant, and other branches, and especially the persistence of reality and doubt, all set the stage for our modern pluralistic world—as the following chapters will explore.

CHAPTER FIVE

GOD BETWEEN THE SHEETS

S ex is wonderful, powerful, terrifying. Sexual desire is one of the primal human drives, paradoxically demanding that we surrender to it while simultaneously insisting that we can master it. No functioning society can permit unrestrained sexual activity, as that leads to anarchy, jealousy, fear, chaos, violence, and war—think of Helen of Troy. All societies therefore set limitations on human sexual activity for the sake of peace and security, limitations that are based on their views about sex. The issue that I want to explore in this chapter is what happens when a religion stipulates that the way we dealt with sex at some particular moment long ago is the only legitimate way to deal with sex for all time.

SEX IN THE SCRIPTURE

The ancient Israelites had a patriarchal but still an overall positive attitude toward sexual activity. They were also quite comfortable with the idea that sexual activity was not limited to reproduction. Even the dour author of Ecclesiastes advised his readers to "enjoy life with a woman whom you love all your days of mere breath that have been given to you under the sun."[1] It was not unusual for an Israelite man to have a concubine—a woman whose relationship with a man was for the specific purpose of providing him with sexual pleasure. A rabbinic commentary on Abraham's concubines doesn't mince words: "Read the word *pilegesh* [concubine] as *peleg ishah* [partial wife]: that is to say, for sexual services and not for procreation."[2] When King David was old and bedridden, his ministers found him a beautiful young virgin, Abishag, whom they hoped would rekindle the king's interest in sex—she would "heat up my lord the king." (She tried, but it didn't work—"the king did not 'know' her.")[3] Though concubinage does not appear to have been practiced much in the Second Temple era, it is not clear that it was ever actually forbidden in Jewish law until modern times.[4]

The patriarchal attitude displayed here doesn't mean that women's sexual desires were always ignored. The Biblical Song of Songs celebrates the woman's sexuality as much as the man's. Joel Hoffman, a Biblical scholar and translator, emphasizes that "the Bible's only full-length examination of sexual relationships hits the reader over the head with the equality of the man and the woman," while the Blochs, in the introduction to their translation of the Song, say that "its theme is the wonder of a woman with a man...with...no motive but pleasure."[5] Indeed, it is so erotic and so openly sexual that one has to wonder how it managed to be left in the Scripture when it contains verses such as: "A sachet of myrrh is my lover to me, all night between my breasts" and "Let my lover come to his garden / And eat its luscious fruit."[6] Biblical scholar and pastor Jennifer Knust singles out that last verse in particular as "a frank invitation to sexual intercourse" in a book that "celebrates pleasure for pleasure's sake." The author "rejects the view that men can or should control women" and "displays no interest whatsoever in defending marriage as the only appropriate setting for love." The woman's brothers and the watchmen of the city tried —and failed—to separate the couple, which they would only have done if the lovers weren't married to each other.[7] So powerful and so physically sexual is the Song of Songs that many Jewish and Christian interpreters have tried to turn it into a spiritual allegory of love between God and Israel or between Jesus and the Church. One has to admire their ability to keep a straight face while insisting that lines such as these are spiritual allegories: "his loins are fine-wrought ivory"; "the curves of your thighs like wrought rings"; and "I am a wall / and my breasts are like towers." The medieval Jewish commentator Rashi rationalized "my breasts" in that last verse as the "prayer halls and study halls that breastfeed Israel with words of Torah." The modern translator Robert Alter, however, sees this as the speech of a "sexually mature woman with palpably prominent breasts of which she is proud."[8]

Even so, early in the Common Era the Talmud would recommend a schedule of sexual activity within marriage based on the man's occupation—generally once a week at a minimum. (For the unemployed, it was every night.) The rabbis would also agree that while a wife could refuse her husband, he could not refuse her.[9]

SEX AMONG THE ESSENES

Sometime in the second or first century BCE, a new sect arose among the Jews: the Essenes. There were never many of them, perhaps because they practiced an extreme asceticism—renunciation of physical pleasure. The Essenes who settled at Qumran near the Dead Sea restricted sexual activity to married persons and for the purpose of procreation only. While the wife was pregnant or once she had passed menopause, the couple was forbidden to have sex. If they did, they were expelled from the community.[10] Writers such as Josephus, Philo, and Pliny the

Elder thought that the leaders of the Essenes were total celibates, though whether that was really so is not known for certain. Josephus wrote of them: "these Essenes reject pleasures as an evil" and generally avoid marriage, thinking women lascivious.[11] He might have added that lifelong asceticism in general and celibacy in particular were to be found nowhere else in Jewish law, custom, history, or tradition.

HISTORICAL CHRISTIAN ATTITUDES TOWARD SEX

The first followers of Jesus, living in Judaea, might well have known about the Essenes. The apostle Paul probably did not, as he was from Greek Asia Minor. But he would have read the Stoic philosophers of the first century CE and been influenced by Stoic asceticism. These Stoics were nowhere near as extreme as the Essene community at Qumran, though some of them did suggest that marriage was not for everyone. Paul went further: he preferred that everyone be celibate. Still, he did accept that not all were capable of it. He advised the Corinthians that if a man "thinks that he is not behaving properly toward his fiancée, if his passions are strong, and so it has to be, let him marry as he wishes; it is no sin." He even acknowledged that some of "the other apostles and the brothers of the Lord and [Peter]" were married.[12]

The evangelists who wrote the four gospels came much closer to the Qumran view that having sex even within marriage could sometimes make one morally impure. A direct link between the Essenes and the Jesus Movement is still a matter of speculation, but the parallels are intriguing. Matthew's Jesus made a strong pitch for avoiding sex: There were eunuchs who were born so or who had been made so, "and there are eunuchs who have made themselves eunuchs for the sake of the kingdom of heaven. Let anyone accept this who can." (He probably meant celibacy, not literal castration.) A few chapters later in Matthew,

Jesus asserted that there would be no sex in the afterlife: "For in the resurrection they neither marry nor are given in marriage, but are like angels in heaven."[13]

As always when reading the New Testament, we have to keep in mind that its writers were expecting the end of the existing world and the coming of the kingdom of God to occur at any moment. This expectation could help explain why Paul and Jesus were opposed to divorce, an antagonism not found in Jewish or Roman law. It fit their general attitude toward sex and marriage: there was no point in getting married and having children, as this was to be the last generation, and all marriages will end soon anyway.

It was not, however, a practical attitude to take in a world that stubbornly refused to end. As the Jesus Movement morphed into Christianity, the early Church Fathers needed to construct a theology that kept Christianity going—but at the same time they couldn't contradict texts that were even then becoming canonized. Debates over the role and proper use of sexuality occupied the Church Fathers for the next few centuries, with celibacy generally being the most favored option. Late in the second century, Clement of Alexandria advised that a man should try to conceive without desire, or any passion at all, in full control of his will.[14] Even this put him at odds with some other early Church Fathers, who believed that "only by rejecting marital intercourse and procreation could people be restored to their original, spiritual condition intended by God the Creator."[15] The *Apocalypse of Paul*, a very popular tract probably written around the fourth century, assigned lifetime virgins a higher place in heaven than married couples who had kept their vows. On the other hand, those who had premarital sex would end up in hell bound with red-hot chains.[16]

Early in the fifth century, Bishop Augustine of Hippo formulated a concept of sex that even today remains central to Catholic doctrine: sex is the mechanism through which everyone inherits Adam's "originating original sin"—the "primal" sin, as Augustinian scholar Jesse Couenhoven calls it.[17] In brief, when God created Adam and Eve, he intended that "the marriage of the first human beings, which was worthy of the delight of paradise, would have produced children to love, but without any lust to be ashamed of."[18] But then Adam and Eve ate the forbidden fruit of the tree of knowledge. This disobedience was the primal sin, and one that was "neither necessary nor reasonable, but perverse," even "inexplicable," to Augustine.[19] It was disobedience to God, and from then on their genitals would disobey them, as it were. Sexual arousal now occurs, or fails to occur, without regard to a person's will. Arousal leads to lust, and lust overcomes the will.[20] Everyone born since Adam's primal sin is conceived in lust, and inherits Adam's sin through that very act of conception. Our *origin* is in sin; hence we are born with an "original sin." Augustine held that every child born of lust (which he called "concupiscence") was "bound by original sin," and the only way to be unbound from that sin was to be "reborn" through baptism in the only person who had ever been conceived without lust—Jesus.[21] Original sin transmits through the father; Jesus's father was God and his mother was a virgin. Augustine did acknowledge that one of the values of marriage was that it was the only legitimate way to relieve the pressures of lust for those who "lack the self-control for celibacy."[22] But this just highlighted the problem that even the children of a legitimate marriage can only be conceived in lust.

Augustine's thinking about sex was nuanced and complex, and it changed from time to time.[23] It also took a while for the Catholic Church to turn his and other theologians' ideas into its official doctrine that yielding to sexual desire, even in marriage, is a sin, and is only to be allowed, reluctantly, as long as there is the possibility of engendering offspring. Though the Vatican has lately modified its stance, Augustine's thinking still permeates the Catholic approach to human sexuality. In 1950, Pius XII allowed a limited study of evolution, but only to the extent that it didn't challenge the story of Adam as the single point of origin of modern man. This prohibition was needed in order to preserve the doctrine of "original sin, which proceeds from a sin actually committed by an individual Adam and which, through generation, is passed on to all and is in everyone as his own." (When Pope Francis spoke about evolution in 2015, he did not address the problem that had troubled Pius.)[24]

Early in the sixteenth century, Martin Luther broke away from the Catholic Church and started the Protestant Reformation. His many objections to Catholic doctrine and practice included some about sex. Luther denounced celibacy, approved of marital sex for pleasure, and allowed divorce and remarriage. He did agree with Augustine that marriage is for the production of offspring and that it requires faithfulness, but he rejected the idea that it was a holy sacrament (Catholic doctrine since around 1215). Instead, he restored marriage to its prior status under Roman and Jewish law as a civil contract.[25]

But Luther still insisted that the primary (if no longer the only) legitimate function of sex remained reproduction, and only within marriage. Sexual pleasure purely for its own sake was too much for him. Similarly, John Calvin, an enormously influential Protestant thinker and younger contemporary of Luther, asserted that the "purity" demanded of the Israelites in the Bible "had to do mainly with sex. Religiously approved sexual behavior was pure... Whence it follows, according to Calvin, that the company of man and woman outside marriage is accursed."[26] Luther, Calvin, and other Protestants could not break away entirely from "the traditional Catholic view on [sic] the human being." Protestants "could condemn monasticism and criticize extreme asceticism as unbiblical, but they were theologically barred from turning the opposite—sexual desire— into a virtue."[27] Indeed, the Puritans of the seventeenth century differed from the Catholic ascetics only in degree; they rejected clerical celibacy, but permitted sex only within marriage and then only with the intention of procreation.[28]

Yet neither Catholic nor Protestant preaching, moralizing, inquisitional tortures, excommunications, threats of damnation, or even executions managed to make their congregants completely conform to Christian limitations on sex. The French kings of the medieval period were so fond of mistresses that young women would vie for the position; Madame de Pompadour was only the most famous and powerful one. King Louis XIII of France preferred male lovers, but the main concern of his chief adviser, Cardinal Richelieu, "was that his lovers be politically innocuous."[29] The medieval Church frequently tolerated prostitution and brothels, the rationale being that, if men are going to have sex for pleasure anyway, it is better than they do so with fallen women rather than corrupt their wives. In her study of medieval prostitution in York, England, Adele Sykes describes how the church authorities in the 1460s looked the other way as a woman named Margaret Clay did business as "pimp, procuress and brothel-keeper."[30] In what was probably his earliest essay, Augustine had reluctantly conceded that prostitution served a necessary function, as otherwise men would turn to their wives for lustful rather than procreative reasons. "Remove prostitutes from the social order, however, and lust will destroy it."[31] The greatest of the medieval theologians, Thomas Aquinas, cited this passage as his authority for allowing lesser evils in order to avoid a greater one. (This is not at all to say that either he or Augustine approved of it.)[32] Early Protestants were stricter, or just more stubborn, on this topic. "Martin Luther...rejected the tacit acceptance of prostitution,"[33] though his opposition does not appear to have had a lasting impact. Since Luther permitted divorce and remarriage, and did not require marital relations to only be intended for procreation, he may have thought that Augustine's rationale for prostitution no longer applied.

In at least one instance, Luther condoned bigamy. He allowed himself to be pressured to find Biblical justification for the bigamous marriage of Landgrave Philip of Hesse, one of his most powerful supporters, who for political reasons was unwilling to divorce his first wife. Luther insisted that his "ad hoc advice" must remain confidential, but Philip's open celebration of his new marriage in 1540 made that a vain request. Luther's reputation was permanently damaged. Meanwhile, Philip had three more children by his first wife as well as seven sons by his second.[34]

We also have some knowledge from church records and other sources of how ordinary people managed to have sex in spite of religious disapproval. "In Concord, Massachusetts, a bastion of Puritan tradition, one-third of all children born during the twenty years prior to the American Revolution were conceived out of wedlock."[35] Premarital intercourse was sometimes an acceptable practice in the early modern era as a way to determine "a couple's sexual compatibility." It was the custom in some parts of Germany for a courting couple to spend some "welcome nights" together under chaperonage. If that showed promise, they would then have some "trial nights" together alone. If it didn't work out—and if no pregnancy resulted—the couple was free to part and seek other possible marriage partners.[36] In sociologist Stephanie Coontz's view, the "straitlaced sexual morality" of England and the United States in the late nineteenth century and again in the 1950s "seems to have been a historical and cultural aberration."[37]

RELIGIOUS IMPACT ON SEX TODAY

It's clear that reality has a habit of refusing to conform to religion. This causes theological problems for those religions who maintain that their members are only following instructions from the creator of reality. Reality would not particularly care, were it not that these religions want to compel reality to obey what they claim is God's will. "As a Family Research Council official put it, 'the truths of Scripture regarding human sexuality are not malleable.'"[38] Call it a case of irresistible force meets immovable object—with the caveat that the modern age is more accepting of the irresistible force of human sexual reality and finds religion quite movable indeed.

Let's examine, in the light of this enlightenment, some of the areas where the immovable object has lately moved, so to speak: repression of sexual knowledge, clerical sex abuse, abortion, birth control, and same-sex relations.

Repression of sexual knowledge. The 1950s—Coontz's "historical and cultural aberration"—was a time of significant sexual repression in the United States. Sex did not stop, of course; it just went underground. The Kinsey Reports on male (1948) and female (1953) sexuality revealed just how many ordinary people were quite sexually adventurous in bed. Kinsey showed "that healthy sex led to healthy marriage," that both men and women were having extramarital sex, and that masturbation, petting, premarital sex, and homosexuality were all far more common than was generally admitted—and he refused to condemn any of it.[39] David Halberstam, a preeminent historian of postwar America, describes Kinsey as "the man who had more than anyone else pointed out the hypocrisy in daily American life, the differences between what Americans said about sex and what they actually did."[40]

Religious authorities, not all of them conservative, reacted with outrage. Evangelist Billy Graham, who warned that Kinsey's revelations of how Americans were actually having sex would further damage "the already deteriorating morals of America," was only one of the many religious figures who denounced the Kinsey Reports.[41] Despite their condemnations,

Kinsey's studies, along with improved birth control, even magazines such as *Playboy*, broke the mid-century code of silence and exposed the damage this silence was doing. Masters and Johnson documented in 1970 how repressive teachings by Catholic and fundamentalist Protestant Christians, as well as by Orthodox Jews, were among the prime causes of sexual unhappiness within marriages. They bluntly assessed the impact of their subjects' "orthodox religious negation of an honorable role for sexual function" and the religious suppression of "objectively meaningful material of sexual content" as having a "derogatory affect [sic] upon the total personality."[42] They described in some detail the impact of religious repression on one of the many married couples they interviewed in these words: "Trained by theological demand to uninformed immaturity in matters of sexual connotation, both marital partners had no concept of how to cope when their sexual dysfunction was manifest... Each partner was intimidated, frustrated, and embarrassed for lack of sexual knowledge."[43]

Reliable information about sex, including realistic sex education in schools, did become more available in late twentieth-century America, but that triggered a virulent and still growing reaction by religious conservatives determined to reverse this accommodation to reality. Yet the unrealistic abstinence-only sex education that they demand has had "no impact of any kind on rates of unintended pregnancy, STDs, and the use of condoms and other contraceptives," according to a survey of studies on this question.[44] One study reports that as many as 80% of young evangelicals engage in premarital sex and sometimes abort their unplanned pregnancies, in spite of continual pressure to maintain sexual abstinence and to reject abortions.[45] On the other hand, these programs have had a significant *negative* impact on gay and lesbian youth. A large-scale 2011 study by the University of Texas established a significant correlation between religious condemnations of homosexuality and young people harming themselves and committing suicide.[46]

In the 1990s, some evangelical Christian churches started a "purity movement," which uses shame, peer and pastoral pressure, intrusions into the public education system, and other techniques to inculcate an abstinence-only, sex-only-within-marriage mindset. They particularly target young women, who are told (as girls have been told since time immemorial) that they are responsible for the purity of the boys around them. Andrew Herrmann, a former "evangelical fundamentalist," describes how "purity culture teaches that men are never responsible [for their sexual behavior] because they are weak, 'visual creatures' that can't control themselves." From this it follows that "since women are the gatekeepers of their virginity and men are animals, sexual encounters before marriage are always the woman's fault."[47] That makes the "purity culture" a perfect petri dish for sexual abuse. Linda Kay Klein, who also grew up in that culture, reports on the psychological and physical damage it has caused. "Evangelical Christianity's sexual purity movement is traumatizing many girls and maturing women haunted by sexual and gender-based anxiety." She supports her argument with "research show[ing] that complementarianism upholds abusive dynamics among conservative, evangelical women whose religious lives are integral to their sense of identity."[48]

Complementarianism is a theological construct currently popular among some evangelicals. It asserts that *all* males and *all* females have identical separate and complementary roles assigned to them by God—an extreme example of the unjustified universalism discussed in the previous chapter. Especially as regards marriage and church, men must be dominant and women submissive. Any deviation from these divinely predetermined roles is a grave sin. Recent studies suggest that insisting on such rigid dominant and submissive roles may be encouraging physical sexual violence in addition to causing psychological damage.[49] Denial of reality doesn't change the reality; it just damages those who are trying to cope with it.

Clerical sex abuse. From the beginning, Christianity has insisted that everyone must stay celibate outside marriage. Clergy should be both unmarried and celibate, said Augustine, though prior to his time and for hundreds of years afterwards priests were often married and had families. The higher orders were not allowed to marry, but bishops lived openly with their mistresses and took care to place their "nephews" in good positions. It was only in 1073 that the Catholic Church, under Pope Gregory VII, formally outlawed priestly marriage and episcopal nepotism.[50] (Orthodox churches to this day allow conjugal rights to married priests; only the higher orders of clergy must be celibate.)

The reality nonetheless is that celibacy is unnatural for most people and its enforcement largely impractical. It took many years for Gregory's prohibitions to be effective, and their main effect was to drive priestly sex underground. We are all too familiar today with the details of sex abuse by supposedly celibate clergy, which has made the Church extremely uncomfortable and cost it the trust of the faithful, not to mention billions of US dollars in settlements.[51]

Clerical sex abuse is by no means limited to Catholic clerics. The hypocrisy of imams, rabbis, and Protestant ministers has been similarly, if sometimes less dramatically, exposed.[52] As I was finalizing this book, the Southern Baptist Convention released an extremely damning report on sexual abuse by SBC pastors and efforts by the leadership to cover it up.[53] Religions tend to confer on their officials a sanctity that tempts them into thinking they are exempt from the strictures that bind ordinary mortals. We increasingly measure a religion's virtue by how effectively it fights that temptation and punishes those who yield to it, and no religion comes off well.

Abortion. These days abortion is one of the most bitterly contested topics in the United States, but I'm not going to get into arguments over the morality of abortion here. For my purposes, the importance of the abortion debate in this country is that it shows the degree to which some religious authorities are willing to ignore political reality, economic reality, and medical and emotional reality in order to impose—by any means necessary—their objections to abortion on the rest of us.

The political reality is that six out of ten Americans have consistently accepted the idea that abortion should remain legal in all or almost all cases. In spite of all the debates and outrages and violence, very few minds have been changed, and the country is generally satisfied that abortion should remain legal for the most part. The largest groups that are most opposed to abortion are the Latter-Day Saints (Mormons) and white evangelical Protestants. Even most Catholics are willing to allow all or almost all abortions.[54] Following the Supreme Court's decision in 2022 that abortion is no longer a protected right, polls have shown that, overall, Americans are opposed to outlawing all abortions by two to one.[55]

The economic reality is that some women who seek abortions cannot afford to have a child or to have another child when they are already struggling to care for the ones they have. The medical and emotional reality is that women have abortions for many reasons, some of them overlapping. Often the pregnancy was unplanned, in many cases because of lack of access to contraceptives. It may be an ectopic or tubal pregnancy, where the fertilized egg lodges outside the uterus. Such a pregnancy can never produce a living child, and is always a serious threat to the life of the mother. Sometimes it happens that a serious or fatal fetal abnormality, such as anencephaly (absence of brain development) is discovered only late in the pregnancy. When a pregnancy results from rape or incest, the woman (or girl, in too many cases) will seek an abortion for her physical or mental health, or even to save her life.

Whether any, some, or all of these are thought to be valid reasons to have an abortion corresponds to a great extent to one's religious views. Many Protestant denominations have come to accept that abortion needs to remain legal and available, albeit with some limits. These include the Episcopal, Evangelical Lutheran, Methodist, and Presbyterian churches. Most branches of Judaism take a similar position, and while many Orthodox Jews oppose abortion in general, even they will make exceptions.[56] (Even the most stringent of the Orthodox agree that the fetus does not have a life (soul) of its own until the head emerges from the womb.[57])

Many evangelical Protestants, the Latter-Day Saints, and the Catholic clergy—though not so much the Catholic laity—remain firmly opposed to all or almost all abortions. The Catholic position in particular shows how early Christian uneasiness over sex continues to impact the world. Every sex act, they say, must be open to the possibility of procreation, the idea being that God will decide whether a pregnancy results. To abort that pregnancy is thus to reject God's decision.

The officials of the Catholic Church immediately organized in opposition to *Roe v. Wade*, the 1973 Supreme Court decision that legalized abortion in the United States. Evangelical Protestants were slower to react, most not even bothering to condemn it at first. "The overwhelming [early] response to *Roe v. Wade* on the part of evangelicals was silence, and the voices that spoke on the matter were ambivalent." Instead, they "considered abortion a 'Catholic issue.'"[58] A report by the Southern Baptist Convention a week after *Roe* was announced declared that the convention "has no official position on abortion." It noted that two years earlier, the convention had called for legislation allowing abortion in cases of rape, incest, and even "clear evidence of severe fetal deformity."[59] Conservative evangelicals had some qualms about abortion, but initially made efforts to find a middle ground.[60] Then, in 1978, the Internal Revenue Service sent a final notice to Bob Jones University, a private evangelical school, that its tax-exempt status was being revoked because of the school's racial segregation policies. Evangelicals were furious over what they saw as "government interference" in their institutions. Some of them, such as Paul Weyrich, who had been trying for years to turn conservative evangelicals and fundamentalists into a political force, saw in the Bob Jones case an opening. But as Randall Balmer, a scholar of the evangelical movement, points out, Weyrich and the others knew that a "defense of racial segregation" was not sufficient to rally their voters.[61] Weyrich admitted to Balmer in a 1990 interview that, during one of their conference calls, someone suggested using abortion. "And that is how abortion was cobbled into the political agenda of the Religious Right" is Balmer's summation.[62] This opportunistic use of abortion to restrain "government interference" in school racial policies then metastasized into a full-blown crusade *for* government interference into one of the most private and personal decisions a woman can make: whether to continue a pregnancy.

These religious groups failed to change the political reality of the United States through debate. Now they have succeeded in exploiting the flaws in our system of governance to begin outlawing abortion anyway. They could fix the economic reality of childhood poverty by offering to support the women whose abortions they want to deny, but I have seen no serious effort to do so. (As an aphorism sometimes attributed to former US Congressman Barney Frank says, they care more about what happens before birth and after death than about what happens in between.) They dismiss the emotional reality of carrying a rapist's child to term. They question the medical reality by exposing doctors to fines and long prison terms when they make a medical judgment call. They will stymie women's ability to function as full citizens, deny them autonomy over their own bodies, and cause doctors to hesitate, sometimes fatally, in providing proper medical care. They will not, however, stop abortions.

Birth control. If these religious groups were really concerned about the problems caused by bringing unwanted children into the world, they would support ensuring that such children are never conceived in the first place. That means birth control—the ability to decide for ourselves if and when to have children. But just as abortion rejects the premise that God decides whether a sex act results in pregnancy, birth control rejects God's right to decide. In the words of Paul VI, artificial contraception "frustrates [God's] design which constitutes the norm of marriage, and contradicts the will of the Author of life."[63]

When researchers and activists began promoting contraception early in the twentieth century, official Catholic reaction moved from vocal objection to calling on the forces of the law. A particularly egregious example was the police breakup of a birth control rally in New York City in November 1921 on the explicit orders of the Catholic archbishop.[64] Ironically, this blatant misappropriation of police power pushed some wavering Protestant leaders—although not the fundamentalists—into supporting birth control.[65]

Starting in the 1960s, new and effective contraceptives for women have come on the market. They all have two things in common: they put the woman in control, and their use is not connected to any one sexual encounter. In other words, the woman now has the power to decide for herself how she will deal with her sexuality, and whether and when she wants to have a child. She also has the ability to make these decisions at her convenience, which reduces the fear of pregnancy influencing her reaction to a sexual invitation.

The cost of contraceptives does pose a problem for poor women, in effect denying them that control. Many women also resent taking on the whole burden of contraception, saying it is something that men should share. There are reports that a male contraceptive pill is being developed.

In 1968, Paul VI responded with *Humanae Vitae*, which is still the Vatican's official statement on contraception. The pope commanded all Catholics to avoid any form of birth control (other than timed abstinence), because otherwise they would be going against God's eternal decree. The laity ignored him; more than that, they began avoiding Church discipline. "The disjunction between church teaching that formally defined using birth control as a sin and an overwhelming majority of couples willing to use birth control acted as a significant deterrent to confession" starting in the 1970s.[66] This attitude has only solidified in the decades since then. In 2014, following a survey conducted among Catholics worldwide, the Vatican conceded that "most Catholics reject its teachings on sex and contraception as intrusive and irrelevant."[67] According to a 2011 survey by the Guttmacher Institute, 98% of "sexually experienced Catholic women" have used artificial contraception.[68] But rather than admit that reality does not agree with Augustine and the other Church Fathers, the Catholic Church has turned to politics and the Supreme Court to try to force all Americans, Catholic or otherwise, to fall in line with its discomfort with sexual pleasure.

Protestants do not even try to speak with one voice, and their attitudes toward contraception tend to correspond, more or less, to their feelings about abortion. Some conservative Protestants, such as the Norwegian Christian People's Party, take the position that contraception is preferable to an unwanted pregnancy that could lead to an abortion. The official arm of the Conservative branch of Judaism follows the same reasoning, also conceding that trying to stop unmarried couples from getting contraceptives is "profoundly ineffective" and even counterproductive.[69] As Coontz has observed, every human society has had some form of birth control and also allows some forms of sexual activity that are not tied to procreation.[70]

Same-sex relations. Most people, most of the time, are mostly more attracted to persons of the opposite sex. But just because this is the most common attraction, that does not make it the only "natural" or "normal" one. To claim otherwise is to impose an unjustified universalism similar to insisting that there is only one route to "salvation." What is "normal" is different for different people.

Historically many, perhaps most, societies have recognized varieties of sexual attraction and response as "normal" and made a place for them. The Hittite law code forbade sex between father and son along with other incestuous couplings, but otherwise had no prohibition of same-sex relations.[71] Greek same-sex relationships centered around the warrior cult, with the older man training the younger man in love as well in hunting and war—although sex between "socially equal partners was...essentially un-Greek."[72] In India, the *Kama Sutra* recommended that same-sex relationships should follow local mores.[73] Overall, "two-thirds of the historical societies for which evidence is available have condoned homosexual relations."[74] Where this is no longer the case, it is largely the result of conservative Christian (or Muslim) influence. Hindus in India, for example, were so influenced by European Christian concerns about sex for pleasure "that they came to be thought of as elements of their own religion." Only in recent years have British-era Indian laws against homosexual relations begun to change.[75]

The reality is that people have always sought sex for pleasure, for the emotional connection, for physical release, without the intent and often without the possibility of procreation. Once this is acknowledged as a legitimate reason for sex, there is really no rational argument for legally restricting same-sex relations to any greater degree than opposite-sex relations.

A growing number of Protestant denominations in the United States have come out in support of same-sex marriage. These include the Episcopal Church, the Evangelical Lutheran Church in America, the Society of Friends, and the United Church of Christ. The Conservative, Reconstructionist, and Reform branches of Judaism all officially support same-sex marriage.[76] Conservative and fundamentalist Protestant denominations such as the American and Southern Baptists, the Methodists, and the Missouri Synod Lutherans, remain mostly in opposition. The same is largely true of Orthodox Jews, the Catholic Church, and Islam. While the Latter-Day Saints still consider same-sex relations to be against God's law, they recently announced that they support codifying the right to same-sex marriage, "preserving the rights of our LGBTQ brothers and sisters" while protecting religious freedoms.[77] The American evangelical leadership is more divided, with some groups actively welcoming civil marriage. A 2017 survey by the Public Religion Research Institute (PRRI) finds majority acceptance of same-sex marriage across the ethnic spectrum and that "even those religious groups most opposed to same-sex marriage have become more accepting of it over the last five years."[78]

One reason for this shift is that the majority of Americans now know someone in their family, their circle of coworkers and friends, sometimes even the person in the mirror, who is not practicing exclusively heterosexual sex. It is much harder to demonize someone who is up close and personal. "Having family members, friends, and people in their congregations come out as gay made the difference to evangelicals, as to other Americans."[79] Another factor is that, since the Supreme Court ruled that states cannot ban same-sex marriage, married gays and married lesbians have become more commonplace and have behaved no better and no worse than straight couples. Since the Supreme Court's ruling, support for same-sex marriage has risen steadily—up to 70% in 2021[80]—and the sky has not fallen.

On that last point: some conservatives preach that accepting same-sex marriage risks bringing down the wrath of an angry God. Evangelical preachers Pat Robertson and Jerry Falwell blamed toleration of homosexuality, as well as abortion and feminism, for the Sept. 11, 2001, attacks on the United States by Al-Qaeda—though they then had to apologize when faced with an angry backlash. Gays have also been blamed for hurricanes, for AIDS, and even for the coronavirus pandemic, with one Israeli rabbi saying that "the coronavirus was divine retribution for [Gay] Pride parades around the world."[81]

It may be pointless to argue with those who view such disasters as signs of divine approbation of their personal prejudices, but indulge me for a moment here. In March 1986 the state of Georgia argued before the US Supreme Court that it had the right to outlaw same-sex relations, and in June the Court agreed. From that March until late that same summer, Georgia suffered one of its worst droughts in its history—"truly remarkable in its severity" is how a meteorological study describes it. It got so bad that at the end of July, the governor of Georgia asked churches to pray for rain. That same day, Georgia got rain, all right—a Biblical deluge of thunderstorms, heavy hail, and hurricane-force winds.[82] On the other hand, Massachusetts, the second state to permit same-sex marriage (in 2004, after Hawai'i), did not thereafter suffer any natural disaster of Biblical or even ordinary proportions. Those who insist that God will "lock up the heavens and there will be no rain" if we continue to allow same-sex marriage have some explaining to do.

THE SECULARIZATION OF SEX

There are a number of reasons for religious resistance to the reality of sex. Marie Griffith writes of conservatives' fear that "women, nonwhites, and homosexuals and other 'nonnormative' sexual actors (the transgendered, the fluid, the flagrant) have repeatedly represented something like the enemy within, shredding the sacred fabric binding together a God-blessed nation."[83] A number of scholars have also taken on the task of examining how the Catholic Church and the religious right are each using abortion, gay marriage, transgender people, and other sexual issues to get and maintain political power.[84] "They may not succeed in making a convert of you," warns historian of religion Dag Øistein Endsjø, "but by controlling your sexual life they can make you live as if you were a believer."[85]

I suggest that there is another factor as well: they worry that reality will prove them wrong. The various contributors to the Bible were all products of the various eras in which they lived. Its texts reflect the prejudices, the limitations, the fears and hopes and desires of those authors and their times. They were also edited and redacted by others who had their own agendas. Centuries later, this work of human hands was decreed to be a sacred text whose author was the all-knowing creator of the world. The creator had given us the Bible to be our handbook telling us how to live in his creation. If the creator said he had created us "male and female" with no exceptions, then there are no exceptions. If he decreed that sex was properly reserved for procreation within marriage, who are we, mere mortals, to gainsay him?

We know better. We have always known better, though we were not always able to say so out loud. The reality of sex is the Song of Songs, not Augustine. It is male, female, mixed male, mixed female, cisgender, transgender, asexual, bisexual, heterosexual, homosexual, polysexual. And variations on all of them. It is not simply "male and female created he them." Just because the male and female cisgender variety is the most common one does not make it the only natural one. Denying that is more than just unjustified universalism. It is a refusal to accept the reality that "the truths of Scripture regarding human sexuality" are malleable indeed.

As I said at the beginning of this chapter, all functioning societies place some limitations on human sexual activity. We must not tolerate rape, incest, forced abortions and sterilizations, forced conception or contraception. Equally, we must not tolerate efforts by some religious leaders and groups to force everyone to adhere to their particular perspective on sex, the more so when that perspective is based on some ancient author's idea of sex and is maintained by denying that we understand sex better now.

The challenge of our time is to prevent a return to the sexually repressive years of the mid-twentieth century, let alone those of centuries before. That includes crafting rules for sexual activity that are realistic and that can be sustained in practice. The greater challenge is whether we will continue to be a pluralistic society where everyone has a voice but where reason decides the issue on the basis of reality. Or will we revert to a society controlled by some branch of some religion whose rules cannot be questioned, no matter how antiquated, repressive, and unrealistic they are. The ongoing battles over sexual identity, sexual activity, and sexual equality are central to this challenge. Yes, human sexuality must obey limits, but they must be reasonable ones that do not promote any one particular religious revelation. Sex is so basic to our conception of ourselves that control over someone's sex life leads to control over the whole person. Our very liberty requires the secularization of sex.

CHAPTER SIX

WHEN GOD GOES OFF TO WAR

We are not a nice species. In five thousand years of recorded history, there have been only a few hundred years without a war, or at any rate without a war worth recording.[1] Put another way, for ninety-five percent of our known history, some part of mankind has been at war. Whether or not war is our natural state of being, it is certainly the most common one.

Almost as numerous as the wars themselves are the reasons why we go to war. These range from the lust for power to the need for land and water, from the desire to enforce an ideology to the fear of ideological opposition. Anger and ignorance, pride, even an unintentional insult, have sent armies off to kill each other. What concerns me in this chapter is what happens when God joins the battle. A command from God to take up arms can become a *causus belli*—a justification for war that eliminates the need for any other reason. *"Deus vult!"* ("God wills it!") was a common battle cry in the Middle Ages. This same God can also demand the annihilation of his enemies—no quarter for heretics, no surrender accepted from the ungodly. God can also promise eternal life in heaven for his holy warriors, which makes him a force multiplier of war. That can lead to catastrophic effects orders of magnitude beyond war's normal destruction.

Of all the consequences of the invention of God, the war and violence done in his name have got to rank among the worst. This has to be one of the most important questions in this book: how can we be so eager to kill and die on the imaginary orders of an invented God?

ISRAELITES AT WAR

As with so much else, the answer starts with the Ancient Near East. The idea that war might be commanded or intended by the gods goes back at least to the Sumerian ruler Eanatum I (c. 2470 BCE). "Eanatum always justifies his military actions as being the will of the gods. He paints himself as a restorer of divine justice for the whole of Sumer."[2] Sumerian tablets and steles announced military victories that were credited to the help of the gods. This same idea made its way to the Assyrians and the Hittites and would later dominate Israelite belief.

In the period when the Israelites were settling down in Canaan, much of the region was frequently at war. Local tribes led by local kings fought each other to expand their territory and to gain mastery over each other. The Israelites, whether as tribes in the book of Judges or as the two kingdoms of Israel and Judah, often fought with their neighbors in Moab and Ammon, as well as with the invading Philistines along the coast. Israel and Judah themselves went to war with each other on more than one occasion. There was little difference between their local wars and those in the rest of the Ancient Near East.

Imperial wars were different. Wars between the empires of Egypt and whatever power was currently dominating Mesopotamia were much more destructive. The Israelites were caught up in those wars because they lived in Canaan, the land bridge between the empires, and thus were as small fish caught between two leviathans. Egypt and its adversaries—the Akkadians, the Assyrians, the Babylonians—variously saw the Israelites as vassals, nuisances, hinderances, but not as major threats or competition. If a vassal state became too much of a problem, the great powers would simply eliminate it: Assyria destroyed Israel in 721 BCE, and the Babylonians ravaged Judah 135 years later.

The prophets and the other authors of Scripture explained the victories and defeats in both local and imperial wars in much the same way others had, going back to Eanatum: it was the will of the gods (or God, in this case). The prophets, as proponents of Yahwism, were particularly focused on battle losses, and especially on Nebuchadnezzar's destruction of the Temple, disasters that they declared were the consequence of the Israelites' failure to worship Yahweh alone.

There was one other type of war found in Scripture: a war commanded not by kings but by God. God was also present in the other types of war, but a war which God had ordained was of a different character. This was not a war of chance or choice; it was war started by God and carried out with God's help to achieve God's purpose. There are two notable instances in Scripture of divinely commanded war: against Amalek in the Torah, and against the inhabitants of Canaan in the book of Joshua.

According to the book of Exodus, when the Israelites left Egypt, a local tribe, the Amalekites, attacked them in a vicious battle. In Deuteronomy, Yahweh reminded the Israelites that Amalek had attacked "all the stragglers at your rear, and when you were tired and weary."[3] In response to this cowardly and unprovoked attack, Yahweh issued a famously paradoxical command: "you shall wipe out the remembrance of Amalek from under the heavens, you shall not forget."[4] Amalek thereafter became a code word for an implacable enemy of Israel, someone who must be killed because that is the only way to stop him from killing. In the early days of the monarchy, the prophet Samuel commanded King Saul, in Yahweh's name, to attack the Amalekites and destroy them all, even their animals. When Saul spared Agag, the Amalekite king, and kept some sheep and cattle, Samuel was furious and told him that Yahweh would take away his kingdom for this disobedience.[5] The theme of Amalek as the eternal enemy of Israel occurs at least once more in Scripture, in the book of Esther, written late in the Persian period. Haman, the villain who wants to have all the Jews in the empire put to death, is described as an "Agagite"—a descendant of Agag the Amalekite. During the Holocaust, the rabbis would often refer to Hitler as "Amalek."

Whether there ever really was an Amalek that behaved so despicably as to deserve extermination is highly questionable. No reference to such a tribe has been found outside of Scripture, and even some of the Biblical references do not portray the Amalekites this way. For example, in the book of Numbers, Moses warned the Israelites they were not yet ready to go into Canaan, "for the Amalekite and the Canaanite are there in front of you," in effect listing the Amalekites as just another ordinary enemy.[6] Nonetheless, "Amalek" has become a metaphor for a savage and remorseless enemy of the good, with whom there can be no compromise, and for whom there is no solution short of extermination.

The second example of divinely ordained war is the Conquest of Canaan, described in the book of Joshua, the next book after the Five Books of Moses. The Israelites, having escaped slavery in Egypt forty years earlier, were now commanded by God to take possession of the Promised Land of Canaan and rid it of all those who worshipped gods other than Yahweh. With Yahweh's help, Joshua and his army of nomadic tribesmen blasted down walls, wiped out whole cities, defeated local kings and their armies, killed or drove off or enslaved much of the local population, and took over their lands. At times Yahweh even placed a Canaanite city under the "ban," meaning that everyone and in most cases everything, including livestock and utensils, were to be burnt as a sacrifice to the Lord. This is the same ban that Samuel would later place on Amalek when he ordered King Saul to do battle with them.

We can be confident that the war of conquest and annihilation described in the book of Joshua never happened that way. Ellen Morris has extensively documented Egyptian military and administrative activities in the region during the eighteenth, nineteenth, and twentieth dynasties of the pharaohs (c. 1550–c. 1140 BCE).[7] During this period, which spans all the possible dates of the Exodus and the Conquest, Egypt stationed garrison troops in parts of Canaan as far north as Akko (near modern Haifa), exacting tribute and vassalage from Canaanite kings in what might be described as "the role of absentee landlord [rather than] homeowner."[8] Yet the writer of the book of Joshua never even hinted the Egyptians were there, nor do Egyptian records make any mention of an Israelite invasion. There have been destruction levels found in archeological excavations at Jericho, Hazor, and other places, but they are dated hundreds of years apart, not close in time as the narrative in the book of Joshua requires. The extensive excavations at Jericho and other places are generally acknowledged to contradict the Joshua story of their destruction. Even the book of Judges is at odds with Joshua.[9]

The author of Joshua wrote in the exaggerated annihilation language that was common in the Ancient Near East.[10] Egyptian pharaohs were particularly fond of such phrases. The Israelites were recorded as having been annihilated by Pharaoh Merenptah (c. 1209 BCE) on one of his campaigns in Canaan: "Israel is laid waste; his seed [or: his grain] is not."[11] Curiously, there is no reference in Scripture to this campaign. King Mesha of Moab boasted that he had killed all the Israelites in the town of Nebo, "for I had put it to the ban of [the god] Aštar Kemoš. And from there, I took the vessels of YHWH, and I hauled them before the face of Kemoš." (The book of Kings does record a campaign against Mesha of Moab.)[12] The book of Joshua describes the conquest of Jericho using this same language: the Israelites "put under the ban everything that was in the town, from man to woman, from lad to elder, and to ox and sheep and donkey, by the edge of the sword."[13]

There is also good reason to argue that the book of Joshua, in the form it had during King Josiah's time (late seventh century BCE), deliberately mimicked and satirized the propaganda of Assyria, at that time the greatest power in the region. Biblical scholar Thomas Römer has a detailed list of parallels between the book and the Assyrian conquest accounts. He also discusses how the sun and moon were major Assyrian deities, such that the story of Joshua's stopping them in the sky was a way of saying that Yahweh was in control of the Assyrian gods.[14] Such a tale would serve to lift the spirits of the Israelites in Judah then under Assyrian domination. Moreover, "the original book of Joshua borrows from royal Assyrian ideology in order to construct a military narrative legitimizing Israel's occupation of the land."[15]

Different rationales attend these two divine commands of annihilation. The extermination of Amalek is presented as a requirement of self-defense, while the campaigns of Joshua are necessary to purify the land and remove any pagan influences that might corrupt the Israelites. That these campaigns never happened doesn't alter the impression they made on subsequent generations.

In the Maccabean revolt of the 160s BCE, the Maccabees committed acts similar to what Joshua was said to have done.[16] But after the military disasters of the Great Revolt (66–73 CE) and the Bar Kochba revolt (132–35 CE), Jewish leaders took pains to play down Maccabean militancy and the Conquest story as well. The rabbis of the Talmud period left the books of the Maccabees out of the Hebrew Scripture. They reoriented the festival of Hannukah, which celebrated the Maccabee recapture of the Temple Mount, to focus on the miracle of the oil instead: when the Maccabees took over the Temple, they found only enough kosher oil to provide light for one day, but it burned for eight days until more oil could be prepared.[17] (This story doesn't appear in the books of the Maccabees; instead, the eight–day celebration is explained as mimicking the harvest festival of Sukkot.[18]) The martial side of the story, while not exactly suppressed, was given far less emphasis. The Talmud even says that Jews should not rebel against the nations of the world, and that Jews should no longer try to reestablish God's rule in Judaea until God decides it is time and sends a messiah.[19] The idea was that the Jews should wait, patient and enduring, until God in his infinite wisdom decided that they had redeemed themselves of whatever sins they had committed. The annihilation language of Joshua was held to be a one-time command, no longer applicable.[20]

This rabbinic passivity may have had its roots in earlier responses to crises. The author of the book of Daniel urged the righteous to stand aside and stay out of the way while the archangel Michael dealt with their enemies. Similarly, the *Psalms of Solomon*, written during the Roman occupation of Judaea, called on God to send a king (a messiah) who would "purge Jerusalem from gentiles" on behalf of the Jews. But he would do this by the strength with which God would "undergird" him.[21] During the Great Revolt, the Pharisees, spiritual predecessors of the rabbis, preached accommodation with Rome (but were shouted down by the Zealots). Unfortunately, nowadays "the book of Joshua...once again serves in certain circles as an ideological weapon in reclaiming the past according to an interpretation of the present."[22] The extremist rabbi Meir Kahane argued for a new Israeli military campaign in the manner of Joshua, "purifying" the land of all non-Jews. Not surprisingly, Joshua (and Ezekiel) were Kahane's favorite books of Scripture.[23] The

Israeli Supreme Court outlawed the Kach party that Kahane had founded, but other political parties with similar ideologies have since arisen. Israeli prime minister Yitzhak Rabin was assassinated by a religious fanatic who believed that Rabin, in signing the Oslo Accords, had violated the command in Deuteronomy (and also Joshua) not to enter into a compact with the people of the land.[24]

EARLY CHRISTIANITY AND WAR

While the early Israelites were often caught up in war, early Christians lived under the harsh but effective *Pax Romana*. They could therefore afford to interpret the command "Thou shalt not kill" as an absolute prohibition.[25] The early Church fathers forbade Christians from joining the Roman army for this reason. This pacifism sometimes led Romans to denounce Christians as cowards who refused to defend the state. The third century Church Father Origen retorted that Christians did indeed serve the state—not through force of arms, but with prayer. "And none fight better for the king than we do. We do not indeed fight under him, although he require it; but we fight on his behalf, forming a special army—an army of piety—by offering our prayers to God." He even predicted that if all Romans become Christians, "they will not war at all, being guarded by that divine power" that would save the world for their sake.[26]

Nevertheless, by the early fourth century there were many Christian soldiers serving in the emperor's armies in spite of theological objections to their doing so.[27] After the Battle of Milvian Bridge in 312, Emperor Constantine accepted Christianity as his personal faith and made Christianity a legal religion. Later, in 380 CE, Theodosius I declared Christianity *the* official religion of the empire. The defense of the empire was now in the hands of a Christian emperor leading an army of

Christians, and pacifism was no longer a practical option. Christianity needed a doctrine of war.

Roman philosophers as far back as Cicero (106–43 BCE) had been exploring the question of what constitutes a just war, which humanities scholar Robert Meagher describes as a "war in which men would risk their lives but not their souls."[28] In the years after 380 CE, Bishop Ambrose of Milan relied heavily on Cicero in particular in his search for a way to allow Christians to kill their enemies in battle.[29] Ambrose, and after him his protégé, Bishop Augustine of Hippo, developed a doctrine that a "just war" must be defensive, with mercy for the defeated. The true evils in war were "the desire to do harm, cruelty in taking vengeance...the lust for domination." One must not wage war with passion but with love.[30] However, Augustine made an exception for wars ordered by God, using Joshua's imaginary conquest as his justification. "By reason of the fact that God had commanded this, it must certainly not be considered cruelty that Joshua left no living thing in the cities that were handed over to him."[31] In Augustine's view, when God commanded a war of annihilation, one must not question the morality of that command.

FROM JUST WAR TO HOLY WAR

The idea of limiting organized violence to "just wars" faced a severe challenge as the western Roman empire disintegrated and was replaced by a feudal structure. Instead of a single army under imperial authority, there arose individual men-at-arms who held sway over their lands and people by their own martial prowess and that of whatever retainers they could attract and peasants they could draft. Their prosperity, even their very survival, depended on their skill at killing people.

Compounding the situation after the seventh century was the rise of Islam. Unlike Christianity, Islam had faced military challenges in its formative years and in response had developed a theology that allowed for offensive war. Islam spread rapidly throughout the Middle East and northern Africa, and for a while it posed a concern to Christian Europe with its conquest of the Iberian Peninsula. But its more serious threat was to the eastern Roman empire, Byzantium.

In 1074, Pope Gregory VII summoned the faithful to defend the Byzantines from the Muslim threat and offered remission of earthly sins if they would go. "Be very strong to fight for that praise and glory which surpass all desire... For through labor that is for a moment you can gain an eternal reward."[32] Gregory had long been at odds with the secular powers of Europe, so it should come as no surprise that they ignored his call.

Two decades later a different pope, Urban II, issued his own call for a crusade, and this time the response was overwhelming. Though the word itself would not come into use for another hundred years, "crusade" means a war inspired or initiated by religion for religious purposes. While later crusades (there were over a dozen in all) had mixed motives at best, the First Crusade of 1096 really was a religious war—"*Deus vult!*" (God wills it!) was the Crusader motto. Arguments that religion was only an excuse overlook how Urban II built on Gregory's concept of penitential war to promise the crusaders remission from sin. The military leaders of the First Crusade were all knights— trained professional killers—but they were also Christians who had heard all their lives that killing was a mortal sin for which they would spend eternity in hell. Urban offered them a chance to avoid that fate: by going to Jerusalem and liberating it, they would be participating in "a penitential war."[33] If, as some scholars suggest, profit motivated the first crusaders, it was far more likely profit of a religious sort than a secular one.[34] Equally significant was the mass of common people moved by religious fervor to leave home and family to go on crusade. With little preparation, weapons, or skills, and with no clue as to what they would encounter, they followed charismatic leaders such as Peter the Hermit in a chaotic, ill-organized, and ultimately ill-fated venture to wrest the Holy Land from the clutches of the Saracen.

The professional knights of the First Crusade did manage to conquer much of Palestine and in July 1099 to take Jerusalem. The crusaders then fell upon the city's inhabitants and massacred them in a three-day orgy of blood so fierce that, in the words of a contemporary chronicler using images reminiscent of the book of Revelation, knights rode through the streets in blood up to their knees—though these reports have been challenged as exaggerations.[35] Hofreiter, in his study of the uses of Scriptural genocide, observes that the Amalek and Joshua stories "furnished [the crusaders] with a framework within which they saw their warfare as pleasing to God"—if not immediately at the time of the Jerusalem massacre, then certainly in the chronicles written shortly thereafter.[36] In his study of morality in war, Meagher asserts that "the Crusades...marked the beginning of Christian total war, wars of annihilation—God's wars, willed by God, fought for God's causes by God's armies."[37]

Subsequent crusades lacked the religious fervor that drove the First Crusade. Some never even came close to Palestine, and one, the Fourth Crusade, was manipulated by the Venetians into attacking their commercial rival, Christian Byzantium. Still, the idea of necessary "just war" that Augustine had established had now been overtaken by the popes' promotion of "holy war." And "holy war" was justification for war as the first option. In the words of military historian Arnaud Blin, "a long series of European armies bent on conquering both souls and territories, Bible in one hand and a sword in the other, might be seen a [sic] starting with the First Crusade."[38]

WAR AGAINST THE HERETICS

At least in theological terms, I would not say that the concept of "just war" was discarded. The greatest theologian of the Middle Ages, Thomas Aquinas, replicated Augustine's ideas in his own, highly influential, writing. But in practical terms it does seem that Christian powers fought fewer "just wars," which might be described as wars of necessity, and engaged more and more in "holy wars," which for contrast can be called wars of choice—though the Church would have vehemently insisted that these wars too were necessary.

This is particularly the case in the wars that the Catholic Church now began to wage against anyone it considered to have heretical ideas. From the beginning, Christians had been intolerant of any deviation from what they had decided was orthodox thinking. Now that the Church had acquired a taste for holy wars, it began to use the power of the state to punish dissent with holy violence. As more of Europe's pagans became Christian, they mixed their old faith in with the new. This in turn led to the need to suppress heresy at any cost. The increased expectation of the Second Coming of Jesus at the end of the millennium was also a factor (see chapter 8). The increasing use of holy wars against military enemies of the Church may well have inspired it to call for a similar war against its spiritual dissidents.

Much of the responsibility for the normalization of physical violence against dissenters from the Church must fall on Pope Innocent III (1199–1216), who started the Albigensian Crusade. This crusade is named after the town of Albi in southern France that was home to many Cathars, a group of Christians who rejected the authority of the pope. Innocent III, possibly the most powerful pope in all history, was not about to let such a challenge pass. There were other factors involved, particularly that the Cathars held valuable land that other Frenchmen coveted, but I want to emphasize a couple of points of religious importance. First is that in 1209 Innocent appointed an abbot, Arnald Amalric, as the general in charge, making it clear that this was to be a war guided by the interests of the Church. Second is that, whatever the motives of Innocent and the French, the Cathars themselves did fight in defense of their religious beliefs. After the final battle of the crusade, Montségur in 1244, the last surviving Cathars were offered their lives if they would recant their heresy. Almost all refused and were burned to death.[39]

(Other massacres in that war, especially Amalric's infamous order to "kill them all! God will know his own," were not examples of religious fervor but were coldly calculated tactics intended to weaken Cathar resistance and to discourage other Frenchmen from coming to their aid.[40])

Innocent's willingness to use violence against heresy not only desensitized Christianity to it, but helped lead to its use by the Inquisition. The Inquisition would not be formally established until around 1230, long after Innocent III had died, but he set much of its mechanism in motion.[41] In 1215, the Fourth Lateran Council, which Innocent had summoned, offered remission of sins to secular heretic hunters, just as if they had gone on crusade. Its third canon states that "Catholics who have girded themselves with the cross for the extermination of the heretics, shall enjoy the indulgences and privileges granted to those who go in defense of the Holy Land."[42] In his history of the inquisition, Jonathan Kirsch calls it "essentially a program of Church- and state-sponsored terrorism."[43] In 1252, Innocent IV formally authorized torture on suspected heretics—provided that no limbs were broken or the victim killed. The stated purpose of this torture was not just to make the suspects confess their own heresy, but to get them to name other heretics as well.[44]

As often happens when an institution has absolute authority

and little oversight, the Inquisition quickly moved beyond any religious impulse to become a tool for the greedy, the vengeful, the jealous, and the prejudiced. The Spanish Inquisition, a body independent of the pope, was especially notorious in this. Even "high rank offered no immunity for the descendants of the *conversos*...if only because they possessed wealth that the inquisitors wanted to seize and posts that Old Christians wanted to hold."[45] (Conversos were Spanish Jews—and Muslims—who converted to Catholicism. Marranos, another word for converted Jews, is a more derogatory term. "Old Christians" claimed their blood was "pure," untainted by any Jewish ancestry.) For hundreds of years in Europe and in the Americas, Spanish Catholics lived in constant terror of being accused of harboring thoughts that the religious authorities did not approve of, against which there was no defense. According to Kirsch, the last victim of the Spanish Inquisition was garroted in 1826, over 600 years after Innocent III started his war against heresy.[46]

CATHOLICS AND PROTESTANTS AT WAR

In the sixteenth century, after Martin Luther broke with the Catholic Church and started the Protestant Reformation, Catholics and Protestants literally went to war with each other over the question of which of them had the true key to heaven. In his study of political persecutions justified by "moral purity," sociologist Barrington Moore observes that "for many Catholics the Huguenots [French Protestants] were a disease or a polluting vermin that threatened to destroy the whole social order. For the Huguenots the entire Catholic ritual...formed a poisonous pollution of the true faith, to be rooted out by any possible means."[47] Moore describes an attempt in 1561 to reconcile French Catholics and Protestants that was "torpedoed" when a Calvinist writer, Theodore de Bèze, speaking on behalf of the Protestants, rejected the concept of the Eucharist—bread and wine transformed by a priest into the body and blood of Jesus. The Catholics in attendance called this blasphemous, making any agreement impossible.[48]

By 1562, France was consumed in religious civil war. In the Saint Bartholomew's Day Massacre of 1572, over three thousand Protestants were killed on one day alone, and the pope struck a medal in commemoration.[49] Eventually three claimants to the French crown, two Catholic and one Protestant, squared off against each other, and when only the Protestant was left standing, he agreed to convert to Catholicism—giving rise to the famous and possibly apocryphal quote that "Paris is well worth a mass"—and became Henri IV of France. Henri then tried to calm religious passions with the Edict of Nantes in 1598, which required French Catholics to tolerate the Protestants living around them. In response, a "demented monk" assassinated Henri in 1610.[50]

France's long recovery after its own wars of religion, as well as its military expenditures in New France (Canada), may be among the reasons why it was late in entering the most important religious war of the era: the Thirty Years' War, from 1618 to 1648. Blin describes it as "initially a localized religious conflict with political overtones [that] became a global political conflict with religious undertones."[51] It started when the fervently Catholic Prince Ferdinand, newly anointed as king of Bohemia, pushed to rescind the protections granted to its Protestants by the Holy Roman Emperor Rudolf II in 1609. When two of Ferdinand's advisers tried to break up a parliamentary meeting in Prague in May 1618, the delegates threw them out the window. (The officials survived the three-story fall. According to some reports, it was because they landed on a dung pile.[52]) The "defenestration of Prague" was the spark which lit the Thirty Years' War. Rulers all over Europe chose sides, whether for theological or political reasons. Some saw Protestantism as a way of getting out from under the Holy See's heavy hand, while others saw the new movement as a threat to their own salvation. The war convulsed continental Europe, destroyed much of Germany, sent millions to their deaths either as direct victims of battle or through disease and starvation, and finally came to an end not because of any decisive victories but because the armies were exhausted.

Even then, the Catholic and Protestant parties had to meet thirty miles apart in separate cities while negotiators shuttled back and forth between them.[53] It took several years to get them to finally make peace. The three treaties that made up the Peace of Westphalia, all signed in 1648, were the first documents I know of since Roman times that committed European rulers to an official policy of religious toleration, one in which they acknowledged, however grudgingly, the validity of religious pluralism. For over a hundred years Catholics and Protestants had each used violence and war to try to purify their lands of the other's version of Christianity, and each had largely failed.

WARS AGAINST RELIGION

There are also wars and other forms of violence that have been described as secular or atheist attacks on religion. A primary example often cited is the French Revolution and the Terror that was so much a part of it. In historian Karen Armstrong's description: "Revolutionary France was secularized by coercion, extortion, and bloodshed; for the first time it mobilized the whole of society for war; and its secularism seemed propelled by an aggression toward religion that is still shared by many Europeans today."[54] But the French Revolution was not an attack on believers in God; it was an attack on the Catholic Church. The bishops of the Church exercised political control over the country for their own benefit, particularly in exemption from taxation, as an expert on Catholic history, John McGreevy, makes clear. "Precisely because church and state in France were so intertwined, resentment grew against the web of taxes, tithes, and fees supporting bishops, abbots, and other clerics who lived in luxury."[55] Another scholar argues that the revolution was mainly trying to disconnect the Church from state politics. "The Civil Constitution of the Clergy (1790) [was] a misconceived attempt to destroy, not the Church, but the Roman absolutist allegiance of the Church," explains Hobsbawm.[56] The revolution wanted to curb the political power of the Catholic bishops, and with some exceptions it left Protestants and Jews alone.[57] In 1791, the National Assembly emancipated the Jews and granted them full citizenship (though it had to work to overcome the prejudices of some of its members).[58]

In 1789 the National Assembly passed the *Declaration of the Rights of Man*, which included this article: "No one shall be disquieted on account of his opinions, including his religious views, provided their manifestation does not disturb the public order established by law"[59]—though the revolutionary governments often ignored this admonition. Some leaders of the revolution also responded to charges of atheism by promoting Deism in the form of a "Supreme Being." Deism is a minimalist version of monotheism, holding that there is a divine being who created the universe, but who does not thereafter intervene in it. (Some of the American founding fathers were Deists.) Georges Danton, the Minister of Justice, explained it this way in a 1793 speech: "The people will have festivals where they will offer up incense to the Supreme Being, Nature's master, for it was never our intention to destroy religion so that atheism could take its place."[60]

The French Revolution descended into the Terror from mid-1793 to July 1794—an orgy of bloodshed which started out of concern for political purity, then the desire to stifle all dissent, and finally as a way of getting revenge on personal and political enemies. Change "political purity" in the previous sentence to "religious purity" and that pretty much describes the Inquisition. We could also use Moore's analogy: "the secular version of purity was as much another worldly goal as its religious variants in the Old Testament tradition and during the religious wars in France."[61] In considering whether the Deists of France were worse than the medieval popes and friars, one has to first acknowledge that all of them justified their actions on the conviction that any challenge to their ideology must be violently suppressed.

Unlike the French Revolution, the Bolshevik takeover of Russia in 1917 was led by outright atheists. Atheism was a prime tenet of Marxism, and the Soviets did go to war against religion in general. A "stubborn religious commitment" was grounds for arrest under Stalin.[62] The main target of their ire was the established church, which had supported the deposed tsarist regime. Then the Soviet leadership discovered that Orthodox Christianity was so ingrained in the Russian psyche that it would take a sustained and determined and violent effort to eradicate it.[63] They hoped to replace it with the new Marxist-Leninist ideology—which itself bore a remarkable resemblance to a revealed religion, a "luminous faith" in the words of Russian historian Yuri Slezkine.[64] Indeed, the purges of the Communist Party, while often reflecting Stalin's paranoia and political maneuvering, operated in much the same manner as the Catholic Church's and the French Revolution's assaults on dissident thought. Kirsch remarks that the religiosity of the cult of Stalin was the "single most striking similarity between the Inquisition and the Great Terror" of 1936–38.[65] Ultimately, the Soviet attempt to replace Orthodox Christianity with Marxism-Leninism failed, and was abandoned well before the Soviet collapse in 1991.

Another ideology of the twentieth century was Nazism, which unlike Marxism was not atheist. Adolf Hitler claimed to be acting on God's behalf in his war against the Jews. He used this argument in his negotiations with the Vatican. "Hitler reminded the bishops that he was a Catholic and that his Jewish policies were those the church had advocated for centuries."[66] On the other hand, while "a Nazi was encouraged to be a *Gottgläubiger*, a believer in God...the term carried no suggestion of Christianity."[67]

Regardless, Hitler did draw on traditional German Christian attitudes toward the Jews. This included the publication and widespread distribution of Luther's 1543 pamphlet *On the Jews and Their Lies*, which the Nazis then used to justify their genocide. Also, while the Nazis persecuted church officials, Catholic and Protestant, who stood up against the Nazi plan, they coopted those who cooperated with them or who were unwilling to speak out. The Nazis relied on religious rituals of their own devising, many derived from German pre-Christian practices, as yet another technique for maintaining cohesion and loyalty. The late Chief Rabbi of England, Jonathan Sacks, charged that "the Nazi ideology was not religious. If anything, it was pagan."[68] But "paganism" does describe a religion, or, rather, a category of religion, just not a monotheistic one. The Nazis were religious in their own way, and that factored into their antipathy toward the Abrahamic religions—Judaism, Christianity, and Islam. The Nazis saw them as ideological competitors, not unlike the way the Soviets did.

SOME FINAL THOUGHTS

There are many other acts of war and violence where religion was a factor that I have left out of this brief recitation: the witch hunts, the Puritan executions of Quakers and the burning of books, the fanaticism of the Almoravids in North Africa and Muslim Spain, the Wahhabis who inspired Osama Bin Laden and the Al-Qaeda terrorist movement, the pogroms against the Jews of eastern Europe, the fights between Hindus and Buddhists, the assassinations of Egypt's Anwar Sadat and

Israel's Yitzhak Rabin, China's suppression of Christianity and Islam. The list, unfortunately, is endless, and I only have this one chapter. But there is enough, even here, for me to make some observations on the impact faith has had on war.

The first observation is that while the Abrahamic religions may not be inherently violent, they are not inherently peaceful either. Rabbinic Judaism foreswore violence at a time when Jews weren't in a position to assert themselves militarily anyway. But now some extremist rabbis in Israel are justifying violence against the Palestinians by citing Joshua's conquest myth as if it were history to be reenacted. Christianity could initially claim that it was entirely pacifist, but it forfeited that claim when it inherited the Roman Empire and had to defend it. Islam started out having to fight for its survival—Muhammed fled Mecca for a refuge in Medina when the Meccan merchants plotted to assassinate him for interfering with their pagan religious sales. A few years later, Muhammed returned to Mecca with an army and conquered it. Ever since then, Islam has held that there are legitimate reasons for violence in the name of God.

Islam only turned from war after it overextended itself in its initial conquests, and after it ran into opposition sufficiently strong for it to call for a truce. (In the early years of Islam, a Muslim ruler was not allowed to make peace with unbelievers, but he could agree to a truce. These were limited to ten years at first, but now "no longer need to be of fixed duration."[69]) Christianity only stopped trying to command states to wage war in its name when the states stopped taking orders from the churches. Judaism after the Roman experience shied away from violence, but there are rabbis today who justify war and violence as needed for the physical survival of Israel. Israel's settlement policy is also troublesome, founded as it is on the insistence that God gave all of the land of Canaan to the Jews. It would therefore be going against God's command to give any of it away. Israeli Prime Minister Yitzhak Rabin was assassinated by a religious fanatic who feared the prime minister was about to do just that.

The attacks on religion by the Nazis and the Soviets actually reinforce the argument that religion cannot be left on its own to ensure peace in the world. What the French revolutionaries, the Communists, and the Nazis have in common with Judaism, Christianity, and Islam is that all of them are based on ideologies that resist dissent. All have factions that seek to use the tools of the state to force everyone to behave the way that Moses or Marx or Mao or Muhammed, Jesus or Stalin or the French Directorate, said they must behave. Barrington Moore's analysis of the French Revolution compares it to "militant monotheism. There was the usual demonization and dehumanization of actual and potential opponents." They were "outsiders, threats to human society who should be expelled and killed."[70] The French and Soviet attacks on the established churches in their countries, the Nazi war against the Jews— these are similar to Christianity's persecutions of Jews and those it labelled heretics. In each case, the target was people who by their very existence raised doubts about the truths of the regime. The world must be purified of the danger that the Other represents—and it makes no difference whether those crying havoc are Marxists or Nazis or French radicals, medieval popes or Saudi Wahhabis or Haredi Jews or Christian Nationalists.

Religions, moreover, are particularly suited to supply motives for war and violence. Haredim throw stones at other Jews for not keeping the Sabbath. Catholics kill Protestants, and Protestants kill Catholics, because each thinks the other is leading them to hell. Wahhabis kill their fellow Muslims for not behaving exactly as Muhammad did. India had to split into two countries at the cost of millions of lives because Hindus and Muslims couldn't live with each other. Anti-abortion extremists murder doctors and bomb clinics and say that Jesus approves.

Atrocities from the massacre in Jerusalem at the end of the First Crusade to shooting up a synagogue in Pittsburgh are justified in the name of the Lord. While many English Protestant settlers in the New World argued for the conversion of the indigenous tribes, others said they were enemies of God who must be eliminated. In a 1689 sermon, Cotton Mather told the Massachusetts Puritans that they were "Israel" and the local tribes were "Amalek" whom they were commanded to exterminate.[71] His sermon "advocates genocide against the Native Americans on the authority of the Old Testament."[72] Earlier, in 1637, a company of Puritan forces and their Indian allies attacked a Pequot village and massacred its 400 inhabitants, who were "mostly women, children, and old men."[73] The second-in-command, John Underhill, justified the slaughter by citing the Biblical King "David's war," insisting that "sometimes the Scripture declareth women and children must perish with their parents... We had sufficient light from the Word of God for our proceedings."[74]

Religion also acts as a force multiplier of war in a way that atheist ideologies cannot. Religion can convince you that not only has God commanded you to go to war, but that he will cancel your sins, welcome you to heaven, reward you with seventy-two virgins if you die in his holy battle. (Whether the Qur'an actually promises "holy virgins" is a disputed issue. The point is that some Muslims believe it and have gone to war sustained by that belief. A fourteen-year-old Palestinian boy who had been recruited as a suicide bomber against an Israeli checkpoint, but couldn't bring himself to do it, told interviewers: "Blowing myself up is the only chance I've got to have sex with 72 virgins in the Garden of Eden."[75])

Christianity in particular has used the fear of hell both as a goad to encourage warriors to fight and as a means of targeting for violence those it deems heretics or apostates. Atheism, on the other hand, cannot promise heavenly reward or escape from hell. No Communist soldier ever ran into battle screaming Marx's name the way the Crusaders shouted *"Deus Vult"* (God wills it) or Al-Qaeda suicide bombers yell out *"Allahu akbar"* (God is great). Soviet soldiers in World War II are known to have shouted "For the Motherland! For Stalin!" during battle, but this is more in line with patriotic fervor and Stalin's personality cult than being the equivalent of a believer's calling on God. Japanese kamikaze pilots may well have called on the name of their emperor as they dove into American warships, but emperor-worship was part of their religion and the Japanese are not atheists.

Those who argue that religions are better equipped to ensure peace than either atheism or secularism also overlook the difference between these two. Atheists such as the Soviets are in their way as dogmatic as Osama Bin Laden, Meir Kahane, and Innocent III, and they are equally likely to resort to violence to preserve the purity of their dogmas. Most secularists, on the other hand, just want religion to leave them alone.

Secularism, specifically *the sort of secularism that is not driven by an ideology and is not interested in purity*, is better positioned to keep the peace among religions. The ability of Catholics to live peacefully with Protestants, Shi'ites with Sunnis, Hindus with Buddhists and Muslims, anybody with Jews and atheists, and for that matter communists with capitalists, is largely contingent on the degree to which secular governments are more interested in keeping the peace than in promoting one ideology over another.

Though church-state separation is not formally stated as such in its founding documents, no country embodies this principle so thoroughly as the United States. The American understanding that its government and its officials will hold themselves neutral in matters of religion is an ideal generally honored even though often breached, and is one main reason why the US has—so far—had relatively little experience with religiously motivated violence compared to Europe.

Secular control of the legitimate use of force is not an ideal solution—the secular United States remains to date the only nation to have used nuclear weapons in war. But one of the problems with ideology is that it often expects that there should be an ideal solution, and that it will, when allowed, kill as necessary to bring about that nonexistent ideal. Even the Enlightenment, for all its devotion to reason, fell victim to that fallacy: it believed in the perfectibility of man.

Even so, the United States, founded on the Enlightenment principle that reason should determine our course of action, has remained a secular government that, for the most part, has resisted the argument that it must act in obedience to the commands of one or another divinity. To the extent that this resistance has succeeded, it has kept the peace among the various religions better than those religions have been able to do themselves. This founding principle is now under sustained and determined assault by various religious groups who are fighting, sometimes literally, to enshrine their views on abortion, on evolution, on marriage, women's rights, race relations, and civil rights as the law of the land. That alone is evidence that we need to rely on a non-ideological secularism to protect us from religiously inspired war.

CHAPTER SEVEN

IT'S ALL ABOUT GETTING
INTO HEAVEN

Death is the universal destination. Whatever is begotten and born, dies. As far back as we can trace, human beings have wondered about death and what might follow. Some of the oldest known religions reserved immortality for the gods and sometimes for kings. Over time, prophets and philosophers began to argue that how one behaved while alive would determine whether and how one would live on after having died. Then Christianity came along and insisted that what one believed was more important than how one behaved. No matter how good a life anyone had lived, it counted for nothing unless they also believed in Jesus as their savior.

The consequence of that construction is that Christians started to focus less about making a good life for themselves on earth and more on what they needed to do to insure their salvation in the afterlife. Many also saw it as their sacred duty to save others from hell by getting them to believe as they themselves did. As the Church grew in strength, it realized that its power to help people get into heaven could also be used to keep them out unless they did as they were told. The question for this chapter, then, is what has been the impact of all this on the world?

LIFE AFTER DEATH AND HOW TO GET IT

In most of the Ancient Near East, life after death was not at first a major concern. Eternal life was reserved for the gods, sometimes for the ruler, and occasionally for an exceptional mortal. If there was any kind of life after death for the rest of humanity, it was a dull and listless existence, a shadow of life on earth.

I described the shift in Jewish thinking about death in chapters 2 and 3. To recapitulate briefly: After the end of the Babylonian exile, the Jews, influenced by Hellenistic and possibly Zoroastrian beliefs, began to use judgment after death to solve the problem of evil prospering in life. This solution relied on the growing belief that an individual's consciousness—call it the spirit or the soul—lived on after the death of the body and therefore could be rewarded or punished for deeds done in life.

Jews argued vociferously over just how this would work and what kind of judgment there would be—for example, whether the idea of a bodily resurrection could be reconciled with a belief in spiritual immortality.[1] Jesus and his followers—the Jesus Movement—certainly took part in those disputes. But the Jesus Movement added a unique twist: to gain eternal life, one had to believe that Jesus had died for everyone's sins. It's not clear (at least in the synoptic gospels) that Jesus himself had made that belief a requirement. His parable of the sheep and the goats sorted them for the kingdom or the fire strictly according to how they behaved in life.[2] The passages in the gospels where Jesus did discuss faith were mostly about faith in God and the coming of God's kingdom. When a rich man asked Jesus what he must do to inherit eternal life, Jesus advised him to sell his possessions and give the money to the poor.[3] He also told his listeners, "do not worry about your life, what you will eat or what you will drink, or about your body, what you will wear." God will feed and clothe you if you "strive first for the kingdom of God."[4] But even if Jesus didn't really mean that the rich man had to sell *everything* and reduce himself to poverty, or that people literally should stop growing food and making clothes, this was still unrealistic advice for anyone living a normal life. It made sense only if life were about to radically change.

That was exactly what Jesus and his first followers expected to happen: the kingdom of God was just about to come. After Jesus was executed, his followers expected him to return at any moment to announce the arrival of the kingdom of God on earth. God in his wrath would then smite the unbelievers, while the believers would enjoy a blessed and eternal life. Even though some of the faithful had already died, not to worry, said the apostle Paul. In his first letter to the Thessalonians, he reassured them that their friends and relatives who had died waiting for Jesus would be the first to be restored to life when the kingdom came. After that, Paul went on, "we who are alive, who are left," will be swept up with them and "will be with the Lord forever."[5]

Paul did make clear that in the meantime he expected the faithful to behave—not for the sake of their life on earth that was ending, but for the sake of their eternal life that was just about to begin. He scolded the Corinthians for "sexual immorality" and urged them to be celibate, or if that was not possible, to marry and stay faithful to their spouses. They "must not put Christ to the test" by pushing the boundaries. Just because "all things are lawful" for them did not mean they were all beneficial. By that, Paul meant beneficial to their salvation. Even though they were now saved, he cautioned them, they had to remember that "wrongdoers will not inherit the kingdom of God."[6]

The kingdom of God is to be established here on earth. Earth will become a paradise where the believers will live forever, just as soon as the second coming happens. But as time passed and the second coming continued not to come, the Jesus Movement had to come up with a better answer than what Paul had given the Thessalonians. Paul himself, imprisoned and facing possible execution, wrote to the Philippians that if he were to die before Jesus returned, he expected his spirit would go to heaven and be with Jesus. Indeed, Paul was looking forward to it. "My desire is to depart and be with Christ," he told the Philippians. But at the same time he knew that they still needed him "in the flesh." He was torn between their needs and his wish, but recognized it was "more necessary" for him to remain.[7]

The gospel writers in their turn tried to accommodate the continuing reality of death. Luke's Jesus assured one of his fellow sufferers on the cross: "Truly I tell you, today you will be with me in Paradise."[8] In the gospel of John, Jesus told the Jews that everyone who believed in him "has eternal life, and does not come under judgment, but *has passed* from death to life." That is, believers have already started their eternal life while still on earth.[9]

Even so, the believers will still die on earth, and these and other passages did not really resolve the confusion over the sequence of events that would follow that death. But they do demonstrate that Christians were coming to accept that the second coming would be delayed, that they would die first and get their eternal reward later. It also reinforced their belief that they needed to devote their whole lives in this world to preparing for life in the next one.

CHRISTIAN ASCETICISM

As I explained in the chapter on human sexuality, Christianity started out as an ascetic religion, meaning that it played down or outright denied the value of earthly pleasures. This was and still is most obvious in its attitude toward sex. In the fourth century, Jerome, one of the most famous ascetics in Christian history, wrote how the fear of eternal damnation had driven him into the desert, where he wore sackcloth, let his skin be burned black by the sun, and rejected cooked food as an indulgence. In spite of all his efforts, he was still tormented by sexual desire and dreamed of lovely girls, leading him to cry aloud all night and beat his breast in misery.[10]

This attitude extended toward earthly life in general. In Romans, Paul's last known letter, he complained that his bodily desires were still trying to lure him into sin. "Wretched man that I am! Who will rescue me from this body of death?" Then he warned his readers that "if you live according to the flesh, you will die; but if by the Spirit you put to death the deeds of the body, you will live."[11] One of the earliest martyrs, Bishop Ignatius of Antioch, wrote to the Christian community in Rome that he was looking forward to his execution there. "For though I am alive while I write to you, yet I am eager to die for the sake of Christ... I have no delight in corruptible food, nor in the pleasures of this life. I desire the bread of God."[12]

In *The Varieties of Religious Experience*, William James presented a sixteenth-century Spanish Catholic mystic, John of the Cross, as another example of asceticism. John, wrote James, had advised that "if anything agreeable offers itself to your senses, yet does not at the same time tend purely to the honor and glory of God, renounce it and separate yourself from it for the love of Christ." James, a psychologist as well as a philosopher, warned that one of the practical consequences of asceticism was that "the self-surrender may become so passionate as to turn into self-immolation"—though a more modest ascetism "might be objectively useful."[13] In a slightly different vein, Jesuit[14] missionaries to the Indians in Canada advised their Huron converts that the diseases (most likely smallpox), wars, and crop failures and famines they were suffering from had been "sent by God for the improvement and redemption of those he had elected to save." Even though their heathen Iroquois neighbors were prospering while the Hurons suffered, "it was certain that, as unbelievers, they would not enjoy the rewards of the next life."[15]

Protestants have always rejected the extremes of Catholic asceticism. From what I have found, they rarely retreat from the world to become a hermit or cloistered monk or nun. But some Protestants, even today, agree with the doctrine of the early Puritans of New England. These Puritans were English Protestants who objected to the way the official Church of England kept too much of the Catholic Church's hierarchy and rituals, and eventually sailed to America to escape them.[16] They practiced what sociologist Max Weber called "worldly asceticism," defined as "asceticism turned with all its force against one thing: the spontaneous enjoyment of life and all it had to offer." This, Weber explained, derived from their belief that "the span of human life is infinitely short and precious to make sure of one's own election." Earthly frivolities such as "sociability, idle talk, luxury...more sleep than is necessary for health" would take precious time away from the essential business of building up credit for eternity. "The salvation of the soul and that alone was the centre of their life and work."[17]

It's all about getting into heaven.

WHAT ABOUT ALL THOSE OTHER SOULS?

Christianity is also about getting *all* souls into heaven. It is possible that in the beginning the Jesus Movement might have thought to confine its activities to other Jews. Matthew's Jesus even hinted at this when he told his disciples he had been sent "only to the lost sheep of the house of Israel."[18] But once Jesus's followers, and especially Paul, decided to take their message out into the Roman world, they necessarily had to make that message a universal one. Paul warned that everyone, "the Jew as well as the Greek," is damned from birth because of Adam's original sin. However, if you accept that, and if you accept that

Jesus sacrificed himself in expiation, then God will forgive you for Adam's sin.

So far, so good. But then they said that believing this was the *only* way to escape damnation. This is the theological foundation of Christianity: only if you believe that Jesus saved you from hell can you be saved from hell.

Let's set aside the problem of how a just God can punish people with hellfire for all eternity who never even got a chance to hear this message. Theologians have wrestled with that conundrum—I would call it a structural flaw—for millennia. My concern here is how the belief that everyone needed to be saved from hell directed Christians' attitude toward Jews, other cultures, and even other Christians.

Jews. By the end of the first millennium, most people in Europe outside of Scandinavia were Christian, except for the Jews. The Catholic Church, which up to that point had largely tolerated the Jews as called for by Augustine's witness doctrine, became concerned that their continued presence among Christians could become a corrupting influence. In the words of medieval scholar Jeremy Cohen, "the Christian fear of heresy and misunderstanding of what was thought to be the Jews' life of perversity came more and more to dominate Europe's conception of its Jewry."[19] Medieval princes and priests organized the burning of the Talmud and other rabbinical books. They forced Jews into public debates with priests and monks trained in dialectic. While Christians were not allowed, theologically, to literally force Jews to convert, they used the power of the state to herd them into churches where a friar (a member of one of the ascetic monastic orders) would hector them about their sins.[20] "Wherever they could, the friars encroached upon the daily religious lives of the Jews," burning their books, invading their synagogues, inciting mob violence, and taking other actions all with the goal of getting the Jews to, finally, believe in Jesus.[21]

By the end of the twelfth century, kings were expelling Jews from their territories—though sometimes they did so in order to avoid paying their debts to the Jews or to seize Jewish wealth, regardless of whatever pious excuses they came up with.[22] At other times, popes and princes herded Jews into ghettos, restricted their movements, limited how they could make a living—all, so they said, to persuade them to save their souls. As we saw earlier in chapter 4, medieval Christian leaders from the Catholic Pope Paul IV to the Protestant Martin Luther demanded ever harsher tactics against the Jews. Paul IV explained that Jews needed to be confined to ghettos and restricted to rag-picking so that, "won over by the piety and kindness of the See, [the Jews] should at long last recognize their erroneous ways, and should lose no time in seeing the true light of the catholic faith."[23] Luther, on the other hand, wanted the Jews driven out of Germany because they wouldn't listen to him.

Other cultures. From the beginning, Christians believed it was their divinely commanded duty to preach the gospel to the whole world. They had mixed success at best in Asia, but when Europeans started coming to the Americas, both Catholics and Protestants saw the indigenous peoples they found there as ripe for their message of salvation. Many factors played a role in the European conquest of the Americas, of which Christianity was only one.[24] And given what we know of the cultural and physical destruction of the indigenous American societies, it may be difficult to take at face value the sincerity of the missionaries toward the Indians. Still, it is possible to make some general observations. One is that many of these missionaries and their supporters believed that if they could convert enough of the indigenous peoples, that would be the signal that Jesus had been waiting for, when he would return to earth and establish the kingdom of God. Catholic friars coming from Spain and Portugal "laboured in the conviction that the conversion of the

Indians heralded the fulfilment of prophecies about the imminent end of the world."[25] We also see that friars did frequently display a genuine concern for the Indians' souls (if not their bodies), sometimes risking their own lives to convert people who were at the point of death.[26] In what may have been a sincere response to hearing about Columbus's adventures, "Ferdinand and Isabella also vowed to convert the Indians to Christianity, dreading that otherwise so many thousands would continue to die in ignorance to spend their eternity in hell."[27]

The same cannot be said of the conquistadors, the soldiers of fortune whom the king and queen of Spain authorized to conquer the Americas in their name and in the name of the Lord. In his study of empires, Timothy Parsons writes that "to the Spanish, indigenous Americans who rejected Christianity were degenerate heathens who needed to be saved from damnation by force." This gave cover to the conquistadors' greed and rapacity, "entail[ing] a higher magnitude of dehumanizingly ruthless exploitation."[28]

Friars as well as conquistadors forced the Indians to do hard labor on the lands they had taken from them. The friars themselves had little understanding of the pragmatic views that Indians generally held of religion and the supernatural, and had no compunctions over beating and enslaving their new converts to prevent them from leaving the missions or from continuing their "pagan" practices. Writing about the friars and the Mayans in the Yucatan, one historian describes the position taken by Fray Diego de Landa, bishop of Yucatan: "There could be no talk of accommodating native culture. It had to be uprooted and destroyed."[29] The Jesuits in French Canada, on the other hand, "combined a policy of coercion with one of relative accommodation."[30] Later Jesuit missionaries in the Pacific Northwest and among the Navajo did make some efforts to adapt local sentiments and rituals into Christian practice—though still with the ultimate aim of eliminating the other religions.[31]

Protestant missionaries have an equally mixed history, though the elements of the mix are somewhat different. In London in 1610, Protestant minister William Crashaw preached a sermon to the "adventurers" who were going to join the Jamestown colony in Virginia and to their investors. He told them their primary duty was "the conversion of the heathen from the devil to God." The settlers were to give them civility "for their bodies" and Christianity "for their souls: The first to make them men: the second happy men; the first to cover their bodies from the shame of the world: the second, to cover their souls from the wrath of God."[32] But in practice Protestant ministers were less active than their Catholic counterparts. "Generally, the closer a Protestant was to the mission field, the less enthusiastic he or she was about it."[33] They were known to refuse to perform deathbed conversions (in contrast to the Catholic friars), believing them to be an act of desperation and not a true expression of love for God.[34] And whatever their clergy may have preached as every Christian's first duty, Protestants in general were more interested in driving Indians off the land.[35] Still, it can be fairly said that some Protestants became at least as interested as Catholics in saving Indian souls by the early nineteenth century.[36]

Both Protestant and Catholic missionaries long viewed any indigenous culture as inherently inferior to theirs. "All missionaries began with the assumption that civilization equaled Christianity and vice versus and that not being a Christian equaled not being civilized and living in a disorganized and savage state." (The founder of Rhode Island, Roger Williams, was an almost singular exception.)[37] This attitude is changing, finally. In 1987, a Seattle group of Catholic and Protestant spiritual leaders issued "a formal apology on behalf of our churches for their long-standing participation in the destruction of traditional Native American spiritual practices." In 2022, Pope Francis apologized to Canada's First Nations for "the role that a number of Catholics, particularly those with educational responsibilities, have had in...the abuses [they] suffered and in the lack of respect shown" toward their culture and their very identity.[38]

Other Christians. Christians also poached on other Christians. In the previous chapter, I went into some detail about the wars of religion between Catholics and Protestants that devastated Europe for more than a hundred years. In the Americas, Crashaw urged his Virginia Protestant colonists to convert the Indians before the Catholics could. "For the *Papists,* we know that they approve nothing that *Protestants* undertake."[39] His sentiment was echoed by other Protestants down to the twentieth century: they had to rescue the Indians not just from their own mistaken beliefs but from those of the Catholics—from "Antichrist."[40] Catholics felt the same about Protestants. Francis Paul Prucha, a Jesuit priest and a major scholar of Native American history, wrote that nineteenth-century Catholic and Protestant missionaries spent more time condemning each other than in converting the indigenous peoples. "Each side held firmly—indeed adamantly—to its revealed truths and eagerly consigned the other to the flames of hell." (They became more cooperative in the twentieth century.)[41] Evangelical Protestants such as the Pentecostals are currently making serious inroads in Catholic Latin America, as are the Latter-Day Saints (Mormons).[42] If many Catholics and Protestants are more reconciled to each other's presence nowadays, that may be a consequence of modern pluralism. But for some, particularly conservative Catholics and fundamentalist Protestants, such reconciliation might be better credited to a tactical willingness to collaborate with each other in resisting pluralism and other common enemies such as secularism and Islam.[43] Theirs may turn out to be little more than a coalition of convenience that will eventually disintegrate as they compete for secular power as well as for immortal souls.

HOW CHRISTIANS CAN STILL GO TO HELL

Believing in Jesus was only the first step to salvation. Christians were constantly warned they could forfeit their salvation if they veered from the narrow path that had been laid out for them. The Church, and the churches, used the ever-present threat of hell to compel the behavior and even the thoughts of their flocks. Three of the most important areas in which they exercised this thought control were heresy, curiosity, and disobedience.

Heresy. The basis of Christianity is that you must believe in Jesus or you will go to hell. But there is a caveat: you must believe in Jesus *in the right way.* At the start of Christianity, New Testament writers warned the faithful that heresy—"asserting your own judgment rather than submitting obediently to the mind of the church"—would damn you to hell.[44] Paul placed a curse on "anyone [who] proclaims to you a gospel contrary to what you received" from him. The gospel of Matthew blasted wolves in sheep's clothing—false prophets who claimed to speak in Jesus's name.[45] The second letter of John warns against "deceivers...who do not confess that Jesus Christ has come in the flesh." This was a reference to Docetism, the belief that Jesus only *appeared* (from the Greek word *dókēsis*: appearance) to be human, and therefore he only *appeared* to have suffered and died on the cross. The author of Second John warned true believers not to offer them the hospitality normally accorded a fellow Christian, "for to welcome is to participate in the evil deeds of such a person." They had gone "beyond" the teaching of Jesus—they believed in him, but not in the right way.[46] To listen to them was to put one's eternal soul in peril. At the end of the second century, Irenaeus, bishop of Lyon, was quite blunt about using the threat of hell to combat this and other dissident ideas. "Let these persons [e.g., Valentinus; disciples of Marcion; the Gnostics]...be recognized as agents of Satan by all those who worship God...who has prepared eternal fire for every kind of apostasy."[47]

After the Emperor Constantine acknowledged Christianity as a legitimate religion in 313, he took a personal interest in Church actions, including the several doctrinal trends then competing to be normative Christianity. Constantine wanted the Christians in his empire to stop fighting over doctrines and settle on one—though he was less interested in which particular doctrine they chose. In 325, he summoned the bishops to Nicaea to settle the issue of Arianism (the belief that the Son had been created by the Father and had not always existed). The council voted to adopt the basics of the Nicene Creed and to declare Arianism a heresy. The emperor then enforced that declaration by first trying to persuade recalcitrant Arian bishops to agree, and then by sending the last two holdouts, along with Arius himself, into exile.[48]

Constantine's interference in Christian doctrinal disputes established the precedent that the newly legitimized Church could call on the power of the state to enforce its theological decisions. This would eventually lead to atrocities such as the Inquisition and the wars between Catholic and Protestant states, all goaded on by the fear that even just being exposed to some heretical thought could send one to the eternal fires of hell. The proponents of these activities were worried, or at least said they were worried, that if they were to let unrepentant heretics live, they could put other Christians in peril of eternal damnation. Best to be ruthless in this world in order to save souls for the next one.

Protestants, being a diverse group to begin with, have a mixed record on questions of heresy. Colonial North America is one example: several of the colonies were established by specific Protestant denominations with the intent of providing their adherents with safe havens to separate them from the heresies of other denominations. "Indeed, at the end of the seventeenth century, most colonies offered *less* religious toleration than did the mother country."[49] This included the removal of nonmembers from their midst lest they corrupt the true believers. In reviewing prosecutions for religious offenses in colonial times, Susan Juster offers this analogy: "religious prejudice functioned in the colonial era much like racial prejudice does in modern America."[50] Puritan Boston's expulsion and occasional execution of Quakers is one notorious example. The Quakers, who had also started in England, "embraced a doctrine of absolute human equality." This doctrine "put the Quakers at odds with both Anglicans (who upheld the sacraments) and with the Puritans (who believed in conformity to church authorities)."[51]

Many Protestants still worry they will be damned to hell for thinking the wrong thoughts. This is sometimes called "salvation anxiety."[52] In the chapter on human sexuality, I introduced Linda Kay Klein, who had grown up in an evangelical church. She describes it as "a religion in which every decision was not only a matter of life or death, but a matter of *eternal* life or *eternal* death." When Klein first sat down to write about the people she had interviewed and the harm that the purity movement had done to their lives, her mother warned her that she was endangering her salvation—even though everything she was writing was true. (Klein adds that a decade later her mother was much more supportive of the book.)[53]

Conservative evangelicals in particular see it as their moral and political duty to rescue America from the dangers of secular ideas, using what Jason Bivins, a specialist in religion and American culture, aptly labels a "Religion of Fear." Hell Houses[54] and the *Left Behind* novels, he argues, are examples of their "intentions to proselytize and save souls they believe are at risk"—and also to destroy the post-war American liberalism they are convinced has put those souls in jeopardy.[55] These evangelicals, Bivins argues, demand the demonization of the "other" even as their identity depends on those they seek to banish. "Those very things which threaten to undermine the purity of identity, and must consequently be driven away, are continually made central to the cultures and symbol systems they are said to oppose. I call this feature of conservative evangelical identity *the demonology within.*"[56]

Curiosity. The threat of hell has long been used to counter the danger that human curiosity, particularly scientific curiosity, might uncover things that contradict the revealed religion. Augustine warned against it back in the late fourth century. "Men are led to investigate the secrets of nature, which are irrelevant to our lives, although such knowledge is of no value to them and they wish to gain it merely for the sake of knowledge." He called curiosity a "poison" that masquerades as science and learning. It distracts us from our prayers, tempts us to take pride in our own learning, endangers our salvation.[57]

The medieval Church was less worried about scientific curiosity than Augustine—but only as long as the science didn't conflict with Church doctrine. Thus, once the Church had decreed that the Earth was the center of the universe and that all heavenly bodies revolved around it, it resisted any challenges to that decree. The Inquisition sent Giordano Bruno to the stake, and put Galileo under house arrest for the rest of his life, for showing that in reality the earth revolves around the sun. (It does bear noting that Bruno's and Galileo's situations were more complex than simple heresy—each man had made political miscalculations and powerful enemies. Their heretical heliocentricity was just another weapon to bring them down.)[58]

Bruno was executed in 1600, Galileo confined in 1633. But in the years after Galileo, the Catholic Church lost much of its power to punish heretical thoughts. In 1687, Isaac Newton had no trouble publishing his *Mathematical Principles of Natural Philosophy* (often called the *Principia),* one of the most important works in the history of science. He proved (to the ten people in the world who could follow his mathematics) not only that the earth and the other planets do revolve around the sun, but also how they manage to do it: the sun's gravity keeps them in orbit. A century later, Pierre Laplace modified Newton's explanation, and in the twentieth century Einstein substituted his theory of gravity—that it operates at the speed of light—for Newton's.

Some Protestants also have problems with scientific "heresies." Take for example Darwin's theory of evolution. Mainline white Protestants generally accept his theory, while others are more likely to reject it unless God is somehow involved.[59] (The Catholic Church, on the other hand, has gradually become more accepting of the theory.[60]) Conservative evangelicals and fundamentalist Protestants have waged outright war against teaching the theory of evolution, along with aspects of geology and other sciences, in American schools for more than a hundred years now.[61]

In 1921, three-time Presidential nominee William Jennings Bryan "encouraged taxpayers to demand that their teachers stop instructing students in scientific ideas that undermined faith." Bryan wasn't a fundamentalist, strictly speaking, but he made common cause with them on evolution.[62] He led the prosecution in the 1925 Scopes trial that tested Tennessee's law forbidding evolution to be taught. Tennessee repealed its law in 1967, and the Supreme Court has declared similar laws to be unconstitutional. But there continue to be legal challenges against the teaching of evolution, which courts continue to dismiss out of hand.[63]

As this isn't a science textbook, it's not the proper forum to go into the details of evolution and natural selection, or why intelligent design and creationism have no scientific foundation. Suffice it to say that the driving force behind science is *doubt*. Science starts with observations which it then subjects to questions: Did we really see what we thought we saw? What's a good explanation for it? Is there a better explanation? If a proposed explanation survives these doubts, it can become a hypothesis, which is then examined by other scientists who have their own doubts about it. If they are satisfied, the hypothesis could become a theory—but even then it is always open to doubt. It can be reevaluated, modified, and even rejected in whole or in part.

Those who hold to intelligent design and other creationist ideas, on the other hand, start with the Bible, then seek out observations that confirm the Bible while rejecting those that do not. The Bible itself—their theory, though they would never call it that—cannot be modified, much less rejected, no matter how much it is contradicted by reality. To allow that would be to allow doubt, and doubt would jeopardize their chance at heaven. In this much, anyway, Augustine was right to fear curiosity.

Disobedience. The Roman emperors' embrace of Christianity opened the way for the Church to use the fear of hell to exert political power. Around 380, when Roman Emperor Theodosius I ordered the abbot of Callinicum (in modern Syria) to restore the synagogue that a mob of monks had destroyed, Bishop Ambrose of Milan condemned him for doing so. "Will you give this triumph over the Church of God to the Jews? this trophy over Christ's people, this exultation, O Emperor, to the unbelievers?" The emperor must rescind this order, Ambrose insisted, warning him that "it is a serious matter to endanger your salvation for the Jews."[64]

Ambrose later claimed the emperor thereupon reversed his decision, though whether Theodosius actually did so is not clear.[65] Regardless, in the eleventh century Gregory VII recommended that the bishop of Metz use the Callinicum case as precedent to threaten secular rulers with the loss of their salvation if they disobeyed the Church. He reminded Bishop Herman that many previous popes had used excommunication to keep kings and emperors in line.[66] Gregory expected this threat to work because by then all of Europe was living in mortal terror of committing sins that would send them to hell forever. Asbridge describes Europe in Gregory's day as a land where "the full pantheon of human experience—birth, love, anger and death—was governed by Christian dogma, and the cornerstone of this system of belief was fear... This universal obsession, shared by king and peasant alike, shaped all custom, morality and law."[67]

The Church also used other weapons such as excommunication, which guaranteed damnation unless the sinner repented and was forgiven by the Church. Gregory VII spent most of his pontificate engaged in a political struggle with the secular rulers of Europe, particularly Henry IV of Germany, and he used threats of excommunication to get his way. Given Henry's attitude toward Gregory, I am doubtful that the king was actually worried the pope could have him sent to hell, but he nonetheless spent three days at Canossa in January 1077 standing in the snow waiting for the pope to hear his confession and forgive him. It was politically necessary, he had learned.[68] Gregory did succeed in humbling the German king to his will (briefly), but he also succeeded in alienating many of Europe's rulers, and when he later summoned them to a crusade, he was ignored.[69]

European secular authorities resented the power of the popes and their bishops to order them around, and seized on any opening to push back. In 1302, Boniface VIII issued the bull *Unam Sanctum*, in which he announced that "we declare, we proclaim, we define that it is absolutely necessary for salvation that every human creature be subject to the Roman Pontiff."[70] This so annoyed Philip IV of France that he had Boniface briefly taken prisoner with the intent of putting him on trial.[71] Around 1530, Clement VII refused to annul Henry VIII of England's marriage to Catherine of Aragon, probably because Catherine's nephew was Charles V of Spain, whose army was occupying Rome just then. Henry then forced the English clergy to acknowledge him as the head of the English church in place of the pope and got rid of Catherine that way. His daughter Elizabeth I later completed the establishment of the Church of England (the Anglican Church) as a Protestant denomination.[72]

Protestants also use the fear of hell to enforce obedience, but have generally been less effective at it than the Catholic Church. For one thing, Protestant leaders rarely if ever claimed the same power as the pope to get people into heaven or to keep them out. Another factor is that there are many branches of Protestantism, so a person excommunicated by one branch might find a welcome in another one. Even in the most authoritarian Protestant domains, dissidents could escape to other Protestant parts of Europe. In colonial Massachusetts, when the Puritans controlled the government, they were able to punish disobedient congregants with the stock, the whipping post, and on occasion by hanging. But they gradually lost that power as other colonies such as next-door Rhode Island (whose charter promised religious liberty for all[73]) were able to offer sanctuary.

INDULGENCES AND THE PROTESTANT REFORMATION

The Protestant Reformation itself had started as an act of disobedience—an objection to the way the Church was playing on people's fears of hell by offering them a chance to buy their way out of it. Using hell as a fundraiser goes back at least as far as the fifth century. Salvian of Marseille "conjured up a gripping vision of the other world" and urged the rich, in particular, to think of the torments that awaited them there. "Only by generous donations to the church...might [the rich] be saved from this grim tribunal... Never before had wealth and the afterlife been brought together in so menacing a manner." By the end of the sixth century, many of "those who gave alms to the poor and endowments to the churches and monasteries did so, quite bluntly, *pro remedio animae*—'to heal and protect their souls' in the afterlife and, above all, at the Last Judgment."[74]

In medieval times, the Church relied heavily on the sale of

indulgences as a way of raising funds. Technically, an indulgence did not rescue one from hell. But it would reduce the amount of time a soul would have to spend in purgatory—a kind of halfway station on the way to heaven where one paid penance for sins even after the Church had granted absolution. Indulgences were once offered for free to anyone who went on crusade. Within a few hundred years, however, their sale had become a major source of income for the Church and its bishops, not to mention itinerant indulgence salesmen. Indulgences were popular with the laity as a form of reassurance in a frighteningly lethal world. In 1515, when Leo X was trying to finish building St. Peter's Basilica in Rome, he turned to indulgences almost as a matter of course. Unfortunately for Leo, his indulgence campaign aroused the ire of one Martin Luther, a hitherto little-known Augustinian friar. "The treasures of indulgences are nets with which one now fishes for the wealth of men," Luther thundered in his 1517 manifesto.[75]

The friar did not initially intend to leave the Church, and the pope did not think the friar much of a threat at first. But as both sides hardened their positions, Luther was able to benefit from the Germans' growing resentment toward the Italians who ran the papal machinery, from the newly invented printing press which publicized his ideas, and from the politics surrounding the election of a new Holy Roman Emperor in 1519. Within a few years, Luther had broken with the pope and started what would become the Protestant Reformation.[76]

Let me pause here to point out that while we sometimes view Protestants and Catholics in binary terms, that is far too simplistic. Catholics are, in theory at least, subject to a unified doctrine and discipline. There is no such unity, even in theory, among Protestants. In Luther's lifetime alone there were significant splits and factions. Those who call themselves Protestants today range from the Anglicans and their American cousins the Episcopalians to the Presbyterians to the Quakers and the

Mennonites, from the Methodists to the Southern Baptists to the Pentecostals and evangelicals, and different groups of Lutherans. Still, there are some things all Protestant denominations have in common. One is that they all reject the authority of the pope. Another is that, while they raise money in many ways, some quite questionable, they have never, so far as I know, offered to free someone from the fear of hell in return for money.

EVEN GOOD CHRISTIANS MIGHT GO TO HELL

Yet one more marker common to Protestants is a belief in justification by faith alone. Catholics believe that faith, while necessary, is not sufficient for salvation; one must also do good works. This is based in part on a passage in the Epistle of James —"You see that faith was active along with [Abraham's] works, and faith was brought to completion by the works"—a passage that so annoyed Luther he almost left James out of his translation of the New Testament.[77] Luther had reasoned that none of us is worthy of salvation, being so depraved by nature that we all deserve to be sent to hell. Instead, he argued, God chooses to "impute" to those who believe in Jesus the merits of Jesus's sacrifice and resurrection as a gift of grace to the undeserving.[78] The value of the doctrine of justification by faith alone, explained Martin Chemnitz, one of the early Protestant commentators, was that it eased the minds of Jesus believers who were terrified that their actions—their works—weren't good enough to let them avoid eternity in hell.[79]

Luther's doctrine immediately led to charges that it allowed the faithful a "license to sin," but Luther dismissed this. In his thinking, God gave us this grace as an act of unconditional love, and by recognizing this, "we will love him unreservedly in return," avoiding sin and doing good works as an act of love.[80]

A problem of a different nature arose a few years later, when

John Calvin of Geneva merged justification by faith with long-standing ideas about predestination into a doctrine of double predestination: God had already decided before we were even born who was destined for hell as well who was destined for heaven. A historian of Protestantism, Alec Ryrie, describes Calvin's doctrine this way: God's "decision to save us is free, sovereign, and inscrutable, and if he does not choose to save us, there is absolutely nothing we can do about it. In other words, our eternal fate is predestined."[81] No matter how good a life anyone had lived *and* no matter how much they believed in Jesus, it counted for nothing if God had already decided otherwise. Even if you firmly believed that Jesus saved you from hell, you might not be saved from hell.

The history of predestination goes back before Augustine and is far too complex to be examined here.[82] My present concern is that Calvin's double predestination posed tremendous spiritual and psychological perils. John Tillotson, the Anglican archbishop of Canterbury in the 1690s, warned that in good men, the doctrine stirred up "groundless fears" and discomfort—the very fears Luther had hoped to assuage. In bad men, the feeling that nothing they did could save them would lead them to "licentiousness."[83] Calvin himself confessed it was a "dreadful" decree, though he hoped that it would reassure the godly by telling them that their doubts and terrors were all part of God's plan.[84] The godly were not always reassured. During the revival movement now known as the "First Great Awakening" that swept colonial America in the 1730s, evangelical preachers insisted that God would bestow his grace "only upon some of those who accepted their own utter helplessness to save themselves" (which was contrary to pure Calvinism). "Seekers then fell into a profound sense of despair, doubting that God would ever save them." Joseph Hawley, whose nephew Jonathan Edwards was the leading preacher of the revival, fell into such despair over his salvation that he cut his own throat; nor was he the only one who killed himself out of dread over eternity. "Such suicides dissipated the enthusiasm that sustained a revival, bringing the zeal and the conversions to a halt."[85] By the end of the nineteenth century, belief in double predestination was fading, at least in the United States.[86]

WHAT PRICE HEAVEN?

The earliest Christians expected that the world as they knew it was about to end at any moment, to be replaced by the kingdom of God on earth. When that failed to happen on schedule, they decided to focus on life after death in heaven as a temporary substitute for the coming kingdom. Either way, whether on earth or in heaven or hell, everyone's eternal fate depended on behaving properly and most importantly on believing properly. Seen in this light, life on earth has value only to the extent that it helps one get into heaven after death.

The consequences of this stance have been enormous. Millions have slaughtered other millions out of fear that allowing those others to live would lead them to question their own beliefs and thus threaten their own salvation. Christians persecuted Jews for centuries because their continued existence as Jews called into doubt Christianity's claim to have super-seded Judaism. That same fear of doubt also encouraged Christians to suppress alternative versions of Christianity and to limit science to that which their theology was prepared to accept. Nothing could be allowed to disturb Christians' certainty that they possessed the only valid path to eternal life.

That path to eternal happiness frequently includes minimizing or outright rejecting the pleasures this world has to offer. "Do not store up for yourselves treasures on earth...but store up for yourselves treasures in heaven," said Jesus in Matthew.[87] Christianity is not the only religion with a tendency to asceti-cism, but it is unusual in the way it has frequently urged its adherents to adopt extremes of denial. It goes to great lengths to encourage sufferers to accept their suffering, promising them they will be compensated for the pain of this life with eternal life in heaven. "For this slight momentary affliction is preparing us for an eternal weight of glory beyond all measure," Paul assured the Corinthians.[88] Augustine counseled against committing suicide to escape the world's suffering. Those who are saved must patiently endure the evils of earthly life, he wrote, for they are made happy by their hope of salvation.[89] Some of the French Jesuit missionaries in seventeenth-century Canada "argued that suffering was necessary in order to reduce the pride and independence that kept [indigenous] people from recognizing the necessity of submission and their obligations to God and the Jesuits."[90]

Early in the 1800s, New England missionaries promoted the idea that slavery was good for the Blacks. In his study of American religious nationalism, historian Sam Haselby quotes from numerous pamphlets of the time, such as *The Negro Servant* by the New England Tract Society (1815), showing that they "represented American slavery as God's way of bringing Africans to salvation." (Haselby also points out that some Christian abolitionists had an "acrimonious falling out" with missionary societies over their pro-slavery stance.) [91]

Slaveholders in the American South had initially resisted exposing their African-American slaves to Christianity, fearing that they might pick up ideas about equality and even rebellion.[92] Then they realized they could use it to their advantage. In the New Testament Epistle to the Colossians we find this admonition: "Slaves, obey your earthly masters in everything...since you know that from the Lord you will receive the inheritance as your reward."[93] In an 1842 pamphlet, Charles Jones used this passage and others from the New Testament in urging his fellow Southerners to preach the gospel to their slaves. "Is not the discharge of duty made more sure and faithful, and respect for authority strengthened by considerations drawn from the omniscience of God and the retributions of eternity?"[94]

At the same time, we need to be clear that Christian beliefs also motivated the abolitionists who pushed successfully for an end to slavery, many of whom had opposed African slavery from the beginning.[95] In the decades leading up to the Civil War, the Presbyterians, Methodists, and Baptists split into northern and southern denominations over the question of slavery.[96]

Another consequence of putting the afterlife ahead of current life is a lack of concern for the physical health of the planet. Some of the fervently religious do read the verses in Genesis as commanding them to be "good stewards" of the earth. A Pentecostal deacon in Louisiana is fighting the polluters of his beloved bayou and is part of a lawsuit to force them to clean it up. Even so, the pollution doesn't concern him as much as "saving all those babies" from abortion. We only have a short time on this earth, he explained to sociologist Arlie Hochschild, "but if we get our souls saved, we go to Heaven, and Heaven is for eternity. We'll never have to worry about the environment from then on. That's the most important thing."[97] Some people approach the ongoing Covid-19 pandemic with similar insouciance. The governor of Mississippi explained his state's poor response to the disease by saying: "When you believe in eternal life—when you believe that living on this earth is but a blip on the screen, then you don't have to be so scared of things"— though he added that "God also tells us to take necessary precautions."[98]

In the chapter on Christianity's impact on human sexuality, I suggested that religious opposition to our modern understanding of sex amounts to a denial of reality. The obsession with life after death even at the expense of life here on earth is not quite the same thing, but it betrays, let us say, a similar distaste for reality. We are being asked to believe that life after death, for which the evidence is at best speculative, is more important than life in this world, which we live in now and which we know is real with every breath we take.

When I wondered as a child what happens when we die, my parents told me to just worry about this world; the next world will take care of itself. This is a very Jewish answer (though, as one might expect, not all Jews will agree). It says to me that we should do what will help us here and now, what will make life better for ourselves, our community, our children, our planet, for our sakes and theirs and not for the sake of heaven. Life on earth matters more than life after death. It is only to be expected that Christians have trouble with this last point, though some denominations in this modern, pluralistic age may be coming around. For example, the current Presbyterian confession of faith (1967) makes only one brief mention of life after death. Presbyterian minister Lewis R. Donelson stresses this, pointing out that "the rest of the confession is devoted to present life on this earth... We all seem to be 48-year-olds, like me, concentrating on the enormous tasks of this life and letting God worry about heaven."[99]

Let me offer one last thought on life and death from the Jewish tradition. There is a tale the rabbis tell that when Moses was about to die and was complaining to God that he was not allowed to enter the Promised Land, God replied that, after all his labors, Moses had earned his rest.[100] This should be the measure of our lives: When it comes our time to die, we should be worthy of rest.

CHAPTER EIGHT

THE WORLD WILL END ON [FILL IN THE BLANK]

The belief that the world as we have known it is just about to end, to be replaced by God's kingdom on earth, is possibly the oldest idea in Christianity. According to Mark's gospel, the first words Jesus preached were: "The time is fulfilled, and the kingdom of God is at hand."[1] To this day, the expectation that Jesus will return any moment now to establish God's kingdom continues to shape Christian thinking and actions. It is the ultimate extrapolation of the belief that God interferes in history. This in turn continues to have a major impact on the world, so much so that I can only give a few examples here, or else it would dominate the book.[2] My intention in this chapter is to briefly examine three questions. First: how did Christianity acquire this expectation? Second: how do Christians cope with the continuing failure of the world to end as expected? Third and most important: why, even now, is this expectation of the end of the world still interfering with the world's efforts to keep going?

THE BEGINNING OF THE END OF DAYS

From early days, Israelites thought of time as linear: it had a beginning and it will have an ending.[3] However, the authors of Scripture were much more specific about what happened when time began—the six days of creation—than about how they expect it will end. There was a general understanding that in "future days," or at the "end of days," or when the "day of the Lord" occurs, the earthly world with all its dangers and disappointments will be replaced by an earthly paradise with God openly in charge. But this was a rather vague belief with no particular schedule or details. Much of it is simply what one might expect to hear from a small nation hoping for a reversal of fortune against its larger and more powerful neighbors. Isaiah, writing in the eighth century BCE when Israel was under Assyrian domination, promised that "in future days" God's house will be well-established and all nations will come to worship there, beating their swords into plowshares as they do so. This vision of a peaceful transformation is even enshrined at the United Nations. Other visions were more vengeful. Early in the Babylonian exile, the prophet Ezekiel hoped for a time when the Temple would be rebuilt and Israel would triumph over its enemies, whereupon Yahweh "will become known before the eyes of many nations, and they shall know that I am the Lord." The last of the Hebrew prophets, Malachi, concluded by predicting that God would soon send Elijah to prepare everyone for the "coming of the day of the Lord, / great and fearsome," when there would be healing for the righteous and destruction of the wicked. Even Isaiah warned that the day of the Lord would come in "anger and smoldering wrath, / to turn the earth into desolation / and expunge its offenses from it."[4]

The author of Daniel, writing in the second century BCE, claimed a similar vision, but unlike his predecessors, he made specific predictions and gave a specific date (several dates, actually). He told his readers that there was about to be a great battle with displays of supernatural power, after which the righteous and the wicked would receive their eternal judgment—and it was all going to happen right away. I explained the reasons why he did this in chapter 2. The point here is that the author of Daniel, writing in a time of an existential war with the Seleucids, predicted a violent ending to the present-day world—what we would now call an apocalypse—that would come to pass inevitably and very soon.

When it didn't come to pass, some Jews continued to believe in Daniel and set about reexamining his predictions looking for a new date. The Qumran community of the first century CE read into Daniel and other books of Scripture a clear description— clear to them, anyway—of the era that they themselves were living in. Roman oppression and Temple corruption were signs that the final war between light and darkness had already begun, that God was preparing to fight on their behalf and would soon send a messiah to reveal the truth at the moment of the establishment of God's kingdom.[5]

There is an academic argument that John the Baptist had some connection with the Qumran community, though he never became an initiate.[6] Whether or not the Baptist got the idea from them, he too believed that the end of days was already here. John went around Galilee telling everyone to "repent, for the kingdom of heaven is at hand." Jesus, whom John had baptized, continued to preach that same message after John's arrest.[7] Then, after Jesus had been crucified and the world hadn't ended, his disciples preached that Jesus had gone to heaven to get the kingdom moving, as it were. Any day now, he would return and bring the kingdom with him. Paul assured the Romans that "now is the moment for you to wake from sleep. For salvation is nearer to us now than when we became believers; the night is far gone, the day is near."[8] The First Letter of Peter similarly exhorted its readers to remember that "the end of all things is near," while the First Letter of John announced that "antichrists" have appeared, and that "from this we know that it is the last hour."[9]

Still the world continued as before. In medieval scholar Richard Landes's pointed observation, "God ha[s] demonstrated...an infuriating reluctance to show up according to the prophetic promises and apocalyptic calculations of humans."[10] By the end of the first century, many Christians had started to come to terms with this delay by reckoning, as the Second Letter of Peter did, that God's idea of "immediately" was different from man's.[11] Even earlier, some of the evangelists had begun to hedge their bets. Matthew, writing around the year 80, had Jesus warn his listeners that "neither the angels of heaven, nor the Son, but only the Father" knows the day and hour when the kingdom will come. The book of Acts, possibly written a decade after Matthew, even turned that warning into an outright prohibition against trying to calculate when Jesus would return. When the disciples asked the risen Jesus when he would restore the kingdom, "he replied, 'It is not for you to know the times or periods that the Father has set by his own authority.'"[12]

Some New Testament authors, however, were still counting on an imminent grand finale. The book of Revelation, most likely written just before the end of the first century, started by warning its readers to pay heed to its prophecy, "for the time is near." Later in the book, an angel called out: "Fear God and give him glory, for the hour of his judgment has come."[13] Revelation —apokalypsis in the original Greek—is also the most violent book in the entire Bible. It is from here that the English word apocalypse acquired the connotation of not just the end of the world and the final judgment of God, but of a violent, world-shattering, supernatural-clash-of-elemental-forces end of the world and the wrath of God.

Revelation, as well as the other books of the New Testament, were all written for the peoples of their time.[14] But as happened with the book of Daniel—also written for that author's own time—when the predicted apocalyptic moment passed uneventfully, some decided that the texts had been misunderstood, that they were really talking about a *different* time still to come. This led to two responses to the problem of why the kingdom hasn't come yet. The first was that it will happen when God decides it will happen. The other was that the Bible does in fact tell us the exact date of the end of the world, if only we can figure it out.

'X' THOUSAND YEARS TO JUDGMENT DAY

In Revelation, John of Patmos described what he saw after God's armies first defeated the devil: the martyrs who had died for the faith "came to life and reigned with Christ a thousand years."[15] This is only one of several mentions in the book of a thousand-year span, from which we get the term *millennialism*, from the Latin *mille annum* (a thousand years). Millennialism denotes a belief that there will be a thousand-year period of divinely directed life, to be followed by the Last Judgment when the fate of all souls will be decided for all eternity. The decision to include Revelation in the New Testament was hotly contested for centuries, but it guaranteed that millennialism would continue to be a major factor in Christian thinking and in its impact on the western world.[16]

God had created the world in six days, it says in Genesis. Around 120 CE, the Epistle of Barnabas explained that, because each of those days represented a thousand years, all things would be completed in six thousand years.[17] Therefore, the day of the Lord would occur sometime around AM (*anno mundi*) 6000—that is to say, 6000 years after the creation of the world.[18] Landes gives a number of examples of various Christian thinkers trying to calculate how many years were left to us before then. For instance, sometime in the third century CE Hippolytus of Rome calculated that Jesus had been born in AM

5500. "From the birth of Christ, then, we must reckon the 500 years that remain to make up the 6000, and thus the end shall be"—meaning that the existing world will end around what we would now label the year 500 CE. Hippolytus explains that this delay is necessary so that "in the remaining half time the gospel might be preached to the whole world, and that when the sixth day was completed He might end the present life."[19] Other Christian thinkers used different dates for the creation of the world and came up with different years for the birth of Jesus, such as AM 5200 and 5325, but all of them placed it in the sixth millennium of the world.[20] (Jews also start with the creation of the world, but calculate it very differently. According to the Jewish calendar, Jesus was born in the fourth millennium, sometime between the Hebrew years 3757 and 3761.)

Landes argues that Hippolytus was actually attempting to tamp down current millennial speculation by moving the date a few centuries beyond his own lifetime.[21] But before long, the institutional Church had become powerful and prosperous and had little wish to see its power and prosperity come to an end any time soon.[22] Bishop Augustine of Hippo tried to put an end to all such speculation by declaring that the current age, the sixth millennium, was in fact the age in which Jesus, through the Church, was already reigning on earth. Moreover, this millennium was not fixed at a thousand years but was of indefinite duration.[23] Indeed, wrote Augustine, Paul's First Letter to the Thessalonians makes it clear that it is not proper for us to even try to calculate when the end of days will arrive.[24] Still, many Christians kept trying to calculate it anyway.[25]

Around 525 CE, the monk Dionysius Exiguus proposed a new type of calendar to set the annual date of Easter, based on *anno domini* (AD: the year of our Lord), in which AD 1 was the year when Jesus was believed to have been born.[26] (It's long been known that he was almost certainly off by four years.) At first, people paid little attention to Dionysius's dating system.[27]

But early in the eighth century CE, the Venerable Bede, a monk in northern England, undertook a detailed recalculation of the age of the world and concluded that "Jesus Christ, the Son of God, allowed the Sixth Age of the world by His coming" in AM 3952, around 1500 years earlier than Hippolytus's date.[28] The chapter of Bede's *The Reckoning of Time* where this quote is taken from is titled "The Six Ages of This World," and Bede was at pains there to make clear that each "age" was defined by the events that happened during that age and not by strict thousand-year spans. The birth (in theological terms, the "incarnation") of Jesus thus marked the start of the Sixth Age. This "millennium" doesn't have a fixed length of time, but will, "like senility...come to an end in the death of the whole world." Bede was even more explicit in the following chapter: "No one should pay heed to those who speculate that the existence of this world was determined from the beginning at 6,000 years."[29] Bede then deliberately used Dionysius's AD dates for the chronology in his *Ecclesiastical History of England* rather than any of the AM versions. In describing the Roman emperor Claudius's war in Britain, Bede wrote: "This war he concluded in the fourth year of his empire, which is the forty-sixth year from the incarnation of our Lord."[30] A historian of the early medieval British period, Maírín MacCarron, argues that Bede did this in order to reinforce the idea that the length of the Sixth Age was unknowable.[31] Bede may also have seen an advantage in using a precisely (even if incorrectly) calculated event—the incarnation of Jesus—rather than the date of the creation of the world, for which there were so many competing calculations.

Thanks in large part to Bede's work, and with the help of the Carolingian kings, over the next few centuries the AD year came to dominate western Europe, which later spread it around the globe.[32] It is ironic that one of the greatest consequences of millennialism has been the near-universal imposition of a dating system intended to put a stop to millennialist speculation: AD (*anno domini*), also known as the Common Era (CE), is the standard year almost everywhere on earth.

MILLENNIUMS OF THE MIDDLE AGES

Despite the efforts of Augustine, Bede, and other theologians and thinkers, many simply could not leave millennialism alone.[33] The idea that the end of the world could be calculated, indeed that it was just about to happen, remained a common and influential belief in medieval Europe. The Venerable Bede's adoption of Dionysius's *anno domini* didn't really solve his problem; it just postponed it. It merely moved the date of the millennium from 6,000 years after the creation of the world to a thousand years after the incarnation of Jesus. As the year AD 1000 drew ever closer, "it seem[ed] as if virtually every Christian tradition reached apocalyptic intensity."[34] In the last decades of the first millennium, there were all the usual famines, fires, plagues, and other disasters, but now people started to wonder if they were the signs that the Last Day was finally approaching. In 989 an apparition now known to be Halley's Comet appeared in the sky for months. Vesuvius, the destroyer of Pompeii, erupted in 993, and perhaps also in 991 and 999. There is evidence of a heightened sense of anticipation, though historians still argue whether there was any widespread terror. Some people gave all their possessions to the poor in the hope that this would gain them merit for Judgment Day. At the midnight mass in St. Peter's in Rome on the last day of the year 999, the basilica was packed with worshipers come to watch Pope Sylvester II, some in fear, some in hope, some perhaps waiting to see if he would sprout horns and a tail.[35]

When AD 1000 came and went and the world went on as usual, some argued that the end of the world had started anyway, while others pushed the date forward a few years, or said it would be 1033, the thousandth anniversary of the crucifixion. The failure of the world to end as it was supposed to on any of these dates made people wonder if some outside malevolent force was interfering with God's plans. Jews in particular fell under suspicion. "Far easier than admitting error, Christians [could] blame the Jews: had they only converted, *then* Jesus would have come," writes Landes, adding: "Hell hath no fury like an apocalyptic lover scorned."[36]

Even in earlier centuries there had been some connection between anti-Jewish sentiment and anxiety over the apocalypse.[37] After AD 1000 this hostility increased even more. There were a number of reasons for this, but the connection to the missed millennium cannot be dismissed as entirely coincidental. There is a reasonably reliable report that in 1007 the king of France tried to force the Jews of Rouen to convert, in violation of Augustine's witness doctrine.[38] Apocalypse historian Martyn Whittock sees "forced baptisms [of Jews] in western German cities...as expressions of fanatical enthusiasm for becoming part of God's end-times judgement."[39] When the caliph of Egypt, al-Hakim bi-Amr Allah, ordered the Church of the Holy Sepulcher burned to the ground in 1009, French Christians blamed the Jews for inciting the destruction and attacked Jewish communities in Orléans and other cities. A historian of the Crusades, Jay Rubenstein, calls Orléans the first of the medieval pogroms against the Jews. "A pattern...had been set—a combination of apocalyptic expectation, anti-Jewish violence, and terrors inspired by news from Jerusalem—that would repeat itself at the time of the First Crusade."[40] Prior to the eleventh century, Jews had survived more or less comfortably in European lands, albeit with some significant exceptions.[41] But by the turn of the millennium, Jews were the only significant group of non-Christians left in Christian Europe, and they were increasingly targeted because of it.

According to some Christian traditions, one of the prerequisites of the millennium was that "misbelief had to be eliminated," which was coming to mean the physical elimination of the misbelievers.[42] The First Crusade, in 1096, was partly inspired by millennial fervor—the need to restore Jerusalem to Christian control in order to hasten the Second Coming. On their way to "liberate" Jerusalem, a horde of peasant crusaders led by Peter the Hermit (the "People's Crusade") massacred Jews in several cities across Europe, in spite of efforts by high churchmen and secular rulers to stop them. The crusade's apocalyptic fervor had led them to attack these "enemies of Christ" living among them.[43] "Conversion of the Jews became a perennial theme of apocalyptic anticipation"[44]—a theme that continues today. And it set the pattern for several hundred years of oppression, persecution, expulsion, and slaughter.

Nor was it just the Jews who felt the wrath of medieval Christendom. Doubt among Christians had to be eliminated as well. The first executions for heresy in over 600 years took place in 1022 at Orléans and at Turin a few years later. "These incidents all hint at an increased and widespread appetite for reform after the millennium," writes medieval historian James Palmer, adding that, to medieval Christians, heresy was "perhaps the greatest apocalyptic concern of all."[45]

Millennial expectations continued throughout the high Middle Ages in spite of Church efforts to suppress them. They were sometimes triggered by calculations, other times by events. Much of this resulted from the influence of Joachim of Fiore, a twelfth-century abbot who held that the millennium was still to come, rejecting Augustine's insistence that the world was already living in it. Joachim (who died in 1202) expected a new age to follow some cataclysmic event he predicted would occur in 1260.[46] By 1240, the Mongols had conquered much of Russia and had started moving into Hungary, leading many to argue that "the appearance and behavior of those ferocious warriors could only make sense in the context of the endtime."[47] For tactical reasons and because of politics back home, in 1242 the

Mongols retreated before they could truly threaten the heart of Catholic Europe, though they continued to launch devastating raids in Poland and Hungary for the rest of the century.[48] In Italy there was famine in 1258 and plague in 1259, plus incessant warfare between Florentine families, all of which so convinced some that the end was near that they became flagellants, going from Italian town to town whipping themselves in public penance. But the Italian "mass flagellant movement soon died of disillusionment" when 1260 came and went.[49]

A hundred years later, in the mid-fourteenth century, events rather than predictions caused an outbreak of apocalyptic concern. The Black Death of 1348–49 killed perhaps one-third or more of Europe; no one knows for sure. Flagellants, many of whom "certainly lived in a world of millenarian phantasy," reappeared all over central Europe.[50] The sense of utter hopelessness convinced many that the plague was a sign of the apocalypse predicted in Revelation. "During the Black Death popular fear was so great that terror of the End Time dominated thinking and writing."[51]

In 1453, the Ottoman Turks captured Constantinople, ending an Orthodox Christian empire that had lasted over a thousand years. Worries that this was a harbinger of the apocalypse were not confined to Catholic Europe. While millennialism had previously been uncommon among the Russian Orthodox, the fall of Constantinople to the Muslims led to much millennial speculation in Russia. That in turn eventually led to a schism in the Russian Orthodox Church, with the breakaway Old Believers in 1666 charging that the tsar or the patriarch was antichrist, that the established church an abomination, and that its changes to the liturgy were a sign that the tribulations had begun. Possibly as many as twenty percent of Russians were Old Believers in the seventeenth century and endured occasional persecution under the tsars.[52] There are still a number of Old Believers around the world today.

Numerous other events in this period were seen as apocalyptic possibilities, even including the ongoing struggles between popes and emperors. "Millenarian beliefs operated at *all levels* of society in the Middle Ages," writes Whittock, even though Catholic Church officials discouraged these popular beliefs, sometimes quite forcefully.[53] When it comes to the Protestants, however, there are whole sects who officially and theologically expect the millennium and even believe they must help to bring it about.

PROTESTANT MILLENNIALISTS

The Catholic Church continues to enforce the view established by Augustine that we are currently living in the millennium preceding Jesus's return, but that it is not a precise period of a thousand years. It's an indefinite span of time during which the Church, by spreading Christianity around the world, will create the conditions for Jesus to return. (This position is called amillennialism.) This is also the position of Protestants such as the Episcopalians. Other Protestants, starting with Luther himself, have embraced the idea of the millennium as something that is yet to happen, and that might even come into being in their own lifetimes. Luther scholar Heiko Oberman writes that Luther saw in the actions of the Catholic Church of his day clear signs that Jesus's prophecy of the Last Days was even now coming to pass. Another scholar adds that later in life Luther (who died in 1546) was increasingly convinced the world would end by 1600.[54]

Protestant millennialists can be broadly divided into two main categories: *premillennialists* and *postmillennialists*. Premillennialists believe that Jesus will come back *before* the millennium, so that the thousand years of God's kingdom on earth start immediately upon his return. Postmillennialists believe that Jesus will return only *after* the kingdom of God has been established on earth for a thousand years. Both do hold that, once the millennium has ended, God will decide everyone's fate for all eternity at the Last Judgment.

Aside from that basic distinction, there are some other characteristics which generally place a person more in one camp than in the other. Premillennialists often expect a "tribulation" —an era of doom, disaster, and despair—for some period of time prior to Jesus's return, and Jesus will start his reign by cleaning it all up. This tends to make them see the world in pessimistic terms: it's not worth the effort to make the world better, at least on a large scale, prior to the Second Coming. It also means that the millennium will begin suddenly, with a supernatural event, a divine manifestation that will uncontestably reveal God's power and will. Many premillennialists calculate and recalculate the exact date when they believe the celestial event will come to pass.

Postmillennialists are generally more optimistic in that they see the problems of the world as things in need of reform *now*, by human beings, in order to bring about the thousand years that must pass before Jesus comes again. Postmillennialists are more likely to look forward to the establishment of the millennial Christian kingdom on earth. For them, the only necessary supernatural event is the one that will happen at the end of those thousand years, because until then God hides his guiding hand by acting through human beings.[55]

These are basic categorizations only. There are many variations, and often people cannot be easily classified as one or the other, as we will shortly see. Some individuals also shift back and forth between pre- and postmillennialism, depending on what happens to them personally and on how they view changes taking place in the world around them.[56]

EARLY MILLENNIALISM IN AMERICA

The English colonials in America were largely Protestants, and many were postmillennialists of some sort. In particular, the Puritans came to the colonies as "God's chosen instruments" to bring about the millennium in the New World, and millennialism "pervaded Puritan life" in New England.[57] "The Calvinist view [was] that the kingdom of God had begun with the resurrection of Christ, and that, consequently, the Calvinists, as the representatives of the true kingdom of God on earth, had authority over civil sovereigns."[58] The Puritans were Calvinists. As such, they undertook to create a Calvinist-style state that would be the first step in the postmillennial process of preparing the world for Jesus to return.

Still, Massachusetts preachers Increase and Cotton Mather, father and son, spent much of the seventeenth century finding in the numerous disasters of their time signs of the approaching end, a premillennialist position.[59] John Cotton, an influential Boston theologian of the middle 1600s, seems to have combined elements of both premillennialism and postmillennialism. He preached that "so far as God helps by Scripture light, about the time 1655. [sic] there will be then such a blow given to this beast, and to the head of this beast, which is *Pontifex maximus* [the pope], as that we shall see a further gradual accomplishment and fulfilling of this Prophecy here." (Cotton, who died in 1652, made this claim around 1640.) [60]

New England's initial millennial fervor appears to have dampened by the middle of the seventeenth century.[61] It flared up again with the First Great Awakening in the 1730s. This was led by Jonathan Edwards, possibly the greatest Protestant theologian in eighteenth century America. He declared that "we can't reasonably think otherwise, than that the beginning of this great work of God [the millennium] must be near. And there are many things that make it probable that this work will begin in

America."[62] Even into the late nineteenth century, many were anticipating "a thousand-year period of peace, prosperity, and righteousness described in the book of Revelation, which they hoped to help inaugurate through their own good works."[63] The westward expansion, the abolitionist movement to get rid of slavery, and especially the concepts of American Exceptionalism and James Polk's "Manifest Destiny," all were driven by or at least strengthened by postmillennialist beliefs.[64] Nineteenth-century "postmillennialism legitimated American civil religion, that durable fusion of patriotism, nondenominational Protestantism, and belief in America's responsibility to conduct an experiment in free government."[65]

The nineteenth century also witnessed a revival of premillennialism, with the Millerites being one of the most famous early instances. In 1831, William Miller, a Baptist layman from upstate New York, published his conclusion, based on "biblical arithmetic," that "Christ would return in glory" between March 1843 and March 1844. Perhaps as many as fifty thousand Americans, mostly in the northeast, were convinced by Miller, who also attracted some believers in Britain. When nothing happened, Miller admitted he had miscalculated, but then allowed himself to be pressured into setting an exact date: October 22, 1844. As that date approached, "thousands of Americans" (there appears to be no reliable number) prepared for the Second Coming by quitting their jobs, selling off their property, leaving crops unharvested, and forgiving debts. The "Great Disappointment" that followed left many Millerites pauperized as well as humiliated. Some Millerites abandoned the whole idea, but "probably a majority" remained convinced that Jesus would have appeared had they not done something wrong. They eventually coalesced into the Seventh-day Adventists, who even now expect the millennium any day.[66]

Postmillennialism was still the order of the day for much of nineteenth century America, but it began losing adherents after the Civil War (1861–65). The Civil War was, in historian Garry Wills's words, an "apocalyptic war," from its (eventual) goal of eliminating slavery to its unofficial anthem, the "Battle Hymn of the Republic," many of whose lines came right out of Revelation. The South, as Wills reminds us, was equally sure that God was on their side in their "cosmic battle."[67] But the destruction the war left behind, especially in the South, caused many to rethink the expected order of events, and to think more in premillennialist terms, in which "tribulation" came first. The North as well looked at the poverty in its cities and the corruption of its leaders and also began to wonder if the premillennialists were right.[68]

Postmillennialism did not lose all influence. Sociologists John R. Hall and Zeke Baker argue that postmillennialism was a major factor in the "Social Gospel" movement of the later nineteenth and most of the twentieth centuries, which drew in Catholics, Jews, and secularists in addition to millennialist Protestants.[69] Still, premillennialism gradually gained the upper hand in the twentieth century. The horrors of World War I and especially World War II, the Holocaust, atomic weapons, dismay at disruptive social changes, and the rising supremacy of secular science were all contributing factors.[70]

AMERICAN MILLENNIALISM TODAY

Jonathan Edwards was the most influential of the early American evangelicals. Evangelicalism, found in Britain but especially in America since the eighteenth century, does not describe a specific Christian sect or group, but rather a section of the Christian spectrum, and one with many colors to it, as it were. In her monumental study of evangelicalism, Frances Fitzgerald offers a basic definition of evangelicals as those who "believed they had been born again in Christ and had a duty to evangelize, or spread the good news of the Gospels in America and abroad."[71] Evangelicalism in America can be traced back to the revivals of the First Great Awakening that Edwards had initiated. Beyond the requirement that everyone must have a "personal experience" and an ongoing relationship with Jesus as their personal savior, one of the few things most evangelicals have in common is a belief in the oncoming millennium. That belief may be premillennial, postmillennial, or some combination or variation thereof. Evangelicals are more likely to be politically conservative, though many express liberal ideas. In 2018, one quarter of all Americans identified as evangelicals of some form. This actually represents a slight decline from previous years, but they have long been and continue to be hugely influential in American politics.[72]

Fundamentalism is a peculiarly American variation of evangelicalism, though it is now being spread around the world. Like evangelicalism, it is a category, not a denomination, and historians generally set its origins in the late nineteenth and early twentieth centuries. It takes its name from *The Fundamentals: A Testimony of Truth*, a set of twelve manifestos published between 1910 and 1915.[73] Those who classify themselves as fundamentalists hold that what Fitzgerald calls the "original autographs" —the "manuscripts that came from the hands of the prophets" —are "inerrant," that is, without error or flaw. She goes on to observe that since these documents "did not, of course, exist," Biblical inerrantism "was safe from biblical scholarship." Nonetheless, she points out, this qualification was a "subtlety lost on most nonscholars," for whom whatever translation they were relying on "was to be taken for fact."[74]

Fundamentalists also resist modernization and "progress," again unlike many evangelicals. And they are almost entirely premillennialist. They are convinced that the world is completely messed up, that the "tribulations" will start any time now—or have already started—and that Jesus will return any moment now bringing with him a flaming sword and exacting retribution on all those who do not believe as they, the fundamentalists, do. A particularly popular belief among fundamentalists is that they will be "raptured"—taken bodily up to heaven just as Jesus comes (though there are disagreements over whether this will happen at the start of the tribulations, during them, or when Jesus puts an end to them.) Believers in the rapture generally can be described as "dispensationalists."[75]

There are some postmillennialist fundamentalists as well, who see it as their duty to help bring about the millennium through preaching the gospel, inspiring holiness, and in the case of Christian Reconstructionists,[76] encouraging governments to enforce "Old Testament principles" of behavior. For Reconstructionists, these include the total absence of government assistance, public schools replaced by private and home schooling, a patriarchal family structure where women stay at home, stoning of Sabbath breakers and non-heterosexuals, and the expulsion of anyone, even other Christians, who do not share their version of the faith. Fitzgerald quotes their founder, R. J. Rushdoony, as rejecting democracy—Christianity is "committed to spiritual aristocracy," he said—and describes his intention to establish Old Testament law, including the death penalty for homosexuality, "incorrigible juvenile delinquency," and blasphemy, among other things.[77] "Christian Reconstructionists are few in number," writes history and religion professor Richard Kyle, "and it is unlikely that they will ever take over America, let alone the world." He admits, however, that it is difficult to accurately assess their influence on American politics.[78] I am not as sanguine as Kyle about the danger they represent, though I will hazard that if the United States were ever in a situation where Reconstructionists or a similar theological autocracy were in a position to take political power, there would be so many competing autocracies vying—probably violently—to challenge their rule that their specific demands would be the least of our problems.

The majority of American millennialists these days, however, are premillennialists, and they are also an immediate concern. This is because premillennialism encourages a dystopian view of the world about which nothing can be done until Jesus straightens it out himself. Alternatively (and sometimes simultaneously), they may actively encourage crises that they believe are signs that the tribulation is finally about to happen. (They may also expect the rapture will let them escape the consequences of their meddling.) This attitude impacts the whole world in many ways.[79] In the interests of space and time, I will limit myself to just two areas where the desire to hasten the coming of the millennium is actively or passively interfering with efforts to find and implement workable solutions: the modern State of Israel, and global climate change.

The State of Israel. This is an enormously complex topic, one involving the enduring desire of Jews to return to their ancestral homeland, the rights of Palestinians living there, European and American designs on the Middle East in general (especially once they discovered oil there), and numerous other religious, political, ethnic, and cultural factors. One such factor is the evangelical Protestant belief in the approaching end-time, and their belief that the restoration of the Jewish state is a sign that the end is just about here.

Until a few decades ago, the Catholic Church was firmly opposed to the Jews' return to the land of Israel, relying on Augustine's witness doctrine that the Jews were to remain scattered and despondent throughout the world as enduring witnesses to the triumph of Christianity. "Non possumus" ("We cannot") was Pius X's retort to Theodore Herzl's request in 1904 for Vatican support for a Jewish homeland.[80] (The Vatican finally recognized the State of Israel in 1993.)

Many Protestants saw it differently. Like the Catholics, they wanted the Jews to acknowledge and accept Jesus, but they also argued for the restoration of the Jews to their ancestral homeland. The earliest proponent of this argument may have been Thomas Brightman, an Englishman whose pamphlet, *Shall They Return to Jerusalem Again?* was published posthumously in 1615.[81] Seventeenth-century Puritans brought this idea with them to New England. In 1669, Massachusetts clergyman (and later president of Harvard) Increase Mather, commenting on the verse in Romans that "all Israel shall be saved," asserted that "after the Iews [sic] are brought into their own Land again," there will be a great battle between the "converted" Israelites and their enemies, and "after this shall begin the resurrection of the dead."[82]

In England, the seventh Earl of Shaftesbury, president from 1848 to 1885 of the London Society for Promoting Christianity Amongst the Jews, was one of the strongest proponents in Parliament for letting the Jews return to Palestine as a necessary precursor to the Second Coming.[83] His efforts and those of the society he headed played a strong role in Britain's 1917 Balfour Declaration, which promised that "His Majesty's Government view with favour the establishment in Palestine of a national home for the Jewish people, and will use their best endeavors to facilitate the achievement of this object."[84] (Whether Balfour himself believed his actions would help Jesus to return is still debated.[85])

The establishment of the State of Israel in 1948 was seen by evangelicals as a sign that the apocalypse was approaching. Israel's capture of the Old City of Jerusalem was, to them, yet another sign of the onrushing end-time. Recent political events have given evangelicals even more encouragement. A prominent Indiana evangelical theologian, Paul Begley, was quoted in 2017 as saying: "When [then-president Donald] Trump promised Evangelicals that he would move the [US] embassy to Jerusalem, it was a Christian move to stand with Israel... When this happens, it will make it easier for Israel to build the Third Temple, fulfilling Bible prophecy for the End of Times."[86]

(Trump's moving the embassy did not thrill all evangelicals, it must be noted.[87]) Now all that was needed was to actually build the new Temple, and Armageddon—the final battle between good and evil when Jesus would come and smite God's enemies —could begin.

Of course, the Dome of the Rock and the Al-Aqsa Mosque, the third holiest shrines in Islam, sit on the site where the Third Temple would have to go. Nothing could be better guaranteed to start all-out war in the Middle East than their destruction and replacement by a Jewish Temple. For some, that's exactly the idea. "Amid US Dispensationalists, speculations about the rapture or other End Time 'joys' greatly increase following crises or outbreaks of violence in the Middle East involving the Zionist state" because "no peace in the Middle East can be realized or even thought of until and unless the Second Coming is reached catastrophically."[88] (These "dispensationalists" expect to be raptured out of the way ahead of the catastrophe.) In 2007, John Hagee, a major evangelical preacher who runs Christians United For Israel (CUFI), wrote that "the final battle for Jerusalem is about to begin," and that "the coming nuclear showdown with Iran is a certainty" that was predicted by Ezekiel.[89] Hagee, who has close ties with Mike Pence, the former vice-president, praised Trump not only for moving the US embassy to Jerusalem, but also for pulling the United States out of the multinational agreement that had restrained Iran from developing a nuclear weapon.[90]

The idea that violence against Jews in the Holy Land is a necessary precursor to the Second Coming has a long history. Almost 400 years ago, Increase Mather wrote that "after the Israelites shall be in their own Land again, they shall be brought into the greatest distress that ever any people were in in this world." To some of the modern premillennialist supporters of the state of Israel, "any attempt to bring a peaceful end to the Arab-Israeli conflict is only likely to be evidence that a promised anti-Christ is behind the effort." A negotiated peace would be an affront to their belief that only Jesus can bring peace to the region. Such a "false" peace would further delay Jesus's return and must therefore be resisted.[91]

There is an additional reason for this resistance. The same people who applauded the birth of Israel also expect that its destruction will be followed (or perhaps preceded) by the surviving Jews—finally!—converting to Christianity. Some of them are furious with Hagee and his CUFI for agreeing *not* to proselytize to the Jews (for now). "If one does not 'preach the gospel' to the Jew, then one is guilty of the WORST kind of 'hatred' towards the Jew!   How can anyone be more 'anti-Semitic' than that? John Hagee (and others) are NOT 'friends of Israel.'"[92] Despite the reality that nothing has ever altered Jewish indifference to Jesus, nothing has changed these Christians' fantasies either.

Global climate change. Since the start of the Industrial Revolution in the eighteenth century, human beings have had such an impact on the environment of the planet that climate changes now threaten to become an extinction event for many species, not least our own.[93] Scientists have been warning about this in increasingly desperate tones since the 1960s. Yet many people in positions of power, in the United States in particular, continue to avoid dealing with the threat even as it wreaks increasing havoc on our only planet. The "general acceptance of global warming as a real phenomenon, coupled with a relative disinterest in addressing it" has been called the "American paradox" because it is so widespread in the country best positioned to lead the fight for the environment if only it had the will.[94] Many factors are to blame for this paradox, including greed and shortsightedness, but the one I want to look at here is how evangelical and fundamentalist beliefs in the end-times are influencing our dealings with global climate change.

In a seminal paper written in 1967, historian Lynn White

predicted that "we shall continue to have a worsening ecologic crisis until we reject the Christian axiom that nature has no reason for existence save to serve man."[95] It has long been recognized that White's thesis was greatly overstating the case, but his point is not without some validity. A 1995 survey article identified whole branches of Christianity, from Roman Catholic to liberal evangelical, that are actively working to protect the environment. But it also found that "theologically conservative Protestants" are generally identified as being more reluctant to admit we are in a climate crisis or, if so, that we can or should do something about it.[96] Recall the Pentecostal deacon in Louisiana who told sociologist Arlie Hochschild that saving his beloved bayou was important—though not as important as stopping abortions and getting into heaven. The deacon's son isn't even that concerned. "We'll probably never see the bayou like God made it in the beginning until He fixes it himself," he told Hochschild. "And that will happen pretty shortly, so it doesn't matter how much man destroys."[97]

Many fundamentalists believe that God, not man, is responsible for what happens to our environment. This leads some of them to the conclusion that God will not let any serious harm come to it, either because he isn't ready to let the world end just yet, or because he wants the earth to become a paradise for the saved. Religion scholar Robin Veldman quotes a speaker at a Jehovah's Witness convention reassuring his audience that God will not let us ruin the planet. "After the earth had been purified and 'kingdom rule' restored, 'everything will be perfectly balanced again as it was in the beginning.'"[98] Others see God as quite deliberately allowing or even causing the environment to fail as the next step toward the end of the world: "Fundamentalist Christian faith may even encourage individuals to welcome growing environmental problems as positive signs of the Second Coming."[99] Andrew Herrmann, who describes himself as a "former evangelical fundamentalist," insists that "from within the fundamentalist evangelical worldview, the degradation of the Earth is one of the necessary requirements for Armageddon."[100] Robin Veldman interviewed members of the Assembly of God and Seventh-day Adventists who are convinced that God, not humanity, is destroying the environment, and because they expect to be spared the effects of this devastation through the rapture, they are largely indifferent to or even excited by the prospect.[101]

However, Veldman argues that her research found most evangelicals to be what she calls "cool millennialists" (as opposed to "hot" ones such as the Assembly of God). They are not fully committed to the idea that end-times are imminent, and are skeptical about the reality of climate change, but they also insist that belief in the end-time is "not a license for environmental irresponsibility." They are willing to respect and repair the environment—but only on an individual or community level, not on the national or worldwide scale most scientists believe is required.[102] This is due both to their distrust of "secular science" and to their opposition to government action generally.

The various premillennialist approaches to global climate change might be categorized in three ways. The first version is that God is in charge of the end-time, not man, so any efforts to reverse global climate change are not only useless but a rejection of God. A second view is that God will not let the planet be destroyed, so any efforts to reverse global climate change are not only unnecessary but a rejection of God. Third, there are those who insist that global climate change is a hoax intended to make us put our trust in science or government instead of God, so any efforts to reverse global climate change are not only foolish but a rejection of God. These positions are not necessarily mutually exclusive.

Many postmillennialists, on the other hand, want to have a nice clean earth ready to welcome Jesus in a thousand years.

Since 2004, the National Association of Evangelicals (NAE) has promoted "creation care," even calling for government action to address global climate change, a postmillennial position. In a 2022 publication, "Loving the Least of These," the NAE explained that it felt Biblically compelled to preserve the environment. "The Bible does not tell us anything directly about how to evaluate scientific reports or how to respond to a changing environment, but it does give several helpful principles: Care for creation, love our neighbors and witness to the world."[103] In response, Christian right leaders such as James Dobson and Charles Colson, who are at least nominally premillennialists, have fought against the NAE's position. They have gotten politicians and preachers who had supported creation care to reverse that stance, and persuaded enough politicians to block climate change legislation in the US Senate in 2009–10.[104] (In August 2022, Congress finally managed to pass, by the narrowest of margins, the first major piece of environmental protection legislation in several decades.) "Evangelical Christians demonstrating a high level of religious observance" have been found to be more likely "to oppose international treaties to address climate change, only supporting low cost environmental policies."[105] Meanwhile the planet and all its inhabitants increasingly suffer from the increasingly disastrous effects of global climate change.

THE PERSISTENCE OF MISBELIEF

Jesus didn't bring about the end of days in Paul's lifetime as the Apostle had promised he would. He didn't come back when John of Patmos or Barnabas or Hippolytus said he would. He didn't come back at the end of the first millennium however one calculates it. He didn't come back after the Mongol invasions in the thirteenth century, nor in the fourteenth century with its Black Death and other horrors, nor after the fall of Constantinople or World Wars I and II, nor after any of the other signs that were supposed to signal the end of the world. He didn't return after the restoration of the State of Israel or at the end of the second millennium of the Common Era. It's no great stretch to apply Hume's Maxim and Occam's Razor and say with confidence that he is never coming back.

Saying that, however, is an admission of doubt about a basic doctrine, and for many Christians doubt is not an option. After the millennialist fires of the first centuries had simmered down, Church Fathers worked out a theology that let them live with an indefinite delay. The Catholic Church adopted that position and then spent the next millennium and more damping down millennial expectations and predictions. Luther, intentionally or otherwise, stirred the fires up again, and ever since then many Protestants have been on the lookout for signs, apocalyptic or otherwise, of the millennium. A 2010 Pew Research poll of Americans found over forty per cent "definitely" or "probably" expect Jesus to return by 2050.[106] Andrew Herrmann warns that "the belief that we're living in the end times with the imminent return of Jesus is *the* core driving force for fundamental evangelicals."[107] *This* time he really means it, they believe.

The earliest expectations of an immediate end of days faded after the generation of Jesus's time, and the first few generations after them, had "fallen asleep," as Paul would say. After that, expectations rose and fell according to calculations of the calendar; we just witnessed this ourselves as the year 2000 came and went. Events also trigger expectations of the imminent demise of the present-day world, from the Black Death to the Jewish capture of Jerusalem. Poverty, war, displacement, even the feeling that the true believers are not accorded proper respect, all of these can bring about not just an expectation of the end of the world, but the hope that, any day now, the faithful will finally get their chance to say, "we told you so."

But the true impact of the end-time believers is not in their anticipated moment of glory (and gloating), but in the here-and-now. They have infected governments to the extent that they can passively, sometimes even actively, interfere with the world's efforts to cope with world-shattering events. They object, for example, to the United Nations because they think it was predicted in verses from John of Patmos's tortured imagination that "ten kings...are to receive authority as kings for one hour, together with the beast. These are united in yielding their power and authority to the beast."[108] Using those same verses, they also objected to the European Union when it was about to expand to ten member countries. (As of this writing, it has 27 members.) The "beast" was the Roman empire of John's time, but that has never stopped millennialists from taking it out of context and applying it to the perceived "antichrist" of the moment.

These are not parlor games or harmless fantasies. The United Nations was not set up to be a one-world government but to provide a forum where nations around the world could meet to try to at least talk out their differences before (and, hopefully, rather than) going to war over them. It has had mixed success at best, but so far there has been no new world war such as the one that was the impetus for the UN's founding. Attempts by fundamentalists to persuade the United States to withdraw from the United Nations, or to minimize our involvement with it, make the already difficult job of keeping the peace all that much harder. Encouraging Israeli hardliners not to trade one hectare of the "Promised Land" for a lasting peace serves only to keep tensions aflame in one of the most volatile regions of the world. And when, once again, the world doesn't end on schedule, millennialists may again decide to blame the Jews for not playing their proper part, same as after the end of the first millennium. Insisting that global climate change is a hoax, or that we can't or shouldn't do anything about it, discourages politicians who depend on evangelical votes from doing anything constructive to clean up our environment. That leads to more sickness and to shortened, miserable lives, and drives whole species to extinction—all in pursuit of a fantasized end-time vaguely promised by a god of our invention. Of all the impacts Christianity has had on the world, this may well be the most dangerous.

CONCLUSION
IN PRAISE OF DOUBT

I wrote this book in order to examine two questions: how did we in the Western world come up with our idea of God, and what has been the impact of that idea? This led me to a realization of just how important a role *doubt* has played in getting us to the present day, and then to a third question: where do we go from here? But before I get into that, let's review what I've learned in posing the first two questions.

HOW DID WE INVENT GOD?

The Sumerians, the various Semites, the Hittites, and the Hurrians, had a number of gods, similar to other belief systems around the ancient world. What was notable about these nations was that they believed their gods had empowered their kings to make laws to govern the people. Furthermore, the gods expected the people to obey the laws of their rulers or else the gods would visit disasters on them.

The ancient Israelites began with a pantheon much like those of their neighbors and relatives, and they may have had similar ideas of the gods interfering in human affairs. They did not, however, begin with a king, but rather with priests and tribal elders. By the time the Israelites settled into their two kingdoms, the priesthoods of the various gods were long established and were able to maintain their independence from the monarchy to a greater degree than may have been the case in other kingdoms of the Ancient Near East. The priests of the god Yahweh used their physical proximity to the king's court in Jerusalem and their popularity among the people to encourage the kings of Israel and especially Judah to rid their kingdoms of all competing priesthoods. Some kings agreed, but many did not. It was only during the Babylonian exile that the Yahwist priesthood finally succeeded in making their god the exclusive god of the Israelites. Even then, the mixed response to the Seleucid attempts to force Greek gods onto the Jews shows that the idea of worship of Yahweh alone was still open to challenge. Only from the time of the Roman occupation can it really be said that belief in Yahweh as God, the one and only, was close to universal among the Jews.

There were several other significant beliefs that gradually became central to the religion of the Second Temple period. One was that Yahweh was not merely the only god of the Israelites but was the one and only God of all, the creator of the universe. The Israelites—the Jews—hoped that all the world would come to understand this someday, however far off that day might be. In the meantime, they would keep themselves holy through worship of God so as to set an example. They also insisted that the laws and customs and rituals that the Israelites had borrowed or developed over the centuries were actually divine ordinances that their god Yahweh had given all at once to Moses on Mount Sinai. These God-given statutes must not be questioned and must be obeyed, or the nation as a whole would suffer God's wrath. During or after the Babylonian exile, the

Yahwists began to say instead that God would judge everyone individually. This led to a belief in judgment after death—and that meant a belief in individual immortality, which was necessary to make such a judgment possible.

After the Romans took over, their rule became so oppressive that many Jews began to wish for a messiah, a man anointed by God, who would drive these oppressors out of Judaea and establish God's kingdom in the land. During the first century of the Common Era, there were a number of individuals who claimed to be the messiah or who had the claim made on their behalf, but none of them was successful in freeing the Jews. If anyone gave the Romans any trouble, they would simply execute him. One such was an itinerant preacher, Jesus of Nazareth. Like some others, he announced that the kingdom of God was at hand. Unlike some, he didn't advocate violence against Rome, but the Roman authorities crucified him anyway. His followers, who weren't expecting him to be killed like that, at first scattered in fear. Then they regrouped and announced that Jesus had gone willingly to his crucifixion as the ultimate sacrifice for sin, that three days later he rose from the dead, and that he, as the messiah, would be returning very soon to establish God's kingdom on earth.

The original followers of Jesus, who were all Jews, took a number of Jewish ideas and modified them. Yahweh of Israel was indeed the God of all the world—and all the world had to obey him now, not in some distant future. *Now* was the end of days, when the kingdom was coming, when everyone would bow and bend the knee to Yahweh. Everyone would be judged when the kingdom came, and those who failed God's judgment would be damned to hell for all eternity. Furthermore, God's judgment would be based on what each person *believed* more than on how each person *behaved*. Only those who believed that Jesus, the messiah, the son of God, had sacrificed himself to free them from sin could enjoy eternal life in paradise.

Adherents of the Jesus Movement wanted and expected their fellow Jews to join them in this new belief. Almost without exception, however, Jews thought that these new ideas, especially the one about having to believe in Jesus, were too far out of line with Jewish traditions to be acceptable. Nor did they have any interest in a dead messiah. It may be that this indifference spurred followers of Jesus to missionize to the Roman world, or perhaps that was their intention all along. Either way, they had to devise a message about an obscure Jew that would appeal to a world that wasn't interested in Jewish ideas about God and his kingdom. They also had to convince Romans that a man Rome had executed as a common criminal was the savior of the world. And they had to explain why the Jews, his own people, didn't believe it.

The Jesus Movement accomplished this by promoting the idea of universal sin and salvation. Sin was a Jewish concept, but the movement's leaders asserted that sin started with Adam, the ancestor of all, and all were bound in sin and damned to eternal punishment because of him. Therefore everyone, Jews and non-Jews alike, needed to believe in Jesus and his sacrifice on the cross in order to be saved from hell. Not only that, they had to believe in Jesus in the right way. Dissent, even disagreement on the details, could not be tolerated, as it could cost believers their salvation.

In advocating this as a universal necessity, Jesus's followers argued that the Jews had known all this but had rejected the truth out of perversity. They further demonized the Jews in order to shift the blame for the crucifixion away from Rome. It was the Jews, they claimed, who had persecuted and killed Jesus and who were now persecuting his followers as well.

As Gentiles—the non-Jews of the Roman world—who believed in Jesus began to outnumber his Jewish followers, the Jesus Movement came to be recognized as a new religion, Christianity. Over the course of the next three centuries, Christians grew numerous enough that their religion eventually became the official religion of the Roman Empire, with Christian bishops and theologians now influencing, even dictating, its policies.

The earliest Israelites had believed in a pantheon of gods who intervened in human affairs, much the same as the Sumerians, the Hittites, the Hurrians, and their Semitic cousins believed. Later Israelites, now known as Jews, gradually developed an idea of one universal God for all that they hoped everyone would eventually believe in, though they didn't try to rush the process. Christians modified this idea of a universal God and sought to impose it on a world they believed was about to end any day now. They also relied on tools such as intolerance of dissent, a persecution complex, divine judgment after death, and demonization. In effect, Christians expanded on mechanisms that Jews had developed in order to cope with natural disasters, military and theological catastrophes, and the indignities of being a small nation belittled by the great powers of the world. This led to major problems when Christianity became one of the great powers of the world but continued to rely on these coping mechanisms anyway.

WHAT HAS BEEN THE IMPACT OF GOD ON THE WORLD?

The impact of Christianity on the western world, and through it the world at large, was my second question. This impact is so pervasive that I had to limit my inquiry to a few selected topics. I chose Christian-Jewish relations, our sexuality, how and when to go to war, our approach to life and death, and the belief that the world as we know it is about to end. In each of these cases, I found that Christian leaders often decided on a course of action *a priori*, that is, based on their predetermined beliefs. Thereafter, they ignored or rejected any evidence or argument that would change that course of action, because to do so would be to cast doubt on those beliefs.

Christians believed that the Jews had persecuted and rejected Jesus, even killed him. They also believed it was necessary for the Jews to admit this and to convert to Christianity as part of God's plan to bring about the end of days. This was their justification for centuries of persecution of the Jews. The Vatican has tried in recent decades to adopt a more conciliatory attitude toward the Jews—but it still expects them to believe in Jesus someday. Protestant denominations, as always, are a mixed bag, some having come to terms with Jewish existence while others continue even now to missionize to the Jews or demonize them (or both).

The reason Jews pose such a problem for Christians is because the continued existence of Jews as Jews casts doubt on Christianity's universalist claim—that belief in Jesus as savior is universally required because he is the only path to salvation. But Christians also took their insistence on universalism—an unjustified universalism, let us be clear—and applied it to many other aspects of humanity, in particular to sex and gender.

The first Christians believed that, with the kingdom of God coming any day, there would be no next generation and thus no further need for sex. Even today, Christian thinking on sex continues to be influenced by that belief. Because sex is necessary for the continuation of our species, the Church Fathers had to allow it, but limited it to that purpose only, and only within such marriages as the religious authorities had approved. Protestants broke with Catholics only to the extent of holding that not every sex act had to be for the purpose of procreation. But sex still had to be within the confines of marriage. However, we have never limited sexual activity that way. Nor are human beings limited to the binary caricature of "male and female he created them." The evidence is overwhelming that human sexuality is far more complex than that. The psychological damage of trying to comply with this unjustified sexual universalism has been well-documented, and is acknowledged by many Christians. Yet the Vatican and many Protestants, as well as some Orthodox Jews and Muslims, continue to demand a binary, unrealistic approach to sex and gender.

Christianity was originally pacifist, its leaders even forbidding Christians from becoming soldiers. But after it became the official religion of the Roman Empire, Church Fathers realized that there had to be a legitimate way for Christians to fight on behalf of the state. Initially, they limited it to a "just war" fought defensively and with mercy for the defeated. By the start of the second millennium, however, the Church was looking for justification to fight "holy wars"—offensive wars waged in pursuit of Christian domination. The Crusades were designated holy wars, as were the hunts for heretics—a heretic being anyone who thought differently from what the religious authorities had decreed they could think.

Christianity's insistence that life after death is more real and more important than life on earth has also justified all kinds of harm. It has been used to excuse slavery, to suppress scientific curiosity, to outlaw dissent, to support exploitation and coerced conversion, and to command secular authorities to do the bidding of religious powers that answer to no one on earth. Belief in the afterlife helped drive the Inquisition, the heresy hunts, and the witch hunts. It still encourages people to put up with earthly suffering by telling them they will be rewarded for it in heaven. It says that failure in life is only temporary and will be rectified by success after death. For many Christians, as well as for many Muslims and Jews, success is defined as reward in heaven, a stipulation that is impossible to prove or disprove.

Even this afterlife is only temporary, a space where the departed faithful wait for the End of Days and the Last Judgment, when the kingdom of God will be established once and for all on earth as Jesus had promised. Back here on earth, many Christians eagerly, or fearfully, expect each generation will be the last. They themselves will witness the millennium, or be raptured out of the way just before the millennium, or even help bring about the millennium. Some find in this a reason not to worry much about damage to the earth, since it won't matter much longer. Others believe they are called on to resist efforts to heal the earth or make peace among the peoples, so as to hurry the millennium along.

RESISTANCE TO DOUBT AND DISSENT

From the perspective of a revealed religion such as Christianity, it's a serious problem when people start to think for themselves. They might start to disagree about the revelation, and disagreement, even on the details, cannot be tolerated. The stated reason is that having the wrong belief, or even getting some of the details wrong, can lead to eternal damnation. *Doubt* cannot be permitted, since doubt can mean questions, questions can mean dissent, and dissent means someone is going to hell. "But ask in faith, never doubting, for one who doubts is like a wave of the sea, driven and tossed by the wind," says the Epistle of James in the New Testament. It cautions that the "doubter...must not expect to receive anything from the Lord."[1]

The Catholic Church spent centuries hunting down doubters to be turned over to the state for execution. Protestants, as always, are too splintered to be easily categorized, but the record—from Puritan Massachusetts to the purity movement—does show that Protestants can be just as repressive of disagreement. The long-running campaign by some evangelical Protestants to block the teaching of evolution because it could cause children to question their faith is a classic instance of intolerance to doubt.

Jews, being Jews, continue to argue.

THE AGE OF DOUBT

The modern age is an age where doubt is not only permitted but encouraged. The scientific revolution is built on doubt. Unlike religious certainty, scientific certainty is never absolute. The conclusions of science are always open to question.

Here, I submit, is the basis of the conflict between revealed religion and science: the former resists doubt, while the latter requires it. Strictly speaking, history belongs to the humanities, but it still obeys this cardinal rule of science: go where the evidence leads and be open to doubt.

Nothing in the Bible, nothing in religion, is exempt from doubt in the eyes of history. At the front of this book is a quote from Oliver Cromwell in 1650, when he was the religious dictator of Puritan England. He was writing to the elders of the Church of Scotland begging them to "think it possible you may be mistaken."[2] Cromwell would undoubtedly not approve of the use I am making of his admonition. Nonetheless, he planted a seed of doubt and, as I have been at pains to point out over the course of this book, doubt is what enables us to grow.

I began this research project when I could no longer ignore my doubts over whether God exists. I have come to accept that the most reasonable explanation of the evidence is that no gods, or God, have ever existed, though I also accept that this is not, in the end, a conclusion subject to reason. However, the evidence for a specific god can be tested by reason, and I have endeavored to do so here. My reasoned conclusion is that the evidence is so conflicted, and so contradicted by other evidence and by what we know of human behavior, that it cannot serve to establish the existence of God as he is traditionally understood by the western world. More than that, the evidence all points against it.

What has become clear to me is that all our ideas of God are human creations invented to explain phenomena that the people of that time could not explain any other way, such as where we came from or what causes the lightning. Gods and God were also useful as means of control: do what the king (or the priest) says or the gods will smite you. But none of the evidence passes the ordinary evidentiary tests of rationality, causality, or provenance, much less the additional requirements of Hume's Maxim. I am satisfied that my doubts are valid.

PLURALISM AND SECULARISM

One of the major factors that allowed doubt to flourish was the growing toleration of multiple different beliefs, each with an equal claim to be revealed truth. This happened despite the vehement and often violent objections of the Catholic Church, which had successfully suppressed variations of the Christian faith, marginalized or expelled the Jews, and kept Islam at bay. What helped Martin Luther's revolt to succeed was the existence of the printing press that spread his ideas faster than the Church could stop them, combined with the increasing willingness of princes to defy the pope for their own political purposes. The years of violent struggle that followed led to a mostly grudging acknowledgment that religion's power to command political obedience had been substantially reduced. We in the West now live in a pluralistic and increasingly secular world.

Pluralism is a political way of structuring religion within society so that all religious beliefs are tolerated and no religion has control. Secularism, a related concept, means that the norms of society are determined by reasons other than religious. I will go further and state that in a secular pluralistic society almost all ideologies, religious or otherwise, are tolerated. The caveat here is that an ideology that will not tolerate competing ideologies will itself not be tolerated.

Note that when I use the word *secularism*, I don't mean atheism, particularly not the modern-day militant atheism that not only denies the existence of any sort of god but that tries to force its "antireligion" on the body politic. That type of atheism is as much an ideology as is fundamentalist Protestantism or Wahhabi Islam or Haredi Judaism. A functioning pluralistic society will tolerate socialism but not communism, Nazism, or fascism. A functioning secular society will tolerate all religions, even all ideologies, but will give power to none. I propose, in effect, a more thorough establishment of the Enlightenment principle that societies are run by consensus based on reality and reason.

I know, good luck with that. Too many people in the present age have a way of disregarding reality and are unwilling to listen to reason. Here too, religions, particularly Christianity in the West, have had a major impact. One of the themes running throughout this book has been the way many Christians have ignored and rejected inconvenient facts and have made faith supreme over reason. (I could say the same about Judaism, Islam, Hinduism, and so on, but in the West it's been Christianity running the show.)

Faith over reason might have worked in past ages when the secular powers based their legitimacy on faith, and when competing faiths could be excluded, expelled, or otherwise ignored. It is much harder to do that in the modern age. This age has seen too many competing religions, each with too many flawed claims to revealed truth, for us to be able to accept any of them on faith. We now know that the "commandments of God" were in fact collections of human laws and customs that were subsequently invested with a divine imprimatur. We have also come to recognize that these laws and customs were first formed during the Bronze Age and reflect that era's limited understanding of the world. While our modern view of life, the universe, and everything is far from perfect, it is still an improvement over what the writers of Scripture and the New Testament, what the thinkers and powers of earlier ages, all thought they knew. We can no longer afford to be held hostage to antiquity. The facts of life, including the dangers of human extinction from disease, climate change, nuclear war, and over-population, all demand that we face reality. Resistance to reality in the name of revealed religion will not make reality go away.

PRIESTS AND POLITICS

Ironically, early Judaism and Christianity each depended on a kind of "separation of church and state" in order to grow. In the Ancient Near East, the priesthood was usually closely tied to the throne, with the king frequently acting as a priest. Outside of Egypt, the only significant exception that I am aware of is that of the early Israelites, whose priesthoods were well-established before they ever had a king. These priesthoods retained much of their independence from the monarchy, and one in particular, the Yahwist sect, sought to use the power of the kings to elimi-nate the other priesthoods. After the monarchy fell to the Baby-lonians, the Yahwists edited the sacred texts to give divine backing to their claims of priestly primacy. Then, after the fall of the Temple and the loss of priestly power that had been tied to it, rabbis (the legal scholars and teachers) gradually became the leaders of the Jewish communities. Their authority over their communities was often recognized by the secular powers, and they rarely faced challenges from other Jews prior to Enlighten-ment days.

Christianity began as a religion totally separate from the state—the Roman empire—and frequently in conflict with it. Only when Christianity gained imperial recognition did the boundary start to fray. Still, the bishops and other religious leaders generally kept their separate status even as they dictated policy to the emperors. In the feudal age that followed the eclipse of Rome, the Church claimed and sometimes exercised the power to command the kings of Europe until after the Protestant Reformation. Some Protestants then sought to merge the state with the church. I mentioned the postmillennialist theocracy the Puritans tried to establish in colonial New England in the previous chapter. However, other than seventeenth-century New England, England under Cromwell, and the domain Calvin himself set up in Geneva, Protestant ministers rarely got to control the state the way medieval popes had been able to do. (The Mormon domination of Utah is a special case.) The crowned heads of Europe, starting with Henry VIII of England, saw to that by making themselves heads of the various Protestant churches or by otherwise putting their national religion under the control of the state. A century later the newly formed United States, with its multitude of competing churches and sects, decided to establish pluralism as a basic principle and to prohibit any religion or sect from dictating to the nation. If these measures have not served to fully keep the peace, they have still done a decent job of it—not simply by the separation of church and state but also by a degree of subordination of church to state.

BUT WHAT GOOD IS RELIGION?

Despite the wishes of some of the militant atheists, religions are not going away. Literally billions of people on this planet turn to their religions for comfort, for shelter, for strength to face the trials of life. Religions offer spiritual help, community, a sense that there is a purpose to our existence, the idea that what we see may not be all there is. Religious groups feed the hungry, shelter the homeless, work with incarcerated prisoners to reform themselves and with recently released ex-cons to re-enter society. Jews feel that God has called on them to repair a broken world—*tikkun olam*. Christian charities help the poor, the outcast, without insisting they accept Jesus first because they believe this is what Jesus has called them to do. If religious believers can offer good counsel, does it matter that much where they believe it comes from?

Religions also do have some valid ethical ideas. The eighth century BCE prophet Amos was furious with those Israelites who cheated at trade and who bought "the indigent with silver and the needy for the price of sandals." The story of David, Bathsheba, and the prophet Nathan promotes the principle that even kings are accountable for their actions. One of my favorite Biblical passages is Isaiah's list of the things he says God wants us to do: free the oppressed, feed the hungry, shelter the poor, clothe the naked, and don't be a stranger to your kin.[3] The truth that this list was invented by a mortal man and not dictated from on high should not detract from the truth of the message.

However, Christians didn't seek and seize power in order to enforce Isaiah's calls to help the poor or Amos's demand of justice for the powerless. It's often been the opposite, in fact: people in power may make protestations of piety, but how many of them have heeded the pleas of the prophets to help the less fortunate among us? Whatever good that religions may want to bring to the world, it is clear that they don't need the power of the state behind them in order to do so. If anything, religions have done far more harm than good when they've had that power.

IN PRAISE OF DOUBT

Revealed religions have a problem with doubt, as we've seen. Some are willing to allow doubts about the details, though even here they will be wary, as allowing some doubts can lead to doubting more important aspects, even the revelation itself and finally God himself. Much of the history I've recounted in this book has been about the efforts of Christianity to suppress doubt and to deny reality, and about reality's resistance to that denial. The battle to be allowed to doubt was won only when Christianity lost the power to stop it. So if we want to ask how religions can do some good in the world, the answer starts with keeping them from suppressing doubt.

The modern world is increasingly secular and pluralistic. This is a good thing overall, as the alternative is a return to authoritarianism; to religious clashes and even war; to oppression, repression, and extermination in the name of a deity who doesn't even exist. If religions want to play a part in this modern world, they must start by accepting that they are only some of the many players, and that neither they nor anyone else has a mandate from heaven. Religious believers must recognize that the only way they can persuade the body politic to agree with them, if at all, is by the power of reason. "God told me so" is not a legitimate political argument.

It's easy enough for me say this. I look at the world from a Jewish perspective, and Jews place a premium on behavior over belief. (Jews have also been out of power most of the time and so have had little choice but to appeal to reason and to hope for pluralism.) The foundation of Christianity is belief over behavior, and universal belief at that. It's not really my place to tell Christians how to solve their dilemma, only to stress that peace in our pluralistic world demands a realistic solution.

So we have come to my final reason for writing this book. It's not just to share what I have learned. It is a plea to acknowledge that everything we think we know about God is a human construct invented to meet purely human needs according to what people at the time understood them to be. Our understanding of the world and of all who dwell therein has much improved since those Biblical days. The commandments of this God of our invention too often bear little relation to the reality of our world, and we have reached the point where the cost of ignoring that reality is becoming too much to bear. The ideologies of millennia past are not only insufficient to meet the challenges of the present, they are actively interfering with our efforts to find workable solutions. Whatever spiritual value and comfort and guidance religion may have to offer has to be grounded in that reality.

APPENDIX: DATING THE BOOK OF DANIEL

The book of Daniel is in two parts. Chapters 1–6 are stories about its protagonist's life in the Babylonian empire, and chapters 7–12 are his predictions about what was going to happen hundreds of years later in the Maccabean period. Modern critical scholarship is essentially unanimous in dating the last six chapters to Maccabean times, specifically between 168/167 and 164 BCE. The first 6 chapters are harder to pin down, though they were not written by someone who actually lived during the Babylonian empire or its conquest by the Persians.

The Catholic Church acknowledges this, as do many Protestants, but some conservative Protestants dispute this dating. Some Orthodox Jews also insist on taking Daniel at face value.[1] I want to take a moment to explain in some detail why I agree with the critical scholarship on the dating of Daniel. This will serve, among other things, as an example of how I used the sources, the scholarship, and the rules of history to reach the conclusions that are the foundation of this book.

Theologians may approach the Bible any way they choose, according to dictates of their theology, but a historian does not have that option. If a passage from the Bible wants to be accepted as historical evidence, it must plead its case in the court of history and show that it conforms to the rules of history. One basic rule of history is that the story has to make sense. Any analysis has to examine its internal structure, its correlation with other documents, how well it fits in the context of its time, confirmation by artefacts that can be definitively dated, and on top of all that our understanding of human nature. Occam's Razor governs here: the simplest explanation that covers all the known evidence is the most likely one.

If historians are to accept Daniel as a historical record of events, it must pass these tests. Here is a sample passage: "On that very night Belshazzar king of the Chaldeans [Babylonians] was slain. And Darius the Mede received the kingdom when he was sixty-two years old."[2] This passage bothered historians even two millennia ago,[3] but only in the nineteenth century did archeologists uncover records from the time of the Persian conquest of Babylonia that could give an eyewitness account of what happened. These discoveries included the Babylonian Chronicles, among which was the Nabonidus Chronicle. This chronicle records how in Nabonidus's seventeenth year (539/538 BCE), Cyrus deposed Nabonidus and took over the Babylonian empire. "On the fourteenth day...Nabonidus fled. On the sixteenth day, Ugbaru, governor of Gutium, and the army of Cyrus, without battle they entered Babylon. Afterwards, after Nabonidus retreated, he was captured in Babylon."[4] Another find, the Cyrus Cylinder, explains that the Babylonian god Marduk had delivered Nabonidus into Cyrus's hands because the Babylonian king didn't honor the god.[5] (Nabonidus had replaced the worship of Marduk with that of Sin, the moon goddess.)

Matthias Henze, a Babylonian scholar, dates these documents to the time "immediately following the demise of the Neo-Babylonian empire in 539 BCE."[6] He describes them as polemics, which actually enhances their evidence of Nabonidus being the last king of Babylon and Cyrus as his conqueror. If there had been no Nabonidus whose kingship was so despised, there would have been no polemic. Also, the name of his conqueror was irrelevant to the polemic; its target was Nabonidus. Thus, its citation of Cyrus as the conqueror of Babylon is credible.

How does the credibility of Daniel's author hold up when compared to the contemporary record? Instead of Cyrus, he names "Darius the Mede," an appellation not mentioned in any other record, though there have been any number of attempts to identify other historic personages—including Cyrus himself—as this Darius.[7]

More serious is that Daniel never mentions Nabonidus, but instead labels Belshazzar "the king of the Chaldeans" and the son of Nebuchadnezzar at the time when Babylon was conquered.[8] "Son" could also mean grandson, but Nabonidus (Belshazzar's father) had usurped the throne and wasn't related to Nebuchadnezzar at all.[9] Cyrus also claimed Nabonidus's infidelity to Marduk as justification for his conquest of Babylon. It is not credible that someone who actually lived through those events would have misidentified so major a figure as Nabonidus.

In evaluating which version—the artefacts or the book of Daniel—to accept as more accurate, we give more weight to the older document, unless there is some reason not to. There is no record of the existence of the book of Daniel prior to the start of the Maccabean period (168/167 BCE). The mention of "Danil" or "Dan'el" in Ezekiel shouldn't mean our Daniel, since Ezekiel groups Danil together with two known non-Jews, Noah and Job. Also, the Hebrew spelling is different—and there is an ancient Ugaritic epic about a Danil.[10] On the other hand, the Nabonidus Chronicles and the Cyrus Cylinder are contemporaneous records, and they also generally correspond to Greek and Persian histories that we know to have been written prior to 250 BCE.

This is only one example of the problems confronting

someone trying to determine whether the book of Daniel is an accurate historical record. (For some thorough and comprehensive scholarly analyses, see John Collins, *Daniel: A Commentary on the Book of Daniel* (1993) and Ernest Lucas, *Daniel* (2002), both of which I am using as major references for this presentation.[11]) The analysis that makes the most sense of all this evidence is that the author knew something about the events of the time when the Persians conquered Babylon, but not to the degree that someone who had lived in that time would know. So I am on solid ground in accepting the overall consensus of modern critical scholars that the stories in chapters 1–6 were most probably "not composed in the sixth century by anyone close to the Babylonian court," in Collins's words. Elias Bickerman goes further, using external events and the absence of any reference to Antiochus IV to suggest that the first six chapters were "published between 245 and 175" BCE. Lucas, though, contends that the arguments in support of historical inaccuracy are not conclusive, and suggests a verdict of "not proven."[12]

That brings us to the date of the rest of the book, chapters 7 to 12. Here the narrative voice changes from third person to first person, as Daniel describes his dreams or visions along with the angel Gabriel's explanations. This is a classic apocalyptic scenario, where a mortal has dreams or visions full of mysterious symbols and actions, and a divine being has to reveal— *apokaluptó* in Greek—what they really mean. Chapters 10–12 are presented as a single vision vouchsafed to Daniel "in the third year of Cyrus" revealing "what will befall your people in the latter time."[13] Chapter 11 then describes what is going to happen: Persian wealth "shall stir up all, even the kingdom of Greece. And a warrior king shall stand forth and rule very dominantly and do as he pleases. And when he stands forth, his kingdom shall be broken and divided to the four winds of the heavens." (Alter's translation deliberately reflects the quality of the Hebrew, which John Collins describes as "exceptionally poor.")[14] Allowing for the apocalyptic language, this is a reasonably accurate description of Alexander of Macedonia's conquest of the Persian empire and his conquests' breakup into four pieces after his death.[15] Two of those pieces were Egypt, taken by General Ptolemy (whom Daniel calls "the king of the south"), and the old Persian empire from modern Syria to Afghanistan, which General Seleucus ruled. Judaea was originally part of the Ptolemaic empire, but the Seleucids took it from them around 200 BCE. The Seleucid capital of Antioch was north of Judaea, so the Seleucid king became "the king of the north" in Daniel.

The bulk of chapter 11 is a cryptic but accurate description of the conflict between the Ptolemies and the Seleucids through Antiochus IV, who usurped the Seleucid throne, and thus is portrayed as "a contemptible man to whom the kingdom has not been given."[16] Verses 21–39 tell what Antiochus did then: He invaded Egypt twice, though the "Kittim" (a code name for Rome) stopped him the second time, in 168 BCE, and brusquely ordered him to go back where he came from. The Roman historian Livy described Antiochus as dumbstruck by this order, but the king then admitted that he had no choice but to obey the Senate's instructions.[17] In a rage against Roman interference (though it's more likely because he needed money), Antiochus sent forces to pillage the Temple on the way back from Egypt. A year later, he forced the Jews in Judaea to abandon circumcision and Sabbath rest, and "set up the desolating abomination"—a statue, probably of Zeus, in the very Temple. The Jews were then divided among themselves over what to do. This is very close to what happened in the years 169 to 167 BCE.[18]

Then the book of Daniel continues: "At the end-time the king of the north" will sweep through Judaea ("the Splendid Land"), and then "he shall rule over the treasures of gold and silver and all the costly things of Egypt" as well as the surrounding regions. After that, "rumors from the east and the north shall alarm him" and he will start off in that direction with his army. But then "he shall pitch the tents of his pavilion between the sea and the splendid holy mountain [that is, on the plain between the Mediterranean and the Temple Mount], and he shall come to his end, with none to help him."[19]

None of this happened. Antiochus never tried to invade Egypt again, or even to march in that direction, nor did he ever get any of Egypt's treasure. Two scholars, Dov Gera and Wayne Horowitz, made a study of the Babylonian Astronomical Diaries from 169 through 163 BCE, including correlations with the versions in First and Second Maccabees and Josephus. According to these diaries, Antiochus went to war against the king of Armenia sometime in 166 or 165 BCE, and after getting Armenia's surrender, he marched his army to Persia. There he caught some sort of fever or disease and died in Kislev (November or December), 164 BCE.[20]

The author of Daniel was clearly unaware of these events.[21] He also didn't know that, around the same time that Antiochus died, Judah the Maccabee and his guerilla forces succeeded in retaking the Temple and cleansing it of the "desolating abomination." The author's awareness of events, and the time when this awareness ends, enable us to date with high probability the final composition of the book of Daniel more precisely than any other part of Scripture. The most straightforward answer that makes the most sense based on all the known evidence is a date sometime between 168/167 BCE, when the persecutions started, and Judah's recapture of the Temple in 164 BCE.

ACKNOWLEDGMENTS

Writing, as writers like to say, is a solitary business, and this is true. Just ask any writer's spouse (including mine). But it's equally true that every writer depends on a support network that supplies encouragement and criticism, often both at once. In the case of serious non-fiction, it's especially important for a writer to be able to rely on help from experts in the field.

I've been fortunate in both respects. A number of scholars have been of great assistance to me in answering questions, pointing out mistakes, explaining details—though, as always, I remain the one responsible for any errors or misunderstandings. In no particular order of gratitude: Paula Fredriksen generously responded to my numerous queries about the New Testament and Augustine and sent me some of her papers. Brenton Dickieson worked with me to clarify some passages of Paul's letters. Bart Ehrman has been very helpful in answering my questions about the New Testament. Bart has also published several articles based on my research on his blog for his premier members to read and comment on. Frank McCluskey advised me on Plato's philosophy and also commented on my work from a Catholic perspective. Bernard Jackson and Bernard Levinson helped me with the ancient Israelite law codes and other matters. I am particularly grateful to both of them, as well as to Richard Robbins and Esther Mordant, for convincing me to make this a book for a general audience and to not get bogged down in academic details; their advice has made this a much better book. Dr. Robbins's encouragement was especially important to me. He also heads the writers' group of the Institute for Historical Study and has been enormously generous with his time and advice, as has Dr. Mordant, another member of the group. The group's numerous critiques and suggestions have gone a long way to improving my work. I owe a special debt to another member of the writers' group, Rose Marie Cleese, for helping me get the manuscript and the prospectus ready for presentation.

Trevor Bryce and David Tabb Stewart generously spent time helping me understand the relationship between the Hittite empire and the Israelites, as did Eckart Otto, who also improved my understanding of Deuteronomy. Erhard Gerstenberger shared his expertise on possible Zoroastrian influence on the Israelites, while Ernest Lucas engaged me in a helpful discussion on the book of Daniel. Daniel Bodi and Brian Doak courteously sent me several articles that were helpful in my research. Bulent Atalay helped me to understand Newton's physics, and David Cheng confirmed my psychological views on sexuality. Nicholas Polk shared his insights on the book of Joshua, while John Cook did the same on Jesus and sedition, and Dag Øistein Endsjø generously provided me a copy of his *Greek Resurrection Beliefs* that I had been unable to locate elsewhere. Andrei Antokhin at the University of San Francisco gave me much valuable advice on aspects of the New Testament and on miracles. The Rev. Joann Lee of the Calvary Presbyterian Church of San Francisco gave me insights into current Presbyterian thinking. Professor Amy-Jill Levine engaged me in an enlightening discussion on the nature of "messiah" in first-century Judaea. Professor John Hall's observations and critiques were extremely helpful to my understanding of the enormously complex topic of apocalypses throughout history. My publisher, John Mabry, and his editor, Janeen Jones, responded to every question and pointed out every flaw (I hope). Dan and Lee Shearer explained to me their work with prison ministries and how they help ex-cons re-enter society. A number of scholars, students, and interested bystanders read drafts of portions of the chapters on academia.edu and made valuable observations and occasional corrections. And I cannot thank enough the staff at the library of Graduate Theological Union, who were generous with their time and advice over the course of the two years or more that I spent with their books before the Covid pandemic forced me to stop going there.

Friends who read parts of the drafts include Leila Marcucci, Ilham Stropes, Annise Brokstein, Bulent Atalay, Pam Pierce, and Randy Fleitman. Above all, my wife Jean not only read multiple versions of each chapter, but kept my spirits up and my determination going whenever the project began to wear me down. Hers was truly a labor of love, and this book is dedicated to her.

CHRONOLOGY OF EVENTS

(Dates in bold are exact; all others are approximations or sometimes just guesses.)

Before the Common Era (BCE)

c. 3400 / Oldest known writing system (cuneiform) is invented in Sumer

c. 2470 / Sumerian ruler Eanatum I justifies war as commanded by the gods.

2300–2100 / Akkadian Empire

c. 2150 / Earliest date for parts of the *Epic of Gilgamesh*.

2000–1200 / Possible dates for *Enuma Elish* (The Epic of Creation).

c. 1930 / Code of Eshnunna

1830–1530 / First Babylonian Empire (major ruler: Hammurabi)

c. 1750 / Code of Hammurabi

c. 1700 / Oldest known version of *Attrahasis*

1650–1200 / Hittite Empire

1550–1140 / Egypt is militarily active in Canaan

1400–1100 / Possible migration dates of Israelites into Canaan.

1207 / Merenptah or Merneptah Stele

1100s / Possible date for the period of the Judges.

1100–600 / Assyrians are the major power in Mesopotamia.

1075 / Code of the Assura

1050 / Possible start of David's kingdom.

1000? / First Temple dedicated in Jerusalem.

950? / By this date, there are two Israelite kingdoms: Israel and Judah.

c. 850 / Mesha Stele (Moabite Stone)

8th cent. / Amos, First Isaiah

721 / Assyria destroys the northern kingdom (Israel).

697–642 / Reign of King Manasseh of Judah.

650–570 / Jeremiah

640–609 / Reign of King Josiah of Judah. Deuteronomy and possibly Joshua were probably written around this time.

626–539 / Neo-Babylonian Empire (major ruler: Nebuchadnezzar)

612 / Babylonians and their allies complete the conquest of the Assyrian Empire.

605–562 / Reign of Nebuchadnezzar II.

592–570 / Probable dates of Ezekiel's prophecies.

586 or 587 / Nebuchadnezzar of Babylon overthrows his vassal, Zedekiah of Judah, burns Jerusalem, and destroys the First Temple.

556–539 / Reign of Nabonidus, last king of Babylonia. His son, Belshazzar, occasionally acts as his father's regent.

539–538 / Cyrus of Persia conquers the Babylonian empire, allows Israelite exiles to return to Jerusalem.

6th cent. / Second Isaiah (Deutero–Isaiah)

515 / The Second Temple is dedicated.

460(?) / Ezra redacts the Torah into (close to) its present form, brings it to Jerusalem.

426–347 / Plato

4th cent. / Possible composition of Song of Songs, Ecclesiastes.

333–330 / Alexander the Great conquers the Persian Empire.

323 / Alexander dies. His empire is divided among his generals, primarily Seleucus (Syria) and Ptolemy (Egypt).

3rd–1st cents. / Septuagint (LXX) translation of the Hebrew Scriptures and other books (apocrypha) into Greek.

200 / Seleucids take Judaea from the Ptolomies.

175–164 / Reign of the Seleucid emperor Antiochus IV Epiphanes.

167 / Antiochus IV orders all Jews in Judaea to stop practicing Jewish rituals.

166 / The Maccabean revolt begins.

167(165?) / The book of Daniel

164 / Judah the Maccabee captures and cleanses the Temple.

160–140? / Most likely date of the book of Jubilees

142 / Simon, Judah's brother, is acknowledged as high priest.

104 / The Hasmoneans declare themselves kings.

63 / Pompey settles a civil war between two Hasmonean brothers by claiming Judaea for Rome.

37 / Emperor Augustus of Rome appoints Herod as king of Judaea.

4 / King Herod dies. Rome divides his kingdom into Judaea, Galilee, and Transjordan. Most likely year of Jesus's birth.

Common Era (CE)

6 / Rome takes direct control of Judaea.

26–36 or 37 / Pontius Pilate is governor of Judaea.

33(30?) / Jesus is crucified.

1st cent. / Psalms of Solomon; Wisdom of Solomon.

50–51 / Paul writes First Thessalonians, the oldest known document written by a follower of Jesus.

56–57 / Paul writes Romans, his last known epistle.

60s? / Gospel of Q

66 / Judaea revolts against Rome.

70 / On the 9th of Av (early August), Roman troops storm Jerusalem and burn it to the ground, including the Second Temple.

67–70? / The gospel of Mark.

73 / Last holdouts of the Jewish revolt commit suicide at Masada rather than surrender to the Romans.

75–79? / Josephus writes *Wars of the Jews*.

80?–90? / The gospels of Matthew and Luke–Acts.

90?–95? / Josephus writes *Antiquities of the Jews*.

90?–110? / The gospel of John.

95?–100? / Revelation.

110 / Pliny the Younger asks the emperor what to do about "Christians" in his jurisdiction.

155–240 / Tertullian

180 / Irenaeus of Lyon assigns names to the four canonical gospels.

185–253 / Origen

200?–500? / Rabbis, mostly in Babylonia, create the Talmud.

248 / Origen writes *Against Celsus*.

257–59 / Emperor Valerian orders an empire–wide persecution of Christians.

303–11 / The "Great Persecution" of Christians.

312 / Battle of Milvian Bridge. Constantine makes Christianity a legal religion.

325 / Council of Nicaea formalizes the official set of Christian beliefs (the Nicaean Creed).

4th cent. / Probable compilation of the *Kāma Sūtra*.

354–430 / Augustine, Bishop of Hippo.

380 / Theodosius I makes Christianity the sole official religion of the empire.

388 / Monks at Callinicum destroy the synagogue there. Ambrose tells the emperor not to rebuild it.

410 / Visigoths led by Alaric sack the city of Rome.

426 / Augustine finishes writing *The City of God*.

622 / Muhammad flees Mecca for Yathrib (Medina). This becomes year 1 of the Islamic calendar.

999 / On New Year's Eve, crowds gather at St. Peter's in Rome expecting the world to end. It doesn't.

1075 / Gregory VII becomes pope, orders universal clerical celibacy, promotes doctrine of holy war.

1096 / Urban II issues his call for the First Crusade.

1099 / Crusaders capture Jerusalem, massacre almost all its inhabitants.

1198-1216 / Innocent III

1209-1229 / Albigensian Crusade (sporadic battles continue until 1244).

1215 / Fourth Lateran Council

1252 / Inquisition is authorized to use torture.

1302 / Boniface VIII issues *Unam Sanctam* proclaiming the absolute supremacy of the Church.

1303 / Troops under the command of Philip IV of France take Boniface captive.

1478 / The Spanish Inquisition is established. It reports to the Spanish monarch, not to the pope.

1517 / Luther publishes his Ninety–Five Theses, challenging the Vatican's use of indulgences.

1523 / Luther publishes *That Jesus Christ Was Born a Jew*.

1533 / England officially rejects the authority of the pope. A year later, the English crown becomes the head of the Church of England.

1543 / Copernicus publishes his argument that the Earth revolves around the Sun; Luther publishes *On the Jews and Their Lies*.

1555 / Paul IV issues *Cum Nimis Absurdum*, restricting the Jews in the Papal States to poverty and forcing them into ghettos.

1562 / Start of France's religious civil wars.

1598 / Henri IV of France issues the Edict of Nantes promoting religious toleration.

1600 / Giordano Bruno is burned at the stake for insisting Copernicus was right.

1618 / The "Defenestration of Prague" triggers the Thirty Years' War.

1633 / The Inquisition confines Galileo to house arrest for the rest of his life for agreeing with Copernicus.

1641 / The major combatants in the Thirty Years' War agree to begin peace negotiations.

1648 / The Peace of Westphalia ends the Thirty Years' War.

1661 / Last execution of a Quaker, William Leddra, for refusing to stay out of Puritan Massachusetts.

1685–1815 / The Age of Enlightenment

1687 / Sir Isaac Newton publishes *Mathematical Principles of Natural Philosophy*, which proves Copernicus was right.

1730s / "First Great Awakening" promotes evangelicalism in colonial America.

1789 / French revolution begins. Declaration of the Rights of Man.

1791 / United States adopts the Bill of Rights, including a provision that there is no national religion.

1793–94 / The Terror convulses France.

1802 / Pierre Laplace publishes corrections to Newton's theory of the solar system, doesn't mention God.

1826 / The Spanish Inquisition executes its final victim.

1844 / The Millerites expect the world to end on October 22nd. It doesn't.

1859 / Charles Darwin publishes *The Origin of Species*.

1910-15 / *The Fundamentals: A Testimony to the Truth* is published.

1915 / Albert Einstein publishes his theory of gravitation.

1917 / Russian revolutions in February and October.

1921 / New York City police, under the direction of the Catholic archdiocese of New York, break up a birth control rally.

1925 / John Scopes is found guilty of teaching evolution in a Tennessee school.

1933–45 / Nazi Germany.

1945 / The buried library at Nag Hamadi is discovered.

1947 / The first of the Dead Sea or Qumran scrolls is found.

1948 / Jewish state of Israel is founded; Jordan captures the Old City of Jerusalem; the Kinsey report on male sexuality.

1953 / The Kinsey report on female sexuality.

1960 / FDA approves the first contraceptive pill.

1965 / Vatican II Council approves *Nostra Aetate*.

1967 / In the Six Day War, Israel captures the Old City of Jerusalem; a new Presbyterian confession of faith makes only a passing reference to judgment after death; Tennessee repeals its law forbidding the teaching of evolution.

1968 / Paul VI issues *Humanae Vitae*.

1970 / Masters and Johnson document the negative impact of religion on human sexuality.

1973 / US Supreme Court allows abortion.

1986 / US Supreme Court upholds Georgia's sodomy laws. Georgia suffers its worst drought in recorded history.

1993 / The Vatican formally recognizes Israel.

2000 / Many expect the world to end. It doesn't.

2015 / US Supreme Court legalizes same-sex marriages.

2022 / US Supreme Court strikes down abortion protections.

NOTES

INTRODUCTION

1. "Vertical" and "horizontal" history are terms used in scholarship from time to time. See, e.g., Ehrman (2009, 21–22). Some evangelicals use these terms in a special way; see Boyer (2000, 315).
2. Hawking (2018, 38).
3. *Teyku* appears frequently in the Babylonian Talmud. See, e.g., *b. Ber.* 8a.
4. Hume *An Inquiry Concerning Human Understanding*, X.91.
5. See Alter (2019a, xiii–xl) on the problems in translating the Hebrew Scripture into English.
6. Alter (2019b, 163), in his introduction to the book of Samuel.
7. Akenson (1998, 530–32).
8. Akenson (1998, 526–36) has a good description of some of these problems and how historians deal with them. For a more detailed explanation, see Barton (2019, 215–307).
9. I follow the standard Jewish convention of referring to the books of First and Second Samuel, Kings, and Chronicles as single books except when making a specific citation. They are not separate documents the way, for example, First and Second Corinthians are. They were simply too long to fit on a standard scroll, and so were divided more or less in half.
10. See especially S. Cohen (2000, 69–106).

1. GODS OF THE ISRAELITES

1. Cline (2015, 91) ; see Junkkaala (2006, 70–74). Redford (1992, 177–91) goes into detail about Egypt's wars with the Hittites.
2. See, e.g., Barton (2019, 27–28), Finkelstein and Silberman (2001, 107–18), and Niditch (1997, 10–14). Junkkaala (2006, 11–34) gives a good critical summary of many of the various archeological positions.
3. Hasel (2008, 59, 52).
4. Faust (2015, 476). Faust is not clear who he thinks these escapees were, other than that they were not "Israel's 'core' group" (477). Na'aman (2015, 529–31) suggests that Egypt's abrupt withdrawal from Canaan around 1130 BCE may have been a factor in shaping the Exodus narrative.
5. *Attrahasis* II, iv.
6. *Attrahasis* III, v. In the Akkadian version, the *Epic of Gilgamesh*, Attrahasis is called Utnapishtim (Dalley 2008, 2).
7. *Attrahasis* III, vii. See Dalley (2008, 8).

8. Batto (2013, 46) has a chart showing a number of points that *Attrahasis* and the creation and Noah stories in Genesis have in common.
9. Mursili II, quoted by P. Sanders (2007, 185), published by Brill. I am indebted to Professor Trevor Bryce for alerting me to Mursili II's plague prayers and to the research by Paul Sanders.
10. Bryce (2002, 143).
11. Bottéro (2004, 205).
12. Assmann (2008, 11–12).
13. Redford (1992, 365–94). See Römer (2017a, 15–16). Assmann (2014, 68) argues that there is "no connection" at all between Akhenaten's version of monotheism and that of Moses.
14. Rollston (2003, 104). In addition to Rollston, I have relied on Bottéro (2004), Greenstein (2015), Finkelstein and Silberman (2001), Niditch (1997), M. Smith (2002), and Zevit (1990 and 2001), among others. Professor Bernard Jackson generously sent me some of his papers, and offered some ideas and suggestions that I greatly appreciate. As always, any mistakes or misinterpretations are mine alone.
15. See especially Hendel (2005, 50–51) and M. Smith (2002, 2, 2n3, 32). See Alter (2019a, 122n29).
16. Stahl (2020, 8). On Yahweh and El, see M. Smith (2002, 32–43 and the citations in 32-33n45); on Yahweh and Baal, see (43–47). There were apparently a number of different gods in and near Canaan called Baal; see (65–79). On Yahweh's probable origin point in Edom, see, e.g., Kelley (2009, 261–63) and Na'aman (2015, 529–30). See Stahl (2020, 8-11) for a summary of current scholarly thinking.
17. Stahl (2020, 7; see 7–8). Greenstein (2015, 54) also finds a correlation between Yahweh and the Ugaritic Baal. For arguments that Yahweh was originally a weather god, see M. Smith (2002, 47n82).
18. The scholarly consensus on the existence of a United Monarchy under Saul, David, and Solomon fractured decades ago. See Knoppers (1997) for a summary of some recent arguments.
19. 2 Kings 17:7-18. See Alter (2019b, 582n7).
20. 2 Kings 21:3-4.
21. 2 Kings 23:4–13. See Alter (2019b, 849–50). Römer (2017b, 333) suggests Josiah's reforms may have been limited to Jerusalem.
22. 2 Kings 23:37 (my translation).
23. M. Smith (2002, 192). See Knoppers (2001, 407).
24. Judg. 10:6.
25. Judg. 8:27, 28.
26. 2 Kings 4:38–42, 2 Kings 3.
27. Jer. 15:4, 2 Kings 23:26–27. But see 2 Chron. 33:10–17, 36:16.
28. Ezek. 16:25–26. Alter observes that Ezekiel seems to have "some sort of morbid obsession with the female body in its sexual aspect" (2019b, 1091n15; see also 1051).
29. 2 Kings 24:1–25:22.

30. Isa. 40:1. On Second Isaiah (or "Deutero–Isaiah"), see, e.g., Alter (2019b, 617–18), Barton (2019, 104–07).

31. See especially M. Smith (2002, 191–99). See also Barton (2019, 105), S. Cohen (2014, 79–80), and Karagiannis (2019, 193–94); but see Brettler (2010, 28–29), Olyan (2012), and Schenker (1997, 448).

32. Ex. 20:3, Ps. 82:1, Ps. 97:7. See Alter (2019c, 200n1, 230n7).

33. Isa. 45:12 (my translation, slightly emended to emphasize that these are the "hosts of heaven.") See Olyan (2012, 200).

34. Isa. 44:6. This is my translation, to emphasize that Isaiah uses a different word (*mi-baladai*—apart from Me) than Exodus 20:3 (*'al-panai* —beside Me).

35. Zech. 14:1–9*.

36. Fredriksen (2022, 23) argues that "'monotheism' fundamentally misdescribes the religious sensibility of antiquity." See also S. Cohen (2014, 80–85), but see Rollston (2003). Still, I don't want to lose the reader with more technical terms such as "henotheism," so this is a compromise phrasing.

37. Karagiannis (2019, 193). Jer. 27:6. Römer (2017a, 22 [my translation]); see also (2013, 2).

38. Olyan (2012, 201).

39. Akenson (1998, 66). See Bickerman (2012, 29–30), Van der Spek (2014, 246, 257–58).

40. Isa. 45:1.

41. 1 Kings 18:36.

42. 2 Kings 5:15, 19:8. Amos 1:3–2:3, Isa. 2:2–4.

43. See, e.g., M. Smith (2002, 191–92), Rollston (2003, 112n49), Römer (2013).

44. *Hittite Laws* §§192, 193; Deut. 25:5–6. Bryce (2002, 131–32).

45. *Hittite Laws* §192; Lev. 18:18.

46. Stewart (2020, 45). I am indebted to Dr. Stewart for sharing several articles and his time with me to help me understand the tenuous but possible Hittite influence on the Israelites.

47. Knust (2012, 144).

48. *Code of the Assura* §1.8; Deut. 25:11–12 (my translation).

49. Deut. 22:23–27; *Hittite Laws* §197. Westbrook (1988, 6).

50. See Matthews and Benjamin (2006, 105–30). See generally Greengus (2019) for more examples and details.

51. Jackson (2006, 280). The verse in question is Exod. 21:35, which states explicitly that the living ox is to be sold, while the Eshnunna version only implies it (see Jackson 2006, 280n124). See also Otto (2015, 498–99).

52. Weinfeld (2004, 47–50; 47–48n27). The *akītu* rituals probably influenced Ezekiel's Passover purification laws; see Ganzel (2021).

53. Lev. 14:1–8; Weinfeld (2004, 46–47 and 46n24).

54. *Code of Hammurabi*, Preamble. Doak (2006, 5).

55. Westbrook (1988, 3), Satlow (2014, 27–28). See Levinson (1992, 39).

56. I am grateful to Trevor Bryce, Bernard Levinson, Eckart Otto, and David Stewart for helping me with the unlikelihood of a direct connection with the Hittite laws.
57. See Holm (2014, 37) on the scarcity of references to Moses; also see Schmid (2016, 136–38). On the probable uses of the word, "Torah," see, e.g., Alter's comments on Psalm 119 (2019c, 279n1), Collins (2017, 45–47), and Jackson (1990, 246–47).
58. Collins (2017, 25).
59. 1 Sam. 28:9–10. Lev. 20:27 prescribes death by stoning for anyone who consults a ghost; see also Deut. 18:10–11.
60. 2 Sam. 12:7–12. See Alter (2019b, 348n11) for some interesting theories on Uriah's responses to David. See also Westbrook (1998, 33).
61. 2 Kings 14:6, quoting Deut. 24:16.
62. Alter (2019b, 574n6).
63. Jackson (1990, 244–45, italics in original).
64. Knoppers (2001, 398).
65. Wazana (2016, 174). Judg. 8:22–23, 1 Sam. 8:4–20, Deut. 17:14–20.
66. 2 Kings 22:8–11. Römer (2017b, 333–35) argues that this story was "revised and expanded" during the exile, but see Otto (2013, 223–28).
67. Knoppers (2001, 404). See Römer (2005, 80 and 2017b, 336).
68. E.g., Knoppers (2001), Levinson (2001), Satlow (2014, 40–48). Professor Levinson also very kindly helped me understand the problems presented by this passage.
69. Otto (2013, 226).
70. See, e.g., Schmid (2016, 141–44).
71. The scholarship on this topic is so extensive as to defy easy summarization. Interested readers might start with Akenson (1998), Barton (2019), Collins (2017, 21–61), Niditch (1997, 28–33), Otto (2013), Römer (2005 and 2015), Satlow (2014), M. Smith (2002), Ulrich (2012), and Weinfeld (2004).
72. Greengus (2019, 4) argues that while an exact count is impossible, the ratio of sacred to secular law is probably between 2.7/1 and 3.5/1.
73. Deut. 17:20, Deut. 13:1 (in some editions, 12:32). Polk (2020, 56–61).
74. Freedman (1990, 323). Batto (2013, 51–52) argues that Babylonian exiles explicitly rejected the Mesopotamian model of the king as God's viceroy on earth or possessing "divinely infused" authority.
75. Freedman (1990, 324).

2. IMMORTALITY AND THE JEWS

1. See Ben Zvi (2016, 108n12).
2. Mal. 2:11, 3:5. See G. Klein (1987, 23–26) on the possible dating of Malachi. Alter suggests that "coupled with" (u-ba'al) "may be referring simply to sexual relations," not necessarily marriage (2019b, 1389n11).
3. E.g., Ben Zvi (2016, 109–13).

4. Josephus, *Antiquities* 11.329–45; see also the Talmud (*b. Yoma* 69a).
5. S. Cohen (2010, 186; see generally 176–86).
6. Collins (2001, 42).
7. See, e.g., Bickerman (1962), Collins (1993, 63–65), Gruen (2016, 333–34, 343), and Lorein (2001, 157). Gruen argues (2016, 357) that "Antiochus victimized the Jews in a Seleucid power play."
8. 2 Macc. 4:24. See Gruen (2016, 337), Mazzucchi (2009, 22–23).
9. 2 Macc. 5:11–16; see Dan. 11:30. See Collins (2001, 43, 49).
10. See especially Gruen (2016, 340–45).
11. 1 Macc. 1:43.
12. S. Cohen (2014, 33; see 33–34). See Gruen (1998, 6).
13. 1 Macc. 2:44.
14. S. Cohen (2014, 3).
15. Goodman (1993, 9).
16. Jer. 31:28–29; Ezek. 18:5. See S. Cohen (2014, 100–01), Gillman (2000, 98–100). Alter translates the proverb differently; see (2019b, 966n28).
17. Ezek. 18:5–29; quote is at 18:30.
18. S. Cohen (2014, 101). See Gillman (2000, 100).
19. See Alter (2019c, 458–59).
20. Assmann (2005, 148).
21. See Assmann (2005, 414, 115–16).
22. Assmann (2005, 10).
23. Bottéro (2004, 106).
24. *Epic of Gilgamesh*, X.iii (Old Babylonian Version).
25. Bottéro (2004, 106, 108).
26. See, e.g., 1 Kings 2:6, Ps. 6:6, Eccl. 9:10, Job 17:13, 16. See Bottéro (2004, 204) on the similarities between Sheol and the Akkadian version. See also Bernstein (1993, 8–11) on the similarities between Babylonian and early Greek and Hebrew ideas. Bryce (2002, 180–81) argues that the Hittites, though they were not Semites, shared the Semitic idea of a shadowy life after death.
27. 1 Kings 2:2.
28. Gillman (2000, 69).
29. Isa. 65:20 (my translation). See, e.g., Alter (2019b, 618) and Barton (2019, 106–07) on the probable dating and authorship of chapters 56–66 of Isaiah.
30. Ezek. 37:1–14; Isa. 26:19. See, e.g., Alter (2019b, 703n19) and Segal (2004, 255–61). There is some argument over when the Isaiah passage was written.
31. See Gerstenberger (2012, 492); I am grateful to Prof. Gerstenberger for bringing his work to my attention. See, e.g., Gillman (2000, 96–98). Shaked (2016, 1531–33) argues for a probable Zoroastrian origin anyway, but doesn't appear to consider the Hellenistic possibility. See also Bernstein (2017, 5–7).
32. Plato *Timaeus*, 42b, Dan. 12:3. See Bedard (2008, 182), Bickerman (2012, 276). Endsjø (2009, 134) offers a more cautious view. For general informa-

tion on the complex relationship between Judaism and Hellenism, see Bedard (2008), Bickerman (2012), S. Cohen (2014), Collins (2001), Gruen (1998), and Mazzucchi (2009) for starters.

33. The arguments for determining the date of Daniel are complex and technical. I explain some of them in an appendix (Dating the Book of Daniel) for those who are interested.
34. Boyer (2000, 31).
35. Dan. 12:1–3.
36. The Epistle of Jude (1:14–15) quotes *1 Enoch* 1:9. See Collins (2016, 178–79) on Qumran; Isaac (2015, 10) on the Ethiopian Church.
37. Isaac (2015, 9).
38. *1 Enoch* 97:3, 103:6, 103:7, 62:1, 62:11–12. See also, e.g., *1 Enoch* 103:14–104:7.
39. *Wisdom* 2:10, 5:1. See, e.g., Vermes (2011a, 88).
40. S. Cohen (2014, 91).
41. 1 Macc. 2:69.
42. Eccl. 3:19. Sir. 10:11, 11:25–28. See the note on Sir. 11:26 (NRSV(HC), 1549). Sirach (Ecclesiasticus) is probably around 200 BCE. Protestant Bibles put this book in the Apocrypha. Ecclesiastes is harder to date; Alter (2019c, 674) suggests a likely date sometime in the early to middle fourth century BCE.
43. Josephus *Antiquities*, 18.16.
44. 2 Macc. 7:9, 14.
45. *Pss. Sol.* 3:11.
46. 4 Macc. 18:23, 18:5, 12:12. See Ehrman (2020, 131–33).
47. *M. Sanh.* 10:1. See Gillman (2000, 128–31).
48. Dan. 8:17.
49. One was for 1150 days—2300 "evenings and mornings" (Dan. 8:14). There was also 490 years, more or less (Dan. 9:24–28), 1290 days (12:12), and 1335 days (12:13). See Collins (2016, 141).
50. Gillihan (2016, 213–14).
51. See, e.g., S. Cohen (2014, 151), Vermes (2011a, 14–15).
52. Vermes (2011a, 49).
53. Collins (2016, 209); see 206–12. See also Vermes (2011a, 163–65). On the Kittim as the Romans, see also Vermes (2011b, 215).
54. *4 Ezra* 12:31, 33; see Metzger (2015, 517).
55. Isa. 45:1.
56. S. Cohen (2014, 98–99).
57. In the introduction to his translation, Wright (2015, 641–42) suggests that the Roman invaders may have been the target. Atkinson (1999, 442–44) argues that the Psalms, especially number 17, are an attack on Herod, who usurped the throne with Roman help.
58. See Collins (2016, 199–201), Vermes (2011a, 86–87).
59. See Fredriksen (2018, 172–75), Porter and Pearson (2000, 97–98, also 98n46 and 111).
60. 2 Sam. 12:14. Jer. 25:6–9. Isa. 40:2, Obad. 1:10.

61. See Alter (2019c, 748).
62. Dan. 11.
63. Miller (2016, 63). See also the note on Tobit 14:4-7 (NRSV(HC), 1457-58). See also Barton (1988, 215-17) on Tobit's use of prophecy.
64. Miller (2016, 64).
65. The scholarly version of this term is *vaticinium ex eventu.*
66. Bodi (2010, 23 [my translation]).
67. Jer. 25:11-12.
68. Jer. 51:11, *Cyrus Cylinder* §17.
69. Dan. 9:2, 24-28.
70. Isa. 40:1. There are various passages identified as the "Songs"; the main one is Isa. 52:13-53:12. See Evans (2012, 146-47). The term "Suffering Servant" is not in Scripture; its first recorded use was in 1892 (Brettler and Levine 2019, 159). I have relied on Brettler and Levine, and also J. Cohen (2007) and Alter (2019b, 801n3, 802n6, and 803n12) for this section. As always, any errors are mine alone.
71. Isa. 53:3, 5, 9, 10. "Disgraceful burial" is Alter's evaluation of the "crabbed" Hebrew in verse 9. I am also relying on Alter's "conjectural" reading of the verbs as conditional (2019b, 803nn9-10). See also Jackson (2008, 40-41) on the difficulties in understanding the language of this passage.
72. See, e.g., Brettler and Levine (2019, 163-64) and Gillman (2000, 95) on some of the possible identities of the servant. The idea that the "suffering servant" might have been the prophet himself dates back to the Middle Ages (Alter 2019b, 801n3).
73. Dan. 12:3 (*matzdikey harabbim*) and Isa. 53:11 (*yatzdik tzadik 'avdi l'rabbim*). See Collins (1993, 393-94), Gillman (2000, 95).
74. Josephus, *Antiquities* 10.276. See Barton (1988, 181).
75. Dan. 6:4, 6.
76. Alter (2019c, 747). Bickerman (2012, 208). Uusimäki (2018, 5-6). I am grateful to Dr. Jed Wyrick for directing me to Uusimäki's article. For more on the connection between Hellenistic and Second Temple Jewish depictions of their heroes, see, e.g., Gruen (1998, 73-109 and 246-91).
77. Sacks (2016, 64).
78. Gen. 12:10-20. *Jub.* 17:17-18. Gruen (1998, 107) on Joseph.
79. *B. Shab.* 56a, but see, e.g., *b. Yoma* 22b.
80. On the Socrates comparison, see Sterling (2001, 401). Also see chapter 3.

3. SALVATION FOR THE CHRISTIANS

1. See especially L. M. White (2005, 122-32). I have relied on Paula Fredriksen's work for parts of this chapter, and also for some explanations and references she graciously provided me in personal communications. Bart Ehrman has also kindly responded to a number of questions I've posted on his blog. In addition, I have also relied on Chazan (2016, 3-46), J. Cohen

(2007), Ehrman (2018), Setzer (1994), and Wilken (1984), among others. As always, any errors and misinterpretations are all mine.

2. On the dating of the gospels, see, for example, Barton (2019, 199–205), Ehrman (2015, 89–92). See Kloppenborg (2008, 9–12) for an explanation of how scholars determined that Mark was written first.

3. Irenaeus *Against Heresies*, 3.1.1. See Ehrman (2009, 111).

4. Acts 9:1; see Gal. 1:12–17.

5. Ehrman (2001, 57–59). See Evans (1994, 457–66).

6. Josephus *Antiquities*, 18.63–64. See Evans (1994, 466–74), Lémonon (1981, 277), and L. M. White (2005, 97–98). See Whealey (2003, 203–07) for a summary of the historical debate over the passage's authenticity.

7. Josephus *Antiquities*, 20.200.

8. Josephus *Antiquities*, 18.118. Mark 6:17, also Luke 3:19–20.

9. Mark 1:15. I have adopted the NRSV(HC)'s suggestion of "is at hand" as an alternate rendering of "has come near." In Matt. 4:17, Jesus used the same words as John the Baptist.

10. On the unlikelihood of Jesus attracting large crowds, see Fredriksen (1999, 215–17).

11. Cook (2011, 213). My thanks to Dr. Cook for his comments to me on the use of *seditio*, which he thinks was the more likely charge (private communication, June 21, 2020).

12. Josephus *War Against the Jews*, 2.253. On Varus, see *Antiquities*, 17.295.

13. Josephus *War Against the Jews*, 5.450–51.

14. Josephus *Antiquities*, 18.88–89. See also Philo *Gaius*, §302 (40 CE). See, e.g., Bond (1998, 32). Lémonon (1981, 273–77) argues that Pilate was not particularly cruel, but he was "lacking in political sense [and] clumsy with the Jews" (274, my translation).

15. Mark 15:2, Matt. 27:11, Luke 23:3. In John 18:33, Pilate asked the same question, but Jesus was more evasive in his answer.

16. Mark 15:27, Matt. 27:38. Jackson (1972, 35). On the meanings and uses of *lēstes* (pl. *lēstai*), see Fredriksen (2018, 46–47), Jackson (1972, 35–40), and the note on John 10:8 (NRSV(HC), 2033).

17. Mark 11:15–17, Matt. 21:12–13, Luke 19:45–46, John 2:14–16. Fredriksen (1999, 207–14) questions whether it was an invented story.

18. For further reading, see, e.g., Vermes (2011b, 38) and (2013, 23–24) for arguments favoring the troublemaking charge, and to Ehrman (2015,122–23) for sedition, which Cook (2011, 197–203) thinks is the more likely charge. See Fredriksen (1999) for the theory that Pilate executed Jesus as a warning to his crowds of followers. Jackson (2008, 33–39) discusses the problems of the trial narratives from the viewpoint of a legal historian.

19. Josephus *Antiquities*, 20.6.

20. Fredriksen (1999, 253).

21. Josephus *Antiquities*, 18.64.

22. Fredriksen (2010, 81; 1999, 107; 2010, 401n2). See Ehrman (2001, 205–06); see also Commission for Religious Relations with the Jews "Notes on the Correct Way to Present Jews and Judaism," §§18–19.

23. Lev. 24:11. See also Jackson (2008, 38n18 and 50–53).
24. E.g., Ps. 2:7 (Alter (2019c, 29n7) explains that "it was a commonplace in the Ancient Near East, adopted by the Israelites, to imagine the king as God's son.") Jer. 31:8—"Ephraim is my firstborn"; Hos. 11:1—"From Egypt I called my son." Around the time of Jesus, some translators of these texts began to change the wording "to deny that God could have a son at all" (Huntress 1935, 119), but that does not make it blasphemy.
25. Josephus *Antiquities*, 13.297.
26. Ehrman (2001, 220).
27. John 8;59, 10:31–39. Ehrman (2020, 203–04).
28. Acts 6:11, 7:1–60.
29. Josephus War Against the Jews, 2.145.
30. Mark 8:31–32, 9:30–32, 14:50, 14:66–72, 15:40–16:8. One man, Joseph of Arimathea, did take the body and bury it.
31. 1 Cor. 1:23.
32. Of the 13 letters in the New Testament attributed to Paul, scholars are generally in accord that he wrote seven: Romans, 1 and 2 Corinthians, Galatians, Philippians, 1 Thessalonians, and Philemon.
33. Rom. 6:9.
34. Rom. 3:25.
35. Rom. 5:12. Rom. 3:9.
36. Mark 10:17–21, Matt. 19:16–21, Luke 18:18–22.
37. Matt. 25:31–46.
38. John 11:25–26.
39. John 1:29.
40. Sterling (2001, 401).
41. See, e.g., the survey in Ehrman (2020, 279–90).
42. See, e.g., Ehrman (2015, 115–16), Fredriksen (1999, 248–49). Wrede (1971, 218, 230) argues that Jesus was probably *not* known as messiah during his lifetime.
43. Irenaeus *Against Heresies*, 3.18.4. The bracketed words are in the translation.
44. Luke 24:26.
45. 1 Cor. 15:3. See Evans (2012, 144) for a full list of New Testament quotes and allusions to the suffering servant. Some of the list may be speculative.
46. Miller (2016, 63).
47. Evans (2012, 149 and 149–50n19).
48. This is the entire thrust of Miller's book, *Helping Jesus Fulfill Prophecy* (2016).
49. John 5:39.
50. See Barton (1988, 179-92; 215).
51. 1 Cor. 15:20; see 12–24. See, e.g., Allison (2000, 283–85, 299) and Fredriksen (2017, 145).
52. 1 Thess. 4:15–17.
53. Rom. 13:11–12. See Fredriksen (1999, 78–81).
54. Mark 1:15, 9:1; Matt. 16:28.

55. Luke 9:27, 9:28–36 (the NRSV(HC) note to verse 27 (1976) connects Jesus's words to the transfiguration that occurs about eight days later). Luke 17:20–37, 21:7–8. See Ehrman (2001, 130).
56. John 6:40. See also John 11:25–26, Ehrman (2001, 131).
57. John 20:31.
58. Fredriksen (1999, 89). 2 Pet. 3:8–10, referencing Ps. 90:4 and also Paul's "thief in the night" (1 Thess. 5:2).
59. I take this point from De Villiers (2002) and the scholars he cites, and also from Bart Ehrman's responses to my questions about Revelation, which I much appreciate. (Dr. Ehrman generously made his upcoming book on Revelation available to me.)
60. Rev. 1:9. See De Villiers (2002 ,59–60).
61. Rev. 22:12.
62. Rev. 1:3, 14:7.
63. See, e.g., Collins (2016, 327–30), Ehrman (2015, 64–69), Huntress (1935).
64. E.g., John 5:26–27, 6:37–40.

4. WHY WON'T THE JEWS BELIEVE IN JESUS?

1. Eliav (2006, 565). Vermes (2013, 2).
2. Josephus Antiquities, 18.63–64. He describes the three groups, as well as a fourth one, an offshoot of the Pharisees, at 18.11–25. On the suspiciously large number of conversions in Acts, see Sim (2005, 420–23). On the probable number of Pharisees (6,000) and Essenes (4,000), see S. Cohen (2014, 144); there were probably a similar number of Sadducees.
3. Sim (2005, 433, 437; see 426, 436, and 437 for his population estimates.) See also Ehrman (2018, 74–76 and 160–73), Goodman (2007, 492), and Stark (1996, 5). Stark argues (1996, 49–71) that Christian efforts prior to the fifth century to convert Jews were far more successful than is generally acknowledged, but see S. Cohen (2014, 167 and 254–58).
4. Endsjø (2009, 135 [italics in original]).
5. Endsjø (2009, 138–39).
6. Atkinson (1999, 445). I am indebted to Dr. Amy-Jill Levine for reminding me that the idea of a militant messiah was not universal.
7. Wright (2015, 643).
8. 1 Cor. 1:23. Fredriksen (2017, 84 [italics in original]). Deut. 21:23 says "a hanged man is God's curse." See Paul's use of it in Gal. 3:13—a "snarled passage," in Fredriksen's apt description (2017, 83).
9. S. Cohen (2014, 101). Fredriksen (2018, 185). See also Goodman (2007, 492), Setzer (1994, 166–68).
10. Gal. 4:4, Ehrman (2001, 96).
11. Matt. 1:18–25, Luke 1:26–27.
12. Matt. 1:23, citing Isa. 7:14.
13. Setzer (1994, 180 and 219n6).

14. E.g., Lev. 21:7-14: An ordinary priest may marry a widow, though not a divorcee, but the high priest is specifically required to marry a virgin (*b'tullah*).
15. Miller (2016, 11).
16. 1 Cor. 1:23, 1 Thess. 2:15. Dickieson asserts (2006, 3) that Paul is using the "Judaistic motif of critique-from-within" in First Thessalonians. See also Porter and Pearson (2000, 91).
17. Mark 15:10, Matt. 27:18. Luke 23:6-12. John 18:38-19:16. Josephus *Antiquities*, 18.61-62.
18. See Josephus *Antiquities*, 18.88-89.
19. Origen *Against Celsus*, 2.75. See Wilken (1984, 115).
20. Matt. 5:10, 1 Pet. 4:14.
21. Fredriksen (2022, 28).
22. See, e.g., Fredriksen (2010, 89) and references cited in (2022, 28n12), Heemstra (2010, 93), Moss (2014, 175-76).
23. Decree of the Emperor Claudius (ruled 41-54 CE), quoted in Josephus *Antiquities*, 19.290. See also Josephus's recording of earlier, similar decrees by Julius Caesar and other Roman officials (*Antiquities*, 14.190-264), and Augustus's acquiescence to the "idiosyncrasies of Jewish ancestral custom" (Fredriksen 2022, 36).
24. See Fredriksen (2017, 38-49; 2022, 28-29).
25. See S. Cohen (2000, 168-74), Fredriksen (2017, 54-60, 76-77), and Heemstra (2010, 47-48). The Greek term was *theosebeis*, for which Cohen's "preferred translation" is "venerators of God" (2000, 171).
26. Acts 13:16. See Fredriksen (2017, 79-81).
27. 1 Cor. 10:20, 21. On demons, see, e.g., Ehrman (2018, 80).
28. Fredriksen (2010, 27).
29. Fredriksen (2018, 151); see also (2010, 36-38).
30. 2 Cor. 11:24, 25, Acts 24-26. Heemstra (2010, 46) suggests the Jews probably realized the danger before the Romans did.
31. 1 Thess. 2:15. See Heemstra (2010, 52n90).
32. See L. M. White (2005, 355-56) on Tacitus and his biases. Also see Heemstra (2010, 87-93) on Nero.
33. See Heemstra (2010, 80-84).
34. Pliny the Younger *Letters*, X.96 (Pliny to Trajan), X.97 (Trajan to Pliny). See Ehrman (2018, 187), Moss (2014, 139-43), Nixey (2017, 74-85), L. M. White (2005, 357-60), and Wilken (1984, 15-30). On the butchers' complaint, see Nixey (2017, 75).
35. Moss (2014, 144).
36. Tertullian *Letter to Scapula*, V. See Moss (2014, 144), Nixey (2017, 77).
37. Goodman (2007, 512).
38. Origen *Against Celsus*, 3.8 [italics in the translation]. See Fredriksen (2010, 88) for the date. See also Ehrman (2018, 157-58), Goodman (2007, 509-12), McLaren (2013), and Praet (2014, 43-45), among others.
39. Moss (2014, 145-53), Praet (2014, 42-43) on the *pax deorum*.

40. Ehrman (2018, 205). Moss (2014, 154–59) has a slightly different understanding of Diocletian's intentions.
41. Ehrman (2018, 205–06).
42. See M. Cohen (1994, 19–20), Wilken (1983, 76–77).
43. All quotations taken from Chrysostom *Against the Jews: Sermon 1* ("Dangers Ahead").
44. See, e.g., Nixey (2018, 143), Wilken (1983, xv).
45. Augustine *City of God*, 18.46.
46. Weiss (1996, 16). See J. Cohen (2009, 577–78).
47. Paul IV *Cum Nimis Absurdum*.
48. Ryrie (2017, 266).
49. MacCulloch (2005, 690).
50. Luther *On the Jews and Their Lies*, 268–74.
51. Goldfarb (2009, 88).
52. Vatican II *Nostra Aetate* §4. See Commission for Religious Relations with the Jews "Notes on the Correct Way to Present Jews and Judaism," §7.
53. Commission for Religious Relations with the Jews "The Gifts and the Calling of God are Irrevocable," §40.
54. Gregerman (2018, 254, 255).
55. Catholic Online, Jan. 14, 2013, https://www.catholic.org/news/hf/faith/story.php?id=49314.
56. "Rick Warren: Churches aren't being persecuted by COVID restrictions." *Baptist News Global*, Dec. 28, 2020. https://baptistnews.com/article/rick-warren-churches-arent-being-persecuted-by-covid-restrictions/
57. "As Persecution Intensifies, 'We Must Pray for Boldness Rather than Safety.'" *The Christian Post*, May 27, 2021. https://www.christianpost.com/spon sored/as-persecution-intensifies-we-must-pray-for-boldness-rather-than-safety.html
58. Veldman (2019, 90, 91).
59. John 12:25.
60. I am grateful to Dr. Dale Allison for helping me understand John's use of *miseo* (hate) in this verse.

5. GOD BETWEEN THE SHEETS

1. Eccl. 9:9; see Bloch and Bloch (1995, 11–12).
2. *Siftei Ḥaḥamim* on Gen. 25:6 (my translation).
3. 1 Kings 1:2, 4 (my translation). See Alter (2019b, 434n4).
4. See *Even HaEzer* 13:7.
5. Hoffman (2016, 239). Bloch and Bloch (1995, 14).
6. Song of Songs 1:13, 4:16.
7. Knust (2012, 26, 25, 29); see Song of Songs 8:8–9, 5:7, also 8:1. See Bloch and Bloch (1995, 13–14).
8. Song of Songs 5:14, 7:2, 8:10. Rashi on Song of Songs 8:10 (my translation). Alter (2019c, 616n10). See Barton (2019, 218–21), Bloch and Bloch

(1995, 217), and Hoffman (2016, 238). On attempts to read the Song as a metaphor, see, e.g., Barton (2019, 345, 375), Bloch and Bloch (1995, 30-35), Knust (2012, 29-33), and Tanner (1997, 26-31). See *m. Yad.* 3:5 for the rabbinic debate over whether to include this book in the canon; also see Bloch and Bloch (1995, 27-29).

9. *B. Ket.* 61b-62a, *b. Eruv.* 100b. Naturally, this excluded the part of the month when she was menstruating.

10. 4Q270 fragment 7:13. See Josephus *War Of the Jews*, 2.161, Vermes (2011a, 38).

11. Josephus *War of the Jews*, 2.120-21.

12. 1 Cor. 7:36, 7:38, 9:5. See, e.g., Huttunen (2010) for more on the Stoic influence on Paul.

13. Matt. 19:12. Matt. 22:30, also Mark 12:25. See, e.g., Endsjø (2011, 208-9).

14. Clement of Alexandria *Stromata*, III.7.58.

15. Hunter (2018, 18). See Hunter generally for a survey and source materials for various attitudes towards marriage and sex among the early Christians.

16. *Apocalypse of Paul*, §§22, 39. See Ehrman (2020, 262-65).

17. Couenhoven (2005, 364).

18. Augustine *City of God,* 14.23.

19. Couenhoven (2005, 366).

20. Augustine *City of God*, 14.16.

21. Augustine *Marriage and Desire*, I.27. Augustine's understanding of concupiscence is complex, extending far beyond sexual lust. See Couenhoven (2005, 372-76) for an explanation.

22. Hunter (1999, 536), with citations to *On the Excellence of Marriage.*

23. E.g., Augustine *Against the Pelagians*, I.33, *On the Excellence of Marriage*, I.11, and *Marriage and Desire* I.16. See, e.g., J. Cohen (1989, 245-59), Couenhoven (2005), and Hunter (1999).

24. Pius XII *Humani Generis*, §§36, 37. Francis *In Honor of Benedict XVI.*

25. Snuth (1990, 135-36). Buitendag (2007) gives a good, if technical, overview on the development of Luther's thoughts on sex and marriage.

26. Moore (2000, 36), citing (137n14) to Calvin's *L'Instutition Chretienne* book 2, ch. 8, §§41, 43. "Accursed" is the usual translation of the French word *maudite*; "damned" or "demonic" are other ways of reading it.

27. Stensvold (2015, 67, 68).

28. Weber (1976, 158).

29. Neill (2009, 405).

30. Sykes (1995, 23).

31. Augustine *De Ordine*, 2.4. The ancient Greeks and Romans had a closely related understanding of the usefulness of prostitution; see Harper (2012, 368-69).

32. Aquinas *Summa Theologica*, II-II.10.11 A1. On their disapproval of prostitution, see Aquinas *Summa Theologica*, II-II.10.11 and Augustine *Against Faustus*, 22.61 and *De Ordine*, 2.4.

33. Endsjø (2011, 99).

34. Oberman (2006, 284-87), Ryrie (2017, 51-52).

35. Coontz (1992, 184). See Ekirch (2005, 200).
36. Ekirch (2005, 202).
37. Coontz (1992, 184).
38. Griffith (2017, vii).
39. Halberstam (1994, 277–78).
40. Halberstam (1994, 573).
41. Halberstam (1994, 280), quoting Rev. Billy Graham.
42. Masters and Johnson (1970, 179).
43. Masters and Johnson (1970, 178).
44. Heels (2019, 10).
45. "With High Premarital Sex And Abortions Rates, Evangelicals Say It's Time To Talk About Sex." *Huffington Post Religion News Service*, Apr. 23, 2012.   https://www.huffpost.com/entry/evangelicals-sex-frank-talk_n_1443062 See Stanger-Hall and Hall (2011).
46. "Association of Religiosity With Sexual Minority Suicide Ideation and Attempt," *American Journal of Preventive Medicine*, Mar. 14, 2018. https://pubmed.ncbi.nlm.nih.gov/29550162/
47. Herrmann (2021, 9).
48. L. Klein (2018, 8, 67).
49. E.g., R. Smith et al. (2018).
50. Cantor (1994, 251).
51. "Sex abuse claims have cost the US Catholic Church almost $4 billion," *Christianity Today*, Nov. 3, 2015. https://www.christiantoday.com/article/sex.abuse.claims.have.cost.the.us.catholic.church.almost.4.billion/69511.htm. See McGreevy (2022, 380–86) on the worldwide problem, particularly in Australia.
52. On evangelicals, see, e.g., "Abuse of Faith: 20 years, 700 victims: Southern Baptist sexual abuse spreads as leaders resist reforms," *Houston Chronicle*, Feb 10, 2019. https://www.houstonchronicle.com/news/investigations/article/Southern-Baptist-sexual-abuse-spreads-as-leaders-13588038.php. For rabbis, see for example Schwab (2002). Some examples of sex abuse in Islam can be found in "'A long time coming': These Muslims are bringing sex abuse by sheikhs out of the shadows," *Religion News Service*, Jan. 15, 2020.   https://religionnews.com/2020/01/15/a-long-time-coming-these-muslims-are-bringing-sex-abuse-by-sheikhs-out-of-the-shadows/
53. "U.S. Southern Baptists release scathing report on sexual abuse." *Reuters*, May 23, 2022. https://www.reuters.com/world/us/us-southern-baptists-release-scathing-report-sexual-abuse-2022-05-22/
54. "About six-in-ten Americans say abortion should be legal in all or most cases," *Pew Research Center*, Jun. 13, 2022. https://www.pewresearch.org/fact-tank/2022/06/13/about-six-in-ten-americans-say-abortion-should-be-legal-in-all-or-most-cases-2/. "American religious groups vary widely in their views of abortion," *Pew Research Center*, Jan. 22, 2018. https://www.pewresearch.org/fact-tank/2018/01/22/american-religious-groups-vary-widely-in-their-views-of-abortion/

55. *Dobbs v. Jackson Women's Health Organization*, No. 19-1392, 597 U.S. ___ (2022). "Most Americans want chance to support abortion rights on state ballot, USA TODAY/Ipsos poll finds." msn.com, Aug. 10, 2022. https://www.msn.com/en-us/news/politics/most-americans-want-chance-to-support-abortion-rights-on-state-ballot-usa-todayipsos-poll-finds/ar-AA10w7gP

56. "Where major religious groups stand on abortion." *Pew Research Center*, Jun. 21, 2016. https://www.pewresearch.org/fact-tank/2016/06/21/where-major-religious-groups-stand-on-abortion/. "Explained: Orthodox Jews Are Not 'Pro-Choice'—But They're Also Not 'Pro-Life.'" *Forward*, Mar. 3, 2019. https://forward.com/news/420165/orthodox-jews-abortion-pro-life-christians/

57. *B. Sanh.* 72b.

58. Balmer (2021, 35, 37); see Stone (2017, 395).

59. "High Court Holds Abortion To Be 'A right of privacy.'" *Baptist Press*, Jan. 31, 1973.

60. Fitzgerald (2017, 254–56).

61. Balmer (2021, 50). I have relied largely on Balmer (2007) and (2021) for the material in this section.

62. Balmer (2007, 16; see 13–17, also 222n21; see 2021, xi–xiv and 45–57). See Stone (2017, 400–40), also Whitehead and Perry (2020, 73–77).

63. Paul VI *Humanae Vitae*, §13.

64. "Birth Control Raid Made by Police on Archbishop's Order." *New York Times*, Nov. 15, 1921. See Griffith (2017, 14), Stone (2017, 203–04).

65. Griffith (2017, 28–32 and 44–45). On the fundamentalist view, see Sutton (2017, 144–47).

66. McGreevy (2022, 343).

67. "Vatican: Many Catholics ignore teachings on sex." *Nationnews.com*, Jun. 26, 2014. https://www.nationnews.com/2014/06/26/vatican-many-catholics-ignore-teachings-on-sex/

68. Jones and Dreweke (2011, 4).

69. Endsjø (2011, 82), Berkowitz and Popovsky (2010, 14–16).

70. Coontz (1992, 191).

71. *Laws of the Hittites* §189. See Bryce (2002, 50–51 and 273n37). Bryce thinks (51) it likely that homosexuality "was so much an accepted activity in Hittite society that there was no need even to refer to it."

72. Endsjø (2011, 127).

73. *Kāma Sūtra* 2.9.44.

74. Coontz (1992, 184; see 336n9).

75. Endsjø (2011, 161). "India's Supreme Court Decriminalizes Homosexuality in a Historic Ruling for the LGBTQ Community." *Time*, Sept. 26, 2018. https://time.com/5388231/india-decriminalizes-homosexuality-section-377/

76. These organizations and others filed supporting briefs in the Supreme Court case that ultimately legitimated same-sex marriage (Griffith 2017, 305–07).

77. Church of the Latter-Day Saints *Statement on the United States Congress Respect for Marriage Act*, Nov. 15, 2022.

78. "Where Christian churches, other religions stand on gay marriage." *Pew Research Group*, Dec. 21. 2015. https://www.pewresearch.org/fact-tank/2015/12/21/where-christian-churches-stand-on-gay-marriage/. See Fitzgerald (2017, 618–23) on the evangelicals. "Emerging Consensus on LGBT Issues: Findings From the 2017 American Values Atlas." *PRRI*, May 1, 2018. https://www.prri.org/research/emerging-consensus-on-lgbt-issues-findings-from-the-2017-american-values-atlas/. See also Robert Jones (2017, 123–31).

79. FitzGerald (2017, 619).

80. "Record-High 70% in U.S. Support Same-Sex Marriage," *Gallup*, Jun. 8, 2021. https://news.gallup.com/poll/350486/record-high-support-same-sex-marriage.aspx

81. "A NATION CHALLENGED: PLACING BLAME; Falwell Apologizes for Saying An Angry God Allowed Attacks." *New York Times*, Sept. 18, 2001. https://www.nytimes.com/2001/09/18/us/nation-challenged-placing-blame-falwell-apologizes-for-saying-angry-god-allowed.html. "Religious figures blame LGBT+ people for coronavirus." *Reuters*, Mar. 9, 2020. https://www.reuters.com/article/us-health-coronavirus-lgbt-idUSKBN20W2HL. See Whitehead and Perry (2020, 131).

82. *Bowers v Hardwick*, 478 U.S. 186 (1986), *rev'd*, 539 U.S. 558 (2003). Karl and Young (1987, 778). "Churchgoers Pray for Rain, Get Some." *Los Angeles Times*, Jul. 28, 1986. https://www.latimes.com/archives/la-xpm-1986-07-28-mn-18396-story.html

83. Griffith (2017, xi).

84. E.g., Griffith (2017), Fitzgerald (2017), Gorski and Perry (2022), Stone (2017), Whitehead and Perry (2020). Robert Jones (2017, 197–239) takes a perhaps overly optimistic view.

85. Endsjø (2011, 13).

6. WHEN GOD GOES OFF TO WAR

1. Bryce (2002, 98).

2. Espak (2019, 163).

3. Deut. 25:18 (my translation).

4. Deut. 25:19. See Kugler (2020, 2) on the paradox.

5. 1 Sam. 15.

6. Num. 14:43. See Kugler (2020, 7n31) for the absence of extrabiblical or archeological references to Amalek, and (7–12) for the inconsistencies in the Scriptural references.

7. Morris (2005, 27–68, 258–72, 691–710 and generally). See also, e.g., Cline (2015, 28–31), Junkkaala (2006, 70–80), Na'aman (1994, 223), and Redford (1992, 192–213).

8. Morris (2005, 113).

9. On Jericho, see, e.g., Finkelstein and Silberman (2001, 81–83), Junkkaala (2006, 252–54 and 308–11), and Morris (2005, 692). For other discrepancies, including those between Joshua and Judges, compare, for example, Josh. 11:1–14 to Judg. 4:2–3; also see Na'aman (1994, 223–25 and 249–79).

10. Younger (1990, 265).

11. Quoted in Cline (2015, 92). Cline quotes the full text of the Merenptah (also known as Merneptah) Stele, which has more examples of annihilation language. See also Pharaoh Kamose's boast of how he destroyed Avaris (Cline 2015, 17). Hasel (2008, 53 and 53n6) explains that scholars have often translated *prt* as "grain" rather than "seed"; this emphasizes the agricultural nature of the term.

12. *Mesha Stele* §7. 2 Kings 3.

13. Josh. 6:21. See Thelle (2007, 63–70) for a detailed examination of how the Joshua story imitates the Mesha stele and other Ancient Near East conquest stories.

14. Römer (2005, 83–90). Josh. 10:12–13 describes Joshua's control over the sun and moon.

15. Römer (2005, 90).

16. See 1 Macc. 5:28.

17. *B. Shab.* 21b.

18. 2 Macc. 10:6.

19. E.g., *b. Ket.* 111a.

20. See Ehrlich (1999, 121), Thelle (2007, 73, 75–76).

21. *Pss. Sol.* 17:22.

22. Ehrlich (1999, 123).

23. "Kahane Won: How the radical rabbi's ideas and disciples took over Israeli politics, and why it's dangerous." *Tabletmag,* Mar. 14, 2019. https://www.tabletmag.com/sections/israel-middle-east/articles/kahane-won . See also Thelle (2007, 76).

24. Thelle (2007, 76). See Deut. 7:2.

25. The Hebrew text, *loh tirtzakh,* is more accurately rendered as "thou shalt not murder," but some of the early translations missed this distinction.

26. Origen *Against Celsus,* 8.73, 8:70.

27. See Sider (2012, 192–95). Sider's 2012 study of ante-Nicene writings on war, *The Early Church on Killing,* is a classic resource for this period. See also Meagher (2014, 59-66).

28. Meagher (2014, 129).

29. See Blin (2019, 63-67), Meagher (2014, 79-80), Swift (1970).

30. Augustine *Against Faustus,* 22:74–75.

31. Augustine *Questions on the Heptateuch,* 6.10. See Hofreiter (2018, 115–16).

32. Gregory VII *Register,* 2.37 [Dec. 16, 1074].

33. Rubenstein (2011, 24, 25); see (23–25).

34. On Urban's offer, see Asbridge (2005, 71). In general, I have relied on Asbridge for the First Crusade, as well as Blin (2019, 151–63), Hofreiter (2018), and Lambert (2016). Armstrong (2015, 212–13) and Pearse (2007,

64–68) argue that greed for money and land motivated many to go on crusade, while Asbridge (2005, 66–70) and Riley-Smith (1997, 75) make a stronger case for "profiting their souls." See also Hofreiter (2018, 168) and Lambert (2016, 74–78).

35. Lambert (2016, 97).
36. Hofreiter (2018, 182).
37. Meagher (2014, 117).
38. Blin (2019, 163).
39. McGlynn (2018, 285–88).
40. McGlynn (2018, 13–14, 64–68).
41. Kirsch (2008, 60–63).
42. *Lateran IV* Canon 3.
43. Kirsch (2008, 63).
44. *Ad Extirpanda* §26.
45. Kirsch (2008, 179 [italics in original]).
46. Kirsch (2008, 204).
47. Moore (2000, 55).
48. Moore (2000, 42).
49. Moore (2000, 48–51), Ryrie (2017, 93).
50. Dunn (1979, 157).
51. Blin (2019, 263).
52. This is the version I heard when visiting Prague Castle.
53. MacCulloch (2005, 485).
54. Armstrong (2015, 398).
55. McGreevy (2022, 16).
56. Hobsbawm (2003, 86).
57. There was a period of about ten months when Protestant worship was also curbed. *https://www.museeprotestant.org/notice/la-revolution-et-les-protestants/*
58. Goldfarb (2009, 83–89).
59. *Declaration of the Rights of Man* §10.
60. Quoted in Hibbert (2002, 234–35). I have relied in large part on De Ladebat (2007), Hibbert (2002), and Hobsbawm (2003, 73–100) for material about the French Revolution.
61. Moore (2000, 72); see generally 59–104.
62. Glover (2012, 239).
63. See Peris (1998, 21–22).
64. Slezkine (2017, 951, quoting the Communist ideologue Valerian Osinsky). See Burleigh (2007, 71–77, 233–37), Miner (2003), Peris (1998), and Slezkine (2017) for more on Soviet uses of religion and opposition to religion. I am indebted to Professor Richard Robbins for introducing me to Slezkine and Peris and for other leads. As always, any errors or misunderstandings are mine alone.
65. Kirsch (2008, 230). Burleigh (2007, 81) compares the operations of the Communist party in the Soviet Union to those of the Spanish Inquisition.
66. Weiss (1996, 314).
67. Glover (2000, 356).

68. Sacks (2016, 54).
69. Ali and Rehman (2005, 334–35). See Ali and Rehman generally on the complex nature of belligerency between Muslim and non-Muslim states.
70. Moore (2000, 103).
71. Mather *Souldiers counselled and comforted*, 37.
72. Thelle (2007, 74).
73. Taylor (2002, 195; see 194–97).
74. John Underhill, quoted by Segal and Stineback (1977, 136–37; see 105–40). See Karr (1998, 877–78).
75. "'Little bomber' fascinates Israeli media," *BBC News*, Mar. 25, 2004. http://news.bbc.co.uk/2/hi/middle_east/3567791.stm. See Thayer and Hudson (2010, 51).

7. IT'S ALL ABOUT GETTING INTO HEAVEN

1. For more on these issues, see, e.g., Ehrman (2020, 103–46) and Gillman (2000, 96–112). I have drawn on Gillman and Ehrman, and also Bernstein (1993), Freeman (2003), Moss (2014), Nixey (2018), Segal (2004), and others as noted, for many of the ideas explored in this chapter. As always, any errors, mistakes, or misinterpretations are my responsibility alone.
2. Matt. 25:31–46.
3. Mark 10:17–22.
4. Matt. 6:25, 33.
5. 1 Thess. 4:13–18.
6. 1 Cor. 5:1, 7:1–16, 10:9, 6:12, 6:9.
7. Phil. 1:21–25. See Ehrman (2020, 186–88).
8. Luke 23:43.
9. John 5:24 (emphasis added). Ehrman (2020, 205, see 203–08).
10. Jerome *Letter XXII to Eustochium*, §7. See Freeman (2003, 236).
11. Rom. 7:24, 8:13.
12. Ignatius of Antioch *Epistle to the Romans*, §7. See Ehrman (2020, 255–56), Segal (2004, 544–46), and L. M. White (2005, 346 (Box 13.6), but see 480n50).
13. James ([1902] 2010, 279, 251, 330).
14. A special order of Catholic priests, officially called the "Society of Jesus," who specialize in spreading Christianity around the world and who operate under the direct orders of the pope.
15. Blackburn (2000, 116, 117).
16. See Taylor (2002, 160–66).
17. Weber (1976, 165, 166, 157–58, 89–90).
18. Matt. 15:24.
19. J. Cohen (1986, 76). See also Chazan (1980, 241–43).
20. Chazan (1980, 255–63) has some documented examples.
21. J. Cohen (1986, 85).

22. See, e.g., Chazan (1980, 310–12) on how Philip Augustus of France used expulsions in 1182 to wipe out his debts to the Jews.
23. Paul IV *Cum Nimis Absurdum*, preface.
24. Many scholars have written on this topic. Among the ones I have consulted, and who might serve as a starting point, are Harris (1994), Kamen (2003), Ryrie (2017), Segal and Stineback (1977), Taylor (2002), and Wills (2007).
25. Kamen (2003, 144–45).
26. Enochs (2006, 66–67), Taylor (2002, 112).
27. Taylor (2002, 36). Possible Portuguese competition was also a factor.
28. Parsons (2010, 117, 118).
29. Kamen (2003, 148).
30. Blackburn (2000, 131).
31. On the Navajo, see, e.g., Enochs (2006, 70–73) and Pavlik (1997, 46). See Prucha (1998, 134–35) on the Pacific Northwest tribes.
32. Crashaw, *A Sermon Preached in London* [spelling and punctuation modernized for clarity]. See Ryrie (2017, 144).
33. Ryrie (2017, 148).
34. Higham (2016, 6).
35. See, e.g., Meacham (2007, 45–46), Segal and Stineback (1977, 27–31), Taylor (2002, 197–99), Wills (2007, 43–50 and 392–93), and especially Ryrie (2017, 144–52).
36. See, e.g., Higham (2016, 6–14).
37. Higham (2016, 13). On Roger Williams, see Warren (2018, 131–33).
38. "A Public Declaration to the Tribal Councils and Traditional Spiritual Leaders of the Indian and Eskimo Peoples of the Pacific Northwest." Seattle WA, Nov. 21, 1987. https://www.healthfreedom.info/Native%20Spiritual%20Practices.htm. "Pope Francis apologizes to Canada's Indigenous Peoples." *Vatican News*, Jul. 25, 2022. https://www.vaticannews.va/en/pope/news/2022-04/pope-francis-meets-with-canadian-indigenous-peoples.html
39. Crashaw, *A Sermon Preached in London* [spelling and punctuation modernized for clarity; italics in original].
40. Wills (2007, 77); see Ryrie (2017, 149–50).
41. Prucha (1988, 133; see generally). See Taylor (2002, 107).
42. "Why has Pentecostalism grown so dramatically in Latin America?" *Pew Research Center*, Nov. 14, 2014. https://www.pewresearch.org/fact-tank/2014/11/14/why-has-pentecostalism-grown-so-dramatically-in-latin-america/. "Stability attracts Latin Americans to Mormonism." *Reuters*, Feb. 5, 2009. https://www.reuters.com/article/us-mormons-latinamerica-idINTRE5150AG20090206
43. See, e.g., FitzGerald (2017, 550), Ryrie (2017, 464–66).
44. Ryrie (2017, 85).
45. Gal. 1:9. Matt. 7:15.
46. 2 John 1:7-11*.

47. Irenaeus *Against Heresies*, 5.26.2. A few sentences earlier, Irenaeus specifically named the people and groups listed in the bracketed text.
48. See Ehrman (2018, 224–27), Fournier (2016, 61–62).
49. Taylor (2002, 339 [italics in original]).
50. Juster (2011, 142).
51. Ryrie (2017, 127), Meacham (2007, 52). See Taylor (2002, 178–85).
52. I am indebted to the Rev. Joanne Lee of the Calvary Presbyterian Church of San Francisco for this term.
53. L. Klein (2018, 46 [emphasis in original], 250, 256–57).
54. A "Hell House" is a kind of "anti-theme park" that shows visitors in graphic terms what punishments they can expect in hell for various sins, abortion being perhaps the most common one.
55. Bivins (2007, 97).
56. Bivins (2007, 101 [italics in original]).
57. Augustine *Confessions*, X.35.
58. On Bruno, see, for example, Rowland (2009), also Grayling (2016, 246–47). For Galileo, see Reston (1994, 221–41 and generally).
59. "How highly religious Americans view evolution depends on how they're asked about it." *Pew Research Center*, Feb. 6, 2019. https://www.pewre search.org/fact-tank/2019/02/06/how-highly-religious-americans-view-evolution-depends-on-how-theyre-asked-about-it/
60. See Pius XII *Humani Generis*, §36, Francis *In Honor of Benedict XVI*.
61. See, e.g., FitzGerald (2017, 527–28), Ryrie (2017, 250–55), Sutton (2017, 158–59).
62. Sutton (2017, 167, see 166–74). See Ryrie (2017, 294).
63. On the Scopes trial, see, e.g., Sutton (2017, 166–74). On the law's repeal, see "50 Years Ago: Repeal of Tennessee's 'Monkey Law,'" *Scientific American*, May 10, 2017. https://blogs.scientificamerican.com/observations/50-years-ago-repeal-of-tennessees-monkey-law/. *Epperson et al. v. Arkansas*, 393 U.S. 97 (1968) voided a similar Arkansas law. For some of the recent court challenges, see "Ten Major Cases about Evolution and Creationism," *National Center for Science Education*, Jun. 6, 2016. https://ncse.ngo/ten-major-court-cases-about-evolution-and-creationism
64. Ambrose *Letter 40 to Theodosius I*, 20, 26. See Freeman (2003, 218–25), Nirenberg (2014, 117–19).
65. See Freeman (2003, 223–24).
66. Gregory VII *Letter to Bishop Herman of Metz*.
67. Asbridge (2005, 6).
68. For more details, see Cantor (1994, 265–73).
69. See Lambert (2016, 66–67) on this point, also Asbridge (2005, 29–30).
70. Boniface VIII *Unam Sanctam*.
71. See Cantor (1994, 494–96), Meagher (2014, 90–91).
72. See Ryrie (2017, 43–46).
73. Warren (2018, 124).
74. Brown (2015, 119, 166; see 20–23).
75. MacCulloch (2005, 120–23). Luther *95 Theses*, §66.

76. See Ryrie (2017, 22–28) on the Church's initial response to Luther. See generally MacCulloch (2005), Oberman (2006), and Ryrie (2017). I have relied on these authors for the material in this section.
77. James 2:22. See Ryrie (2017, 30–31) on Luther's reaction to James.
78. See, e.g., MacCulloch (2005, 119–20).
79. Fernández-Armesto and Wilson (1997, 82), quoting Chemnitz (1522–86).
80. Ryrie (2017, 21).
81. Ryrie (2017, 79).
82. See, e.g., Fernández-Armesto and Wilson (1997, 87–90), MacCulloch (2005, 106–15) on Augustine's influence, Ryrie (2017, 78–81) on Calvinist predestination.
83. Winship (1996, 46), quoting Tillotson.
84. Winship (1996, 12–13).
85. Taylor (2002, 346; 345-46 on Hawley). See Sederholm (2012) for an analysis of Edward's handling of the "possible social ramifications of his uncle's suicide" (333).
86. Ahlstrom (1972, 844–45).
87. Matt. 6:19–20.
88. 2 Cor. 4:17.
89. Augustine *City of God*, §19.4. See Moss (2014, 189–96), Straw (1999, 840).
90. Blackburn (2000, 105).
91. Haselby (2017, 272–73n67).
92. Baptist (2016, 206, see generally 200–13).
93. Col. 3:22, 24.
94. C. Jones (1842, 201). Jones listed and responded to slaveholders' objections (175–205). See also Ryrie (2017, 190–93).
95. See, e.g., Ahlstrom (1972, 650–53), Ryrie (2017, 183–208).
96. Wills (2007, 307–11).
97. Hochschild (2018, 54).
98. "Tate Reeves Says Mississippians 'Less Scared' of COVID Because They 'Believe in Eternal Life.'" *Newsweek*, Aug. 28, 2021. https://www.newsweek.com/tate-reeves-says-mississippians-less-scared-covid-because-they-believe-eternal-life-1624014
99. *"Do we still believe in heaven? Does it make a difference if we do?" Presbyterians Today* (April 1998). Reposted on the Presbyterian mission website: www.presbyterianmission.org/what-we-believe/life-after-death/
100. *Sifrei Bamidbar*, 135 (c. 200 CE).

8. THE WORLD WILL END ON [FILL IN THE BLANK]

1. Mark 1:15.
2. The collection of scholarly and popular studies of end-time belief would fill a library. Here are some that I have relied on for this chapter that the interested reader can use as a start for further reading: Baumgartner (1999),

Boyer (2000), Cohn (1970), Court (2008), Kyle (2012), Sutton (2017), and Whittock (2021), as well as others mentioned in the endnotes for specific citations. As always, any errors or misrepresentations are mine alone.

3. For more on the Israelite concept of linear time, see, e.g., Boyer (2000, 22–24), Gillman (2000, 21–25), and Whittock (2021, 14–18).

4. Isa. 2:1 (see Alter 2019b, 626n2); other translations say "in days to come." Ezek. 38:23. Mal. 3:23 (my translation). Isa. 13:9.

5. 1QM I.11; see the War Scroll generally. See also S. Cohen (2014, 98), Collins (2016, 206–12), and Vermes (2011a, 71, 84–87). On Second Temple eschatology in general, see, e.g., Baumgartner (1999, 15–16), S. Cohen (2014, 97–100), Segal (2004, 303).

6. Charlesworth (1999). See also Whittock (2021, 32). Also see Porter and Pearson (2000, 111–13).

7. Matt. 3:2, 4:17; see Mark 1:14–15.

8. Rom. 13:11–12.

9. 1 Pet. 4:7, 1 John 2:18.

10. Landes (2002, 254).

11. 2 Pet. 3:3–9.

12. Matt. 24:36. Acts 1:7; see Landes (1988, 142 and n16).

13. Rev. 1:3; 14:7.

14. Dr. Bart Ehrman was kind enough to let me read his upcoming book on Revelation and to let me credit it for some of the insights and references in this chapter. He is one of many scholars who have made convincing arguments that Revelation was written to and for Christians around the end of the first century CE. See Ehrman (2020, 214), also Boyer (2000, 43–44); cf. De Villiers (2002). I am also relying on Baumgartner (1999), Court (2008), and Sutton (2017), among others.

15. Rev. 20:4.

16. Baumgartner (1999, 4).

17. *Epistle of Barnabas* §15.4 (referring to 2 Pet. 3:8, who in turn refers to Ps. 90:4). See Landes (1988, 141–44). I am indebted to Dr. Ehrman's manuscript for alerting me to Landes's work, and also to Barnabas and Hippolytus. Barnabas was named as an apostle in Acts (14:14).

18. See, e.g., Dixon (2012, 38) and Landes (1988, 138).

19. Hippolytus, *Commentary on Daniel* II.6. See Landes (1988, 144–49), also Baumgartner (1999, 40).

20. Landes (1988, 138–41). See also Kyle (2012, 22–24).

21. Landes (1988, 148–49). See Fredriksen (1991, 153–54).

22. See Cohn (1970, 29).

23. Augustine, *City of God* 20.9, 20.7. See, e.g., Fredriksen (1991, 157–63), Landes (1988, 157–58), and Whittock (2021, 62–63), but see Court (2008, 59).

24. Augustine, *Exposition on Psalm 6* §1; see also *City of God* 18.53. See Landes (1988, 157), also Kyle (2012, 25–27).

25. Landes (1988, 200). See Palmer (2014, 233).

26. Declercq (2002, 165–66). See Court (2008, 18), MacCarron (2014, 168–70).
27. MacCarron (2012, 124) notes that Dionysius's dating system was little used prior to Bede. Rothwangl (2016, 7) argues that Dionysius invented AD "because of the imminent arrival of the cosmic year 6000 in the first Christian chronology, called anno mundi (AM)." I have some difficulty with this hypothesis. Nonetheless, I am indebted to his essays for some of the ideas and references they gave me that I used in this chapter.
28. Bede, The Reckoning of Time §66. See Dixon (2012, 38) for an explanation of the difference, and also why Bede's calculation differs by 192 years from the Jewish calculation of 3760.
29. Bede, The Reckoning of Time §66; §67. See Palmer (2014, 100–01).
30. Bede, Ecclesiastical History of England, §I.3.
31. MacCarron (2014, 167). MacCarron further argues (168–71) that Bede used the incarnation of Jesus as his starting date to emphasize its importance to Christianity and to refute certain heresies.
32. Landes (1988, 178–79; 2005, para. 5). See Lacey and Danziger (2000, 12–15).
33. Cohn (1970, 30). I have relied on Cohn, and also Baumgartner (1999), Court (2008), Erdoes (1988), Landes (2005), and Palmer (2014), for much of the material in this section.
34. Landes (2002, 249).
35. This description is drawn primarily from Erdoes (1988, 1–8, 193), along with Baumgartner (1999, 55–58), Court (2008, 62–68), and Lacey and Danziger (1999, 179–92). See Court (2008, 65) and Lacey and Danziger (2000, 180–81) for Halley's Comet. On Vesuvius, see Erdoes (1988, 3) and the article in Progetto Didattico Le Lave Del Vesuvio (https://www.beic.it/it/content/activity-vesuvius-writers-and-chronicles ; undated). Palmer (2014, 227–30) explains why we cannot dismiss belief in the apocalypse circa AD 1000 as earlier historians had done.
36. Landes (2002, 261 [italics in original]). See also Chazan (2016, 110–11).
37. Palmer (2014, 184).
38. See M. Cohen (1994, 178), Palmer (2014, 219).
39. Whittock (2021, 99).
40. Rubenstein (2011, 7–8; see (5–7) for the sacking of the Holy Sepulcher and the French reaction). Also see Palmer (2014, 219).
41. See Cantor (1994, 365).
42. Cohn (1970, 75).
43. Chazan (1996, 64–70), Whittock (2021, 98–99). On the apocalyptic influence on the First Crusade, see Rubenstein (2011). Chazan (1996) goes into great detail on the complexities of Jewish-Christian relations in the First Crusade. See also Cantor (1994, 293), Cohn (1970, 74–79), Hall (2009, 55–57), and Rubenstein (2011, 49–53).
44. Hall (2009, 57).
45. Palmer (2014, 218, 232).

46. Hall (2009, 62–64), Landes (2005, para. 9–10). See also Court (2008, 71–80).
47. Baumgartner (1999, 69).
48. Weatherford (2004, 152-59).
49. Cohn (1970, 128-29).
50. Cohn (1970, 136; see 131-34).
51. Court (2008, 90; see 84–91).
52. Baumgartner (1999, 112-15). For the population percentage, see Cherniavsky (1966, 4 and 4n13). I am indebted to Professor Robbins for bringing the Old Believers, and Cherniavksy's article, to my attention.
53. Whittock (2021, 109 [italics in original]; see 95–110). See, e.g., Baumgartner (1999, 63–80), Cohn (1970, 281–85), Court (2008, 93–102), and Hall (2009, 65–67).
54. Oberman (2006, 70–71). Baumgartner (1999, 84). See Forell's argument (1969) that Luther's doctrine of justification by faith can only be properly understood in the context of an expectation of the end-times.
55. This overview is based on Balmer (2008), Court (2008, 41–45), Howe (2009, 285–89), Kyle (2012, 41–42), Palmer (2014, 12–13), Sutton (2017, 14–17), and Whittock (2021, 64–65). For other ideas about the millennium, see, e.g., Cohn (1970, 13–14), Court (2008, 1–8), and Landes (1988, 206–08).
56. See, e.g., Boyer (2000, 74–77), Ryrie (2017, 262). Evangelical minister and TV host Pat Robertson "vacillated between premillennialism" and "fundamentalist postmillennialism" for a while (Boyer 2000, 303–04).
57. Baumgartner (1999, 124, 125).
58. Almond (2016, 107).
59. Boyer (2000, 75), Wills (2007, 33-34; see 107).
60. Cotton, *An Exposition Upon the Thirteenth Chapter*, page 88 (italics in original). See Maclear (1975, 233).
61. See, e.g., Hall and Baker (2021, 230), Maclear (1975, 257-60).
62. Edwards, *The Millennium Probably to Dawn in America, WJE* 4:353. See Balmer (2008, para. 4), Koester (1995, 138–39), Wills (2007, 100–17).
63. Sutton (2017, 14). See Kyle (2012, 47–53).
64. See, e.g., Boyer (2000, 80–81), Hall and Baker (2021, 235–36), Howe (2009, 304, 702–05), Koester (1995, 140–42).
65. Howe (2009, 289).
66. Baumgartner (1999, 167–70), with input from Court (2008, 119–22), Festinger et al. (2009, 12–23), Howe (2009, 289–92), Kyle (2012, 61–65), and Ryrie (2017, 212–17).
67. Wills (2007, 317, 318).
68. Koester (1995, 142–43).
69. Hall and Baker (2021, 236-37). See Koester (1995, 143).
70. See, e.g., Baumgartner (1999, 214–16), Ryrie (2017, 262–64, 291).
71. Fitzgerald (2017, 2).
72. Pew Research Center, "5 facts about U.S. evangelical Protestants," March 1, 2018.

73. Boyer (2000, 93), Ryrie (2017, 292). See Fitzgerald (2017, 71–72).
74. Fitzgerald (2017, 78–79, see also 644n38). A challenge to "original auto-graph" inerrancy in the 1960s and '70s led to a split at some seminaries (258–60).
75. On the rapture, see Baumgartner (1999, 158–60), Frykholm (2007, 15–17, especially 16 for the etymology of "rapture"), Sutton (2017, 16–19). Rapture is also known as "dispensational premillennialism" or sometimes "premillennial dispensationalism." I have relied for this outline of evangel-icalism and fundamentalism on Boyer (2000), Fitzgerald (2017), Ryrie (2017), Sutton (2017), and Wills (2007). Bart Ehrman also graciously helped me out on these definitions in answering a question I posted on his blog.
76. Christian Reconstructionist ideology is a version of "Dominion theology," from the passage in Genesis (1:28) where God tells Adam and Eve to have dominion over all living things. There is no connection whatever to the Reconstructionist branch of Judaism founded by Mordechai Kaplan.
77. Fitzgerald (2017, 342-43).
78. Kyle (2012, 215; see 210–17). See Boyer (2000, 303–04), Fitzgerald (2017, 337–47).
79. One of the more tragic impacts of belief in the imminence of the apoca-lypse is the rise in mass suicides, such as the Heaven's Gate cult in 1997 or the Branch Davidians (an offshoot of the Seventh-day Adventists) at Waco, Texas, in 1993.
80. "Zionism, Christian history, and the pope." Boston: Boston Globe, Dec. 28, 2015. https://www.bostonglobe.com/opinion/2015/12/28/zionism-christ ian-history-and-pope/igt5VHIwh8WiQ9gx1Uv3NI/story.html
81. Whittock (2021, 121).
82. I. Mather, *The Mystery of Israel's Salvation Explained and Applyed* 8. (See Boyer 2000, 183). The verse is Rom. 11:26.
83. Boyer (2000, 183–84).
84. *Balfour Declaration*. See Willetts (2016). I have relied on Boyer (2000, 181–224), Church (2009), Friedman (1918), Rowe (2013), and Sutton (2017), among others, for material in this section.
85. Church (2009, 382).
86. "Christians Must Help Trump Move Embassy to Bring Third Temple." Israel365news.com, Feb. 9, 2017. https://www.israel365news.com/83386/ mk-glicks-multi-faith-effort-move-embassy-first-step-building-temple-says-pastor/
87. Burge (2017).
88. Aldrovandi (2011, 254; 255).
89. Hagee (2007, 39; 53).
90. "The Evangelicals Who Pray for War With Iran." *The New Republic*, Jan. 9, 2020. https://newrepublic.com/article/156166/pence-pompeo-evanglicals-war-iran-christian-zionism
91. I. Mather, *The Mystery of Israel's Salvation Explained and Applyed* 35. Rowe (2013, 74; see generally). See Aldrovandi (2011, 198–205), on how some

messianic Jews are also hoping to thwart the peace process.

92. "What's Wrong with John Hagee??" *Who Is Israel: Yesterday, To Day, and For Ever*, Mar. 25, 2015 (capitalization in original). https://whoisisrael.org/john-hagee/
93. See, e.g., Bjork-James (2020,11–12) and references cited.
94. Barker and Bearce (2013, 267).
95. Lynn White (1967, 1207).
96. Guth et. al. (1995, 366). On White, see e.g., Guth et. al. (1995, 377), Hope and Jones (2014, 49), Schwadel and Johnson (2017, 22), and especially Veldman (2019, 12–13).
97. Hochschild (2018, 53).
98. Veldman (2019, 84).
99. Hope and Jones (2014, 49).
100. Herrmann (2021, 7). See Boyer (2000, 331–36). See also Guth et. al. (1995, 368), Schwadel and Johnson (2017, 4), Veldman (2019, 72). Herrmann (2021, 7) says that 77% of evangelicals interpret global warming as a sign of the end times. Other polls give much lower figures: a 2016 poll by Yale puts the number at 24%. https://climatecommunication.yale.edu/publications/global-warming-god-end-times/. It may depend on one's definition of an "evangelical."
101. Veldman (2019, 69–70).
102. Veldman (2019, 79; see 75–80, 100). See (250n1) for the source of Veldman's "hot" and "cool" terminology.
103. "Loving the Least of These: Addressing a Changing Environment." 2022. https://www.nae.org/loving-the-least-of-these/
104. Bean and Teles (2015, 7–9). See Veldman (2019, 154). See generally Bjork-James (2020). Balmer (2008, para. 23) opines that Dobson, along with some others, would claim to be premillennialist, but that some of their actions "suggest a disposition toward postmillennialism."
105. Hope and Jones (2014, 49).
106. "Jesus Christ's Return to Earth," Pew Research Center, July 14, 2010. http://pewrsr.ch/T4uCxO
107. Herrmann (2021, 2 [italics in original]).
108. Rev. 17:12–13.

CONCLUSION

1. James 1:6, 8 (1:6,7 in some versions).
2. Cromwell "To the General Assembly of the Kirk of Scotland."
3. Amos 8:6, 2 Sam. 11:2–12:14, Isa. 58:6–7.

APPENDIX: DATING THE BOOK OF DANIEL

1. See Collins (1993, 25–33, 26nn256–57) for some of the conservative Protestant objections to the late dating of Daniel, and Collins's responses. The Catholic New American Bible, St. Joseph Edition, issued under the imprimatur of Paul VI, agrees (1970, 1021) that Daniel was composed between 167 and 164 BCE. The Orthodox Jewish organization Chabad states unequivocally that Daniel lived from 457 to 362 BCE. https://www.chabad.org/library/article_cdo/aid/3630049/jewish/Daniel-the-Prophet-of-the-Bible-His-Life-and-Accomplishments.htm

2. Dan. 5:31–6:1.

3. E.g., Josephus *Antiquities*, 10.248.

4. *Nabonidus Chronicles* iii.14–16.

5. *Cyrus Cylinder* §17.

6. Henze (1999, 61).

7. Collins (1993, 30–32 and 31n304), Lucas (2002, 134–37).

8. Dan. 6:1. Daniel calls Nebuchadnezzar the king's father at 5:18. See Bickerman (2012, 60).

9. See Henze (1999, 58), quoting the Babylonian historian Berossus (c. 280 BCE).

10. Ezek. 14:14, 20. See Alter (2019b, 1087n14).

11. I want to express my appreciation to Dr. Lucas for his helpful questions and observations. As always, any errors or mistakes are mine alone.

12. Collins (1993, 33). Bickerman (2012, 63). Lucas (2002, 306–07).

13. Dan. 10:1, 14.

14. Dan. 11:2–4. Collins (1993, 377).

15. See, e.g., Lucas (2002, 39–40), Collins (1993, 377).

16. Dan. 11:21. See Collins (1993, 382) for the story of how Antiochus took power.

17. Livy *History of Rome*, 45.12.

18. Dan. 11:21–39. For its correlation to known history, see Collins (1993, 382–88), Lucas (2002, 41–42, 283–90).

19. Dan. 11:40–45.

20. Gera and Horowitz (1997, 244–49 on the Armenian and Persian campaigns; 249–50 on the death of Antiochus). See also Collins (1993, 389), Lorein (2001, 166–69), and Lucas (2002, 291–92).

21. See Collins (1993, 390).

PRIMARY SOURCES

Where the source is given as (author date), see the References for the full citation.

ANCIENT NEAR EAST SOURCES

Epic of Gilgamesh [late second millennium BCE]. Stephanie Dalley, translator. (Dalley 2008)

Attrahasis [eighteenth century BCE]. Stephanie Dalley, translator. (Dalley 2008)

Code of Hammurabi [c. 1754 BCE]. L. W. King, translator, 1915. https://source books.fordham.edu/ancient/hamcode.asp

Laws of the Hittites [c. 1650–1500 BCE]. https://e-edu.nbu.bg/pluginfile.php/ 743607/mod_resource/content/1/Hittite%20Laws.pdf

Code of the Assura [c. 1075 BCE] (excerpts). https://sourcebooks.fordham.edu/ ancient/1075assyriancode.asp. Scanned by J. S. Arkenberg, who modernized the text.

Mesha Stele [c. 840 BCE]. Translator not stated. https://www.livius.org/sources/content/anet/320-the-stele-of-mesha/

Nabonidus Chronicle [c. 538 BCE]. A. K. Greyson, translator (with some changes, by Livius(?)). https://www.livius.org/sources/content/mesopotamian-chroni cles-content/abc-7-nabonidus-chronicle/

Cyrus Cylinder [c. 538 BCE]. Translation based on Mordechai Cogan's, published in W.H. Hallo and K.L. Younger, *The Context of Scripture. Vol. II: Monumental Inscriptions from the Biblical World* (2003, Leiden and Boston), but has been adapted to Schaudig's edition with the help of Bert van der Spek. https:// www.livius.org/sources/content/cyrus-cylinder/cyrus-cylinder-translation/

Plato. *Timeaus* [c. 360 BCE]. Benjamin Jowett, translator, In Hamilton, Edith, and Huntington Cairns, editors. *Plato: The Collected Dialogues*, 1151–1211. New York: Pantheon Books.

CANONICAL AND NEAR-CANONICAL SOURCES

Scripture (Old Testament). (Alter 2019a, 2019b, 2019c), except as noted.

Septuagint. https://www.ellopos.net/elpenor/greek-texts/septuagint/default.asp

Apocrypha and New Testament. *The HarperCollins Study Bible*. New York: Harper-Collins Publishers, 1989. It uses the New Revised Standard Version text with added notes and commentary. NRSV(HC) is used to mean this edition.

Gospel of Q. No extant copy exists; I use this reconstruction by John Kloppenborg: www.baytagoodah.com/uploads/9/5/6/0/95600058/john-s-kloppenborg-q-the-earliest-gospel-christian-pdf.pdf, 124–44.

Pseudepigrapha. (Charlesworth 2015):

- *1 Enoch*—The First Apocalypse of Enoch [second century BCE–first century CE].
- *Jub*—Jubilees [second century BCE].
- *Pss. Sol.*—The Psalms of Solomon [first century BCE?].
- *4 Erza*—The Fourth Book of Ezra [late first century CE].

Qumran Scrolls. (Vermes 2011a). Almost all citations to the scrolls use the standard notation: nQxxx

JEWISH SOURCES

Philo. *Embassy to Gaius* [40 CE]. F. H. Colson, translator. In *Philo, Vol. X.* Cambridge, MA: Harvard University Press, 1962.

Josephus, Flavius. *The Complete Works.* William Wriston, translator. (1737). Nashville, TN: Thomas Nelson, 1998.

- *Wars of the Jews* [c. 75 CE].
- *Antiquities of the Jews* [c. 95 CE].

Rabbinical texts:

- Talmud [c. 200 CE–c. 500 CE] (*m.xxx* for Mishneh, and *b.xxx* for the Babylonian Talmud, where *xxx* is the standard abbreviation for the volume name)
- *Sifrei Bamidbar* [c. 200 CE].
- *Rashi on Song of Songs* [c. 1090].
- *Even HaEzer*, by Joseph Caro [c. 1560].
- *Siftei Ḥaḥamim*, by Shabbetai ben Joseph Bass [c. 1660–80].

Rabbinical texts are available online at https://www.sefaria.org/texts

ROMAN SOURCES

Livy. *History of Rome* [c. 30 BCE ?–9 BCE ?]. Alfred C. Schlesinger, translator. Cambridge MA: Harvard University Press, 1951, 1989.

Pliny the Younger. *Letters* [c. 100–120 CE]. Cambridge MA: Harvard University Press, 1915, 1958. William McLemoth, translator, revised by W. M. L. Hutchinson.

EARLY CHRISTIAN SOURCES

Epistle of Barnbas [c. 120 CE]. Bart D. Ehrman, translator. In Ehrman, Bart, *Lost Scriptures: Books That Did Not Make It into the New Testament*, 219-35. Oxford UK: Oxford University Press, 2005.

Apocalypse of Paul [c. 250–400]. M. R. James, translator (1924). http://wesley. nnu.edu/sermons-essays-books/noncanonical-literature/noncanonical-litera ture-apocryphal-nt-apocalypse/apocalypse-of-paul-summary/

ANTE-NICENE FATHERS

Sources found in *The Ante-Nicene Fathers, Vols. I-V*. Rev. Alexander Roberts, D.D., and James Donaldson, LL. D., editors. Grand Rapids MI: Wm. B. Eerdmans Publishing Company, 1896:

- Ignatius of Antioch. *Epistle to the Romans* [c 110 CE]. Translator not stated.
- Irenaeus. *Against Heresies* [c. 180]. Translator not stated.
- Hippolytus, Bishop of Rome [c. 205]. *Commentary on Daniel*, in *The Extant Works and Fragments*. Rev. S. D. F. Salmond, translator.
- Tertullian. *Letter to Scapula* [c. 215]. S. Thelwall, translator.
- Origen. *Against Celsus* [c. 248]. Rev. Frederick Crombie, D.D., translator.

Clement of Alexandria. *Stromata* [c. 185]. John Ernest Leonard Oulton, D.D., and Henry Chadwick, B.D., translators. Philadelphia: Westminster Press, 1954. http://www.earlychristianwritings.com/text/clement-stromata-book3-english.html

AUGUSTINE, BISHOP OF HIPPO (354–430)

Against Two Letters of the Pelagians [c. 420]. 1885. Peter Holmes and Robert Ernest Wallis, translators, revised by Benjamin B. Warfield. https://www.newadvent. org/fathers/1509.htm

All other works by Augustine are from *The Works of Saint Augustine: A Translation for the 21st Century*. Hyde Park NY: New City Press:

- *Confessions* [397]. 1997. *The Confessions of Saint Augustine*. Maria Boulding, O.S.B., translator.

- *On the Excellence of Marriage* [401]. 1999. Ray Kearney, translator.

- *Against Faustus* [c. 410]. 2007. *Answer to Faustus, a Manichean*. Roland Teske, S.J., translator.

- *Questions on the Heptateuch* [419]. 2016. Joseph T. Lienhardt and Sean Doyle, translators.

- *Marriage and Desire* [419]. In *Answer to the Pelagians II*, 1998. Roland J. Teske, S.J., translator.

- *City of God* [426]. 2012–13. William Babcock, translator.

OTHER POST-NICENE FATHERS

Chrysostom, John. *Against the Jews: Sermon 1 ("Dangers Ahead")* [386 or 387 CE]. C. Mervyn Maxwell, translator, from his PhD dissertation, *Chrysostom's Homilies Against the Jews: An English Translation*. University of Chicago, 1966. PDF provided by ProQuest.

Jerome. *Letter XXII to Eustochium* [384]. Translator not stated. https://source books.fordham.edu/basis/jerome-letter22.asp

Ambrose. *Letter 40 to Theodosius I* [388 CE]. In *Nicene and Post-Nicene Fathers of the Christian Church, Vol. X*. Rev. H. de Romestin, translator. Oxford, UK: James Parker and Company, 1896.

PAPAL BULLS, LETTERS, AND CHURCH COUNCILS

Gregory VII. *Letter to Bishop Herman of Metz* [Mar. 15, 1081]. "To Herman of Metz, in Defense of the Papal Policy toward Henry IV." In *The Correspondence of Pope Gregory VII: Selected Letters from the Registrum*, Ephraim Emerton, translator, Book VIII, 21. New York: Columbia University Press, 1932.

Lateran IV. Fourth Lateran Council [1215]. https://sourcebooks.fordham.edu/basis/lateran4.asp

Innocent IV. *Ad Extirpanda* [1252]. http://www.documentacatholicaomnia.eu/01p/1252-05-15,_SS_Innocentius_IV,_Bulla_%27Ad_Extirpanda%27,_EN.pdf

Boniface VIII. *Unam Sanctam* "One God, One Faith, One Spiritual Authority" [1302]. https://sourcebooks.fordham.edu/source/b8-unam.txt

Paul IV. *Cum Nimis Absurdum* [1555]. Translator unknown. https://www.ccjr.us/dialogika-resources/primary-texts-from-the-history-of-the-relationship/paul-iv

Pius XII. *Humani Generis* [Aug. 12, 1950]. http://w2.vatican.va/content/pius-xii/en/encyclicals/documents/hf_p-xii_enc_12081950_humani-generis.html

Vatican II. *Nostra Aetate*: Declaration on the Relation of the Church to Non-Christian Religions [1965]. http://www.vatican.va/archive/hist_councils/ii_vatican_council/documents/vat-ii_decl_19651028_nostra-aetate_en.html

Paul VI. *Humanae Vitae* "Humanae Vitae: Encyclical Letter of His Holiness Pope Paul VI, on the Regulation of Births" [1968]. http://w2.vatican.va/content/paul-vi/en/encyclicals/documents/hf_p-vi_enc_25071968_humanae-vitae.html

Commission for Religious Relations with the Jews (CRRJ). "Notes on the Correct Way to Present Jews and Judaism in Preaching and Catechesis in the Roman Catholic Church." 2005. http://www.christianunity.va/content/unitacristiani/en/commissione-per-i-rapporti-religiosi-con-l-ebraismo/commissione-per-i-rapporti-religiosi-con-l-ebraismo-crre/documenti-della-commissione/en2.html

Francis. *In Honor of Benedict XVI*. Oct. 27 2014. "Address of His Holiness Pope Francis on the Occasion of the Inauguration of the Bust in Honour of Pope Benedict XVI." http://m2.vatican.va/content/francesco/en/speeches/2014/october/documents/papa-francesco_20141027_plenaria-accademia-scienze.html

Commission for Religious Relations with the Jews (CRRJ). "The Gifts and the Calling of God are Irrevocable." 2015. http://www.christianunity.va/content/unitacristiani/it/commissione-per-i-rapporti-religiosi-con-l-ebraismo/commissione-per-i-rapporti-religiosi-con-l-ebraismo-crre/documenti-della-commissione/_perche-i-doni-e-la-chiamata-di-dio-sono-irrevocabili--rm-11-29-/en.html

WORKS BY MARTIN LUTHER

95 Theses. The Ninety-Five Theses [1517]. https://sourcebooks.fordham.edu/source/luther95.txt

On The Jews and Their Lies [1543] in *Luther's Works Vol. 47*, 137-306. Philadelphia: Fortress Press, 1971. Martin H. Bertram, translator.

MISCELLANEOUS SOURCES

Kama Sutra [4th Cent. CE]. See Daniélou (1994).

Bede, *The Reckoning of Time [De temporum ratione]* [725 CE]. Liverpool, UK: Liverpool University Press, 1999. Faith Wallis, translator.

Bede, *Ecclesiastical History of England* [c 731]. London: Henry G. Bohn, 1849. J. A. Giles, D.C.L., editor.

Aquinas, Thomas. *Summa Theologica*. 1265–74. http://www.newadvent.org/summa/index.html

Crashaw, William. A sermon preached in London before the right honorable the Lord Lavvarre, Lord Gouernour and Captaine Generall of Virginea, and others of his Maiesties Counsell for that kingdome, and the rest of the aduenturers in that plantation At the said Lord Generall his leaue taking of England his natiue countrey, and departure for Virginea [Feb. 21, 1609]. Ann Arbor, MI: Text Creation Partnership, 2003 https://quod.lib.umich.edu/e/eebo/A19590.0001.001/1:5?rgn=div1;view=fulltext

Cromwell, Oliver. *To the General Assembly of the Kirk of Scotland* [Aug. 3, 1650]. https://quod.lib.umich.edu/e/eebo2/A37365.0001.001/1:2.2?c=eebo;c=eebo2;g=eebogroup;rgn=div2;view=fulltext;xc=1;rgn1=title;q1=To+the+General+Assembly+of+the+Kirk+of+Scotland

Cotton, John. *An Exposition Upon the Thirteenth Chapter of the Revelation* [1655]. https://quod.lib.umich.edu/e/eebo/A34679.0001.001?view=toc

Mather, Increase. *The mystery of Israel's salvation, explained and applyed: or, A discourse concerning the general conversion of the Israelitish nation* [1669]. https://quod.lib.umich.edu/e/evans/N00091.0001.001/1:8?rgn=div1;view=fulltext#DLPS132

Edwards, Jonathan. *The Millennium Probably to Dawn in America* [1743]. In *Works of Jonathan Edwards, Volume 4 [WJE 4], Great Awakening*, ed. C.C. Goen (New Haven Yale University Press, 1970), 353–58. http://edwards.yale.edu/archive?path=aHR0cDovL2Vkd2FyZHMueWFsZS5lZHUvY2dpLWJpbi9ZXdhGlsby9nZXRRvYmplY3QucGw/Yy4zOjYud2plbw==

Hume, David. *An Inquiry Concerning Human Understanding* (Section X) [1748]. www3.nd.edu/~afreddos/courses/43811/hume-on-miracles.htm

Declaration of the Rights of Man [Aug. 26, 1789]. https://avalon.law.yale.edu/18th_century/rightsof.asp

Balfour Declaration [1917]. Letter from British Foreign Secretary Lord Arthur Balfour to Lord Walter Rothschild, a leader of the London Jewish community. https://www.jewishvirtuallibrary.org/text-of-the-balfour-declaration

REFERENCES

Ahlstrom, Sidney. 1972. *A Religious History of the American People*. New Haven, CT: Yale University Press.

Akenson, Donald Harman. 1998. *Surpassing Wonder: The Invention of the Bible and the Talmuds*. New York: Harcourt Brace and Co.

Aldrovandi, Carlo. 2011. *Apocalyptic Movements in Contemporary Politics: Christian Zionism and Jewish Religious Zionism* (PhD Thesis). University of Bradford. https://core.ac.uk/reader/9636888

Ali, Shaheen Sardar and Javaid Rehman. 2005. "The Concept of *Jihad* in Islamic International Law." In *Journal of Conflict and Security Law (2005)*, Vol. 10 No. 3, 321–43. https://securitypolicylaw.syr.edu/wp-content/uploads/2013/03/Sadaar-Ali-Rehman.2005.Jihad-in-IR-law.pdf

Allison, Dale C. 2000. "The Eschatology of Jesus." *The Encyclopedia of Apocalypticism* 1 (2000): 267-302. http://www.marquette.edu/maqom/allison.pdf.

Almond, Philip C. 2016. *Afterlife: A History of Life After Death*. Ithaca, NY: Cornell University Press.

Alter, Robert. 2019a. *The Hebrew Bible Volume 1 The Five Books of Moses: A Translation and Commentary*. New York: W. W. Norton & Company.

———. 2019b. *The Hebrew Bible Volume 2 Prophets: A Translation and Commentary*. New York: W. W. Norton & Company.

———. 2019c. *The Hebrew Bible Volume 3 The Writings: A Translation and Commentary*. New York: W. W. Norton & Company.

Armstrong, Karen. 2015. *Fields of Blood: Religion and the History of Violence*. New York: Anchor Books.

Asbridge, Thomas. 2005. *The First Crusade: A New History*. Oxford UK: Oxford University Press.

Assmann, Jan. 2005. *Death and Salvation in Ancient Egypt*. Ithaca, NY: Cornell University Press.

———. 2008. *Of God and Gods: Egypt, Israel, and the Rise of Monotheism*. Madison, WI: The University of Wisconsin Press.

———. 2014. *From Akhenaten to Moses: Ancient Egypt and Religious Change*. Cairo: The American University in Cairo Press.

Atkinson, Kenneth. 1999. "On the Herodian Origin of Militant Davidic Messianism at Qumran: New Light from Psalm of Solomon 17." *Journal of Biblical Literature* 118, no. 3: 435–60. https://doi.org/10.2307/3268183

Balmer, Randall. 2007. *Thy Kingdom Come: How the Religious Right Distorts the Faith and Threatens America (An Evangelical's Lament)*. New York: Basic Books.

———. 2008. "Apocalypticism in American Culture." Divining America, TeacherServe©. National Humanities Center. Accessed Feb. 24, 2022. http://nationalhumanitiescenter.org/tserve/twenty/tkeyinfo/apocal.htm

———, 2021. *Bad Faith: Race and the Rise of the Religious Right*. Grand Rapids MI: Wm. B. Eerdmans Publishing Co.

Baptist, Edward E. 2016. *The Half Has Never Been Told: Slavery and the Making of American Capitalism*. New York: Basic Books.

Barker, David C., and David H. Bearce. 2013. "End-Times Theology, the Shadow of the Future, and Public Resistance to Addressing Global Climate Change." *Political Research Quarterly* 66, no. 2 (2013): 267–79. http://www.jstor.org/stable/23563143

Barton, John. 1988. *Oracles of God: Perceptions of Ancient Prophecy in Israel after the Exile*. New York: Oxford University Press.

———. 2019. *A History of the Bible: The Story of the World's Most Influential Book*. N.p.: Viking.

Batto, Bernard F. 2013. *In the Beginning: Essays on Creation Motifs in the Ancient Near East and the Bible*. Winona Lake, IN: Eisenbrauns 13.

Baumgartner, Frederic J. 1999. *Longing For The End: A History of Millennialism in Western Civilization*. New York: St. Martin's Press.

Bean, Lydia and Steve Teles. 2015. "Spreading the Gospel of Climate Change: An Evangelical Battleground." *New America's Strange Bedfellows Series*, November 2015. https://static.newamerica.org/attachments/11649-spreading-the-gospel-of-climate-change/climate_care11.9.4f0142a50aa24a2ba65020f7929f6fd7.pdf

Bedard, Stephen J. 2008. "Hellenistic Influence on the Idea of Resurrection in Jewish Apocalyptic Literature." In *Journal of Greco–Roman Christianity and Judaism* [JGRChJ], Vol. 5 (2008), 174–89. http://jgrchj.net/volume5/JGRChJ5-9_Bedard.pdf .

Ben Zvi, Ehud. 2016. "Rejection of the Foreign Wives in Ezra–Nehemiah," in Steven J. Schweitzer and Frauke Uhlenbruch, editors. *Worlds that Could Not Be. Utopia in Chronicles, Ezra and Nehemiah*, 105–28. London: Bloomsbury T&T Clark. bloomsburycp3.codemantra.com/viewer/5b1d0ebcc15c52da1d921587

Berkowitz, Miriam, and Mark Popovsky. 2010. "Contraception." Responsum approved by the Committee on Jewish Law and Standards (CJLS), Dec. 14, 2010, and published by the Rabbinical Assembly. http://www.rabbinicalassembly.org/sites/default/files/public/halakhah/teshuvot/20052010/Contraception%20Berkowitz%20and%20Popovsky.pdf

Bernstein, Alan E. 1993. *The Formation of Hell: Death and Retribution in the Ancient and Early Christian Worlds*. Ithaca, NY: Cornell University Press.

———. 2017. *Hell and Its Rivals: Death and Retribution Among Christians, Jews, and Muslims in the Early Middle Ages*. Ithaca, NY: Cornell University Press.

Bickerman, Elias. 1962. *From Ezra to the Last of the Maccabees: Foundations of Postbiblical Judaism*. New York: Schocken Books.

———. 2012. *The Jews in the Greek Age*. Cambridge, MA: Harvard University Press.

Bivins, Jason C. 2007. "The Religion of Fear: Conservative Evangelicals, Identity, and Antiliberal Pop." Journal for Cultural and Religious Theory vol. 8 no. 2 (Spring 2007), 81–103. http://www.jcrt.org/archives/08.2/bivins.pdf

Bjork-James, S. 2020. "Lifeboat Theology: White Evangelicalism, Apocalyptic Chronotypes, and Environmental Poltics." *Ethnos: Journal of Anthropology* 2020, 1-36. https://www.academia.edu/download/64835148/Lifeboat_ethics.pdf

Blackburn, Carole. 2000. *Harvest of Souls: The Jesuit Missions and Colonialism in North America, 1632-1650*. Montreal, Quebec: McGill-Queen's University Press.

Blin, Arnaud. 2019. *War and Religion: Europe and the Mediterranean from the First through the Twenty-first Centuries*. Oakland, CA: University of California Press.

Bloch, Chana and Ariel Bloch. 1995. *The Song of Songs: A New Translation With an Introduction and Commentary*. New York: Random House.

Bodi, Daniel. 2010. "Les apocalypses akkadiennes et bibliques: quelques points communs." *Revue des Études Juives* 169 (2010), 13-36. https://www.academia.edu/8587869/

Bond, Helen K. 1998. *Pontius Pilate in history and interpretation*. Cambridge, UK: Cambridge University Press.

Bottéro, Jean. 2004. *Religion in Ancient Mesopotamia*. Chicago: University of Chicago Press. Teresa Lavender Fagan, transl. First published 1998.

Boyer, Paul. 2000. *When Time Shall Be No More: Prophecy Belief in Modern American Culture*. Cambridge MA: The Belknap Press of Harvard University Press.

Brettler, Marc Zvi. 2010. "The Hebrew Bible and the Early History of Israel." In Baskin, Judith R. and Kenneth Seeskin, eds. *The Cambridge Guide to Jewish History, Religion, and Culture*. Cambridge UK Cambridge University Press. www.academia.edu/8301364/

Brettler, Marc and Amy-Jill Levine. 2019. "Isaiah's Suffering Servant: Before and After Christianity." In *Interpretation: A Journal of Bible and Theology* 2019, Vol. 73(2), 158–73. www.academia.edu/38683951/

Brown, Peter. 2015. *The Ransom of the Soul: Afterlife and Wealth in Early Western Christianity*. Cambridge MA: Harvard University Press.

Bryce, Trevor. 2002. *Life and Society in Hittite World*. Oxford, UK: Oxford University Press.

Buitendag, Johan. 2007. "Marriage in the theology of Martin Luther—worldly yet sacred: An option between secularism and clericalism." Pretoria, South Africa: HTS Theological Studies 63(2), 445–61. hts.org.za/index.php/hts/article/view/228/162

Burge, Gary M. 2017. "You Can Be an Evangelical and Reject Trump's Jerusalem Decision." In *The Atlantic*, Dec. 6, 2017.

Burleigh, Michael. 2007. *Sacred Causes: The Clash of Religion and Politics from The Great War to The War on Terror*. New York: HarperCollins.

Cantor, Norman F. 1994. *The Civilization of the Middle Ages*. New York: Harper Collins.

Charlesworth, James H. 1999. "John the Baptizer and Qumran Barriers in Light of the *Rule of the Community*." In Parry, Donald W. and Eugene Ulrich, editors. *The Provo International Conference on the Dead Sea Scrolls: Technological Innovations, New Texts, and Reformulated Issues*. Leiden, Netherlands: Brill.

———, ed. 2015. *The Old Testament Pseudepigrapha (Vols. I and II)*. Peabody, MA: Hendrickson Publishers.

Chazan, Robert, ed. 1980. *Church, State, and Jew in the Middle Ages*. West Orange, NJ: Behrman House.

———. 1996. *In the Year 1096: The First Crusade and the Jews*. Philadelphia: Jewish Publication Society.

———. 2016. *From Anti-Judaism to Anti-Semitism: Ancient and Medieval Christian Constructions of Jewish History*. New York: Cambridge University Press.

Cherniavsky, Michael. 1966. "The Old Believers and the New Religion." *Slavic Review* 25, no. 1 (1966): 1–39. https://doi.org/10.2307/2492649

Church, Philip A. F. 2009. "Dispensational Christian Zionism: A Strange But Acceptable Aberration or a Deviant Heresy?" In *Westminster Theological Journal* 71 (2009), 375-98. www.academia.edu/6011082/

Cline, Eric H. 2015. *1177 B.C.: The Year Civilization Collapsed*. Princeton, NJ: Princeton University Press.

Cohen, Jeremy. 1986. *The Friars and the Jews: The Evolution of Medieval Anti-Judaism*. Ithaca, NY: Cornell University Press.

———. 1989. *"Be Fertile and Increase, Fill the Earth and Master It": The Ancient and Medieval Career of a Biblical Text*. Ithaca, NY: Cornell University Press.

———. 2007. *Christ Killers: The Jews and the passion from the Bible to the big screen*. Oxford, UK: Oxford University Press.

———. 2009. "Revisiting Augustine's Doctrine of Jewish Witness," review of *Augustine and the Jews*, by Paula Fredriksen. *Journal of Religion* 89:4 (October 2009): 564–78. www.academia.edu/36098291/

Cohen, Mark R. 1994. *Under Crescent and Cross: The Jews in the Middle Ages*. Princeton, NJ: Princeton University Press.

Cohen, Shaye J. D. 2000. *The Beginnings of Jewishness: Boundaries, Varieties, Uncertainties*. Berkeley, CA: University of California Press.

———. 2010. *The Significance of Yavneh and Other Essays in Jewish Hellenism*. Tübingen, Germany: Mohr Siebeck.

———. 2014. *From the Maccabees to the Mishnah*, 3rd ed. Louisville, KY: Westminster John Knox Press.

Cohn, Norman. 1970. *The Pursuit of the Millennium: Revolutionary Anarchists and Mystical Anarchists of the Middle Ages*. New York: Oxford University Press.

Collins, John J. 1993. *Daniel: A Commentary on the Book of Daniel*. Minneapolis: Fortress Press.

———. 2001. "Cult and Culture: The Limits of Hellenization in Judea." In Collins, John J. and Gregory E. Sterling, editors. *Hellenism in the Land of Israel*, 38–61. Notre Dame, IN: University of Notre Dame Press.

———. 2016. *The Apocalyptic Imagination: An Introduction to Jewish Apocalyptic Literature (3rd ed.)*. Grand Rapids MI: William B. Eerdmans Publishing Company.

———. 2017. *The Invention of Judaism: Torah and Jewish Identity from Deuteronomy to Paul*. Oakland CA: University of California Press.

Cook, John Granger. 2011. "Crucifixion and Burial." In *New Test. Stud. 57*, 193–213. Cambridge, UK: Cambridge University Press. DOI: doi.org/10.1017/S0028688510000214

Coontz, Stephanie. 1992. *The Way We Never Were: American Families and the Nostalgia Trip*. New York: BasicBooks.

Couenhoven, Jesse. 2005. "St. Augustine's Doctrine of Original Sin." *Augustinian Studies 36*, no. 2 (2005): 359–96. www.academia.edu/1958072/

Court, John M. 2008. *Approaching the Apocalypse: A Short History of Christian Millennialism*. London: I. B. Tauris.

Dalley, Stephanie. 2008. *Myths from Mesopotamia: Creation, The Flood, Gilgamesh, and Others*. Translation and introduction. Oxford, UK: Oxford University Press.

Daniélou, Alain. 1994. Introduction to *The Complete Kāma Sūtra*. Rochester, VT: Park Street Press.

De Ladebat, Philippe. 2007. "Les protestants dans la Révolution française." www.histoire-genealogie.com/Les-protestants-dans-la-Revolution?lang=fr

De Villiers, P. G. R. 2002. "Persecution in the Book of Revelation." *Acta Theologica 2002:2*, 47–70. https://journals.ufs.ac.za/index.php/at/article/download/1555/1530

Declercq, Georges. 2002. "Dionysius Exiguus and the Introduction of the Christian Era." In *Sacris Erudiri* Volume 41 (2002), p. 165-246. www.academia.edu/43960999/

Dickieson, Brenton D. G. 2006. "Antisemitism and the Judaistic Paul: a study of I Thessalonians 2:14–16 in light of Paul's social and rhetorical contexts and the contemporary question of antisemitism." www.academia.edu/4033038/

Dixon, Laurence. 2012. "Why Change a Calendar?—Which year did Bede think he lived in?" *Chronology & Catastrophism REVIEW* 2010 [corrected in the PDF version, 2012], 35-39. https://www.sis-group.org.uk/files/docs/2010-why-change-a-calendar.pdf

Doak, Brian R. 2006. "The Origins of Social Justice in the Ancient Mesopotamian Religious Traditions" (2006). Faculty Publications—College of Christian Studies. Paper 185. http://digitalcommons.georgefox.edu/ccs/185

Dunn, Richard S. 1979. *The Age of Religious Wars: 1559–1715.* 2nd ed. New York: W. W. Norton and Company.

Ehrlich, Carl S. 1999. "Joshua, Judaism, and Genocide." In Borrás, Judit Targarona and Angel Sáenz-Badillos, eds. Jewish Studies at the Turn of the Twentieth Century: Proceedings of the 6th EAJS Congress, Toledo, July 1998. Volume I: Biblical, Rabbinical, and Medieval Studies. Leiden, Netherlands: Brill.

Ehrman, Bart D. 2001. *Jesus: Apocalyptic Prophet of the New Millennium.* Oxford: Oxford University Press.

———. 2009. *Jesus, Interrupted: Revealing the Hidden Contradictions in the Bible (and Why We Don't Know About Them).* New York: Harper One.

———. 2015. *How Jesus Became God: The Evolution of a Jewish Preacher from Galilee.* New York: Harper One.

———. 2018. *The Triumph of Christianity: How a Forbidden Religion Swept the World.* New York: Simon & Schuster.

———. 2020. *Heaven and Hell: A History of the Afterlife.* New York: Simon & Schuster.

Ekirch, A. Roger. 2005. At Day's Close: Night in Times Past. New York: W. W. Norton & Company.

Eliav, Yaron Z. 2006. "Jews and Judaism 70–429 CE." In Potter, David S., ed. *A Companion to the Roman Empire*, 565–86. Malden MA: Blackwell Publishing. www.academia.edu/16373990/

Endsjø, Dag Øistein. 2009. *Greek Resurrection Beliefs and the Success of Christianity.* New York: Palgrave Macmillan. Accessed as PDF graciously provided by the author.

———. 2011. Sex and Religion: Teachings and Taboos in the History of World Faiths. London: Reaktion Books. Peter Graves, transl.

Enochs, Ross. 2006. "The Franciscan Mission to the Navajos: Mission Method and Indigenous Religion, 1898-1940." *The Catholic Historical Review* 92, no. 1 (2006): 46–73. http://www.jstor.org/stable/25027012

Erdoes, Richard. 1988. *AD 1000: Living on the Brink of the Apocalypse.* San Francisco: Harper and Row.

Espak, Peeter. 2019. "The Emergence of the Concept of Divine Warfare and Theology of War in the Ancient Near East." In *Estonian Study of Religion. A Reader*, 155–71. www.academia.edu/40123605/

Evans, Craig A. 1994. "Jesus in Non-Christian Sources." In Chilton, Bruce and Craig A. Evans, eds., *Studying the Historical Jesus: Evaluations of the State of Current Research*, 443-78. Leiden, Netherlands: E. J. Brill.

———. 2012. "Isaiah 53 in the Letters of Peter, Paul, Hebrews, and John." In Bock, Darrel L. and Mitch Glaser, eds., *The Gospel According to Isaiah 53: Encoun-*

tering the Suffering Servant in Jewish and Christian Theology, 145–70. Grand Rapids, MI: Kregel Publications. www.academia.edu/9929626/

Faust, Avraham. 2015. "The Emergence of Iron Age Israel: On Origins and Habitus." In T.E. Levy, T. Schneider and W.H.C. Propp (eds.), *Israel's Exodus in Transdisciplinary Perspective: Text, Archeology, Culture and Geoscience*, 467–82. Heidelberg, Germany: Springer. www.academia.edu/11906343/

Fernández-Armesto, Felipe and Derek Wilson. 1997. *Reformations: A Radical Interpretation of Christianity and the World 1500-2000*. New York: Scribner.

Festinger, Leon, Henry W. Riecken, and Stanley Schachter. [1956] 2009. *When Prophecy Fails: A Social and Psychological Study of a Modern Group That Predicted the Destruction of the World*. Mansfield Center CT: Martino Publishing.

Finkelstein, Israel, and Neil Asher Silberman. 2001. *The Bible Unearthed: Archelogy's New Vision of Ancient Israel and the Origin of Its Sacred Texts*. New York: The Free Press.

FitzGerald, Frances. 2017. *The Evangelicals: The Struggle to Shape America*. New York: Simon & Schuster.

Forell, George Wolfgang. 1969. "Justification and Eschatology in Luther's Thought." *Church History* 38, no. 2 (1969): 164–74. https://doi.org/10.2307/3162704

Fournier, Éric. 2016. "Constantine and Episcopal Banishment: Continuity and Change in the Settlement of Christian Disputes." In Hillner, Julia, Jörg Enberg, and Jakob Ulrich, eds. *Clerical Exile in Late Antiquity*, 47–66. Frankfurt: Peter Lang. www.academia.edu/21291266/

Fredriksen, Paula. 1991. "Apocalypse and Redemption in Early Christianity: From John of Patmos to Augustine of Hippo." *Vigiliae Christianae*, Vol. 45, No. 2 (Jun., 1991), 151–83. www.academia.edu/15574587/

———. 1999. *Jesus of Nazareth, King of the Jews: A Jewish Life and the Emergence of Christianity*. New York: Vintage Books.

———. 2010. *Augustine and the Jews: A Christian Defense of Judaism*. New Haven CT: Yale University Press.

———. 2014. "How Later Contexts Affect Pauline Context, or: Retrospect is the Mother of Anachronism." In Tomson, Peter J. and Joshua Schwartz, eds. *Jews and Christians in the First and Second Centuries: How to Write Their History*, 17–51. Leiden, Netherlands: Koninklijke Brill NV. DOI: 10.1163/9789004279_003

———. 2017. *Paul: The Pagans' Apostle*. New Haven Ct: Yale University Press.

———. 2018. *When Christians Were Jews: The First Generation*. New Haven CT: Yale University Press.

———. 2022. "Philo, Herod, Paul, and the Many Gods of Ancient Jewish 'Monotheism.'" In *Harvard Theological Review* 115:1 (2022), 23–45. Accessed as PDF graciously provided by the author.

Freedman, David Noel. 1990. "The Formation of the Canon of the Old Testament." In Firmage, Edwin B., Bernard G. Weiss, and John W. Welch, eds.

Religion and Law: Biblical-Judaic and Islamic Perspectives. Winona Lake, IN: Eisenbrauns.

Freeman, Charles. 2003. *The Closing of the Western Mind: The Rise of Faith and the Fall of Reason.* New York: Alfred A. Knopf.

Friedman, Lee M. 1918. "Cotton Mather and the Jews." *Publications of the American Jewish Historical Society,* no. 26 (1918): 201–10. http://www.jstor.org/stable/43059308

Frykholm, Amy Johnson. 2007. *Rapture Culture: Left Behind in Evangelical America.* Oxford, UK: Oxford University Press.

Ganzel, Tova. 2021. "First-Month Rituals in Ezekiel's Temple Vision: A Pentateuchal and Babylonian Comparison." *The Catholic Biblical Quarterly,* Volume 83, Number 3, July 2021, pp. 390-406. www.academia.edu/50538130/

Gera, Dov, and Wayne Horowitz. 1997. "Antiochus IV in Life and Death: Evidence from the Babylonian Astronomical Diaries." *Journal of the American Oriental Society* 117, no. 2 (1997), 240–52. https://www.jstor.org/stable/605488

Gerstenberger, Erhard S. 2012. *Israel in the Persian Period: The Fifth and Fourth Centuries B.C.E.* Leiden, Netherlands: Brill. Siegfried S, Schatzmann, transl.

Gillihan, Yonder Moynihan. 2016. "Apocalyptic Elements in Hasmonean Propaganda: Civic Ideology and the Struggle for Political Legitimation." In Lester L. Grabbe and Gabrielle Boccaccini with Jason M. Zurawski, editors. *The Seleucid and Hasmonean Periods and the Apocalyptic Worldview,* 213–23. London: Bloomsbury T&T Clark.

Gillman, Neil. 2000. *The Death of Death: Resurrection and Immortality in Jewish Thought.* Woodstock, VT: Jewish Lights Publishing.

Glover, Jonathan. 2012. *Humanity: A Moral History of the Twentieth Century.* 2nd ed. New Haven Ct: Yale University Press.

Goldfarb, Michael. 2009. *Emancipation: How Liberating Europe's Jews from the Ghetto Led to Revolution and Renaissance.* New York: Simon and Schuster.

Goodman, Martin. 1993. *The Ruling Class of Judaea: The Origins of the Jewish Revolt against Rome AD 66-70.* Cambridge, UK: Cambridge University Press.

———. 2007. *Rome and Jerusalem.* New York: Vintage Books.

Gorski, Philip S. and Samuel L. Perry. 2022. *The Flag and the Cross: White Christian Nationalism and the Threat to American Democracy.* New York: Oxford University Press.

Grayling, A. C. 2016. *The Age of Genius: The Seventeenth Century and the Birth of the Modern Mind.* London: Bloomsbury.

Greengus, Samuel. 2019. "Laws in the Hebrew Bible/Old Testament." In *Oxford Research Encyclopedia of Religion.* Online publication date: Dec. 2019. DOI: 10.1093/acrefore/9780199340378.013.159 www.academia.edu/41535683/

Greenstein, Edward L. 2015. "The God of Israel and the Gods of Canaan: How Different Were They?" In *Proceedings of the World Congress of Jewish Studies, Vol.*

Division A: The Bible and Its World (1997), 47–58. www.academia.e-du/13176902 (http://www.jstor.org/stable/23537959)

Gregerman, Adam. 2018. "The Desirability of Jewish Conversion to Christianity in Contemporary Catholic Thought." In *Horizons* 45, 249–86. www.academia. edu/38219646/

Griffith, R. Marie. 2017. *Moral Combat: How Sex Divided American Christians and Fractured American Politics*. New York: Basic Books.

Gruen, Erich S. 1998. *Heritage and Hellenism: The Reinvention of Jewish Tradition*. Berkeley, CA: University of California Press.

———. 2016. *The Conduct of Identity in Hellenistic Judaism: Essays in Early Jewish Literature and History*. Berlin: De Gruyter. www.degruyter.com/view/product/ 431615 .

Guth, James L., John C. Green, Lyman A. Kellstedt, and Corwin E. Smidt. 1995. "Faith and the Environment: Religious Beliefs and Attitudes on Environmental Policy." *American Journal of Political Science* 39, no. 2 (1995), 364–82. doi:10.2307/2111617.

Hagee, John. 2007. *Jerusalem Countdown* (Revised and Updated). Lake Mary FL: FrontLine.

Halberstam, David. 1994. *The Fifties*. New York: Fawcett Columbine.

Hall, John R. 2000. The apocalypse at Jonestown, ch. 1 of *Apocalypse Observed: Religious Movements and Violence in North America, Europe, and Japan*, 27-73. With Philip D. Schuyler and Sylvaine Trinh. London: Routledge. https://www. researchgate.net/publication/ 286920601_The_apocalypse_at_Jonestown_ch_1_of_Apocalypse_Ob served_Routledge_2000

———. 2009. *Apocalypse: From Antiquity to the Empire of Modernity*. Cambridge, UK: Polity Press.

Hall, John R. and Zeke Baker. 2021. "Climate Change, Apocalypse, and the Future of Salvation." In *Oxford Handbooks Online: Scholarly Research Reviews*, Feb. 2021, 226-42. DOI: 10.1093/oxfordhb/9780198806820.013.14

Harper, Kyle. 2012. *"Porneia*: The Making of a Christian Sexual Norm." In *Journal of Biblical Literature* 131/2 (2012), 363-83. https://www.academia.edu/ 1368753/

Harris, Paul. 1994. "David Brainerd and the Indians: Cultural Interaction and Protestant Missionary Ideology." *American Presbyterians* 72, no. 1 (1994): 1–9. http://www.jstor.org/stable/23332745

Hasel, Michael G. 2008. "Merenptah's Reference to Israel: Critical Issues for the Origin of Israel." Pp. 47-59 In *Critical Issues in Early Israelite History*, ed. Richard S. Hess, Gerald A. Klingbeil, and Paul J. Ray Jr., 47–59. Winona Lake, IN: Eisenbrauns. www.academia.edu/37317424/

Haselby, Sam. 2017. *The Origins of American Religious Nationalism*. Oxford UK: Oxford University Press.

Hawking, Stephen. 2018. *Brief Answers to the Big Questions.* New York: Bantam Books.

Heels, Sonja W. 2019. "The Impact of Abstinence-Only Sex Education Programs in the United States on Adolescent Sexual Outcomes," *Perspectives:* Vol. 11 : Iss. 1 , Article 3. https://scholars.unh.edu/perspectives/vol11/iss1/3

Heemstra, Marius. 2010. *The* Fiscus Judaicus *and the Parting of the Ways.* Tübingen, Germany: Mohr Siebeck.

Hendel, Ronald. 2005. *Remembering Abraham: Culture, Memory, and History in the Hebrew Bible.* Oxford UK: Oxford University Press. www.academia.edu/ 837448/

Henze, Matthias. 1999. *The Madness of King Nebuchadnezzar: The Ancient Near Eastern Origins and Interpretation of Daniel 4.* Leiden, Netherlands: Brill.

Herrmann, Andrew F. 2021. "Purity, Nationalism, and Whiteness: The Fracturing of Fundamentalist Evangelicalism." In *International Review of Qualitative Research* 00(0) 1-19. https://www.researchgate.net/profile/Andrew-Herrmann/publication/343292366_Purity_Nationalism_and_Whiteness_The_Fracturing_of_Fundamentalist_Evangelicalism/links/5faf f6f492851cf24cce825b/Purity-Nationalism-and-Whiteness-The-Fracturing-of-Fundamentalist-Evangelicalism.pdf

Hibbert, Christopher. 2002. *The Days of the French Revolution.* New York: Perennial.

Higham, Carol L. 2016. "Christian Missions to American Indians." Oxford Research Encyclopedias, May 2016. https://doi.org/10.1093/acrefore/ 9780199329175.013.323

Hobsbawm, Eric. 2003. *The Age of Revolution: Europe 1789–1848.* London: Abacus.

Hochschild, Arlie Russell. 2018. *Strangers in Their Own Land: Anger and Mourning on the American Right.* New York: The New Press.

Hoffman, Joel M. 2016. *The Bible Doesn't Say That: 40 Biblical Mistranslations, Misconceptions, and Other Misunderstandings.* New York: Thomas Dunne Books. Kindle.

Hofreiter, Christian. 2018. *Making Sense of Old Testament Genocide: Christian Interpretations of Herem Passages.* Oxford UK: Oxford University Press.

Holm, Tawny L. 2014. "Moses in the Prophets and the Writings of the Hebrew Bible." In Beal, Jane, ed., *Illuminating Moses: A History of Reception from Exodus to the Renaissance,* 37–57. Leiden, Netherlands: Brill. www.academia.edu/1826730/

Hope, Aimie L. B. and Christopher R. Jones. 2014. "The impact of religious faith on attitudes to environmental issues and Carbon Capture and Storage (CCS) technologies: A mixed methods study." In *Technology in Society* 38 (2014), 38-59. https://www.sciencedirect.com/science/article/pii/ S0160791X14000177?via%3Dihub

Howe, Daniel Walker. 2009. *What Hath God Wrought: The Transformation of America 1815-1848.* Oxford, UK: Oxford University Press.

Hunter, David G. 1999. "Marriage." In *Augustine Through the Ages: An Encyclopedia*, edited by Allan D. Fitzgerald, 535–37. Grand Rapids MI: William B. Eerdmans Publishing Company.

———. 2018. *Marriage and Sexuality in Early Christianity*. Minneapolis, MN: Fortress Press.

Huntress, Erminie. 1935. ""Son of God" in Jewish Writings Prior to the Christian Era." *Journal of Biblical Literature* 54, no. 2 (1935): 117–23. doi:10.2307/3259680

Huttunen, Niko. 2010. "Stoic Law in Paul?" In Rasimus, Tuomas, Troels Engberg-Pedersen and Ismo Dunderberg, eds. *Stoicism in Early Christianity*, 39–56. Grand Rapids, MI: Baker Academic.

Isaac, E. 2015. "1 (Ethiopic Apocalypse of) Enoch: A New Translation and Introduction." In *The Old Testament Pseudepigrapha, Vol. 1*, pp 5–89. Peabody. MA: Hendrickson Publishers.

Jackson, Bernard. 1972. *Theft in Early Jewish Law*. Oxford, UK: The Clarendon Press. Photocopied excerpt graciously provided by the author.

———. 1990. "Legalism and Spirituality: Historical, Philosophical, and Semiotic Notes on Legislators, Adjudicators, and Subjects." In *Religion and Law: Biblical-Judaic and Islamic Perspectives*, edited by Edwin B. Firmage et al., 243–61. Winona Lake, IN: Eisenbrauns. Accessed as PDF graciously provided by the author.

———. 2008. *Essays on Halakhah in the New Testament*. Leiden, Netherlands: Brill. Chapters 2 and 3 graciously provided by the author as PDF.

———. 2006. *Wisdom-Laws: A Study of the Mishpatim of Exodus 21:1–22:16*. Oxford UK: Oxford University Press. Chapter 8 graciously provided by the author as a PDF.

James, William. (1902) 2010. *The Varieties of Religious Experience*. Library of America Paperback Classics.

Jones, Charles C. 1842. *The Religious Instruction of the Negroes. In the United States*. Savannah, GA: Thomas Purse. Digitized electronic edition by University of North Carolina at Chapel Hill: https://docsouth.unc.edu/church/jones/jones.html

Jones, Rachel K. and Joerg Dreweke. 2011. "Countering Conventional Wisdom: New Evidence on Religion and Contraceptive Use." Guttmacher Institute. https://grist.org/wp-content/uploads/2012/01/religion-and-contraceptive-use.pdf

Jones, Robert P. 2017. *The End of White Christian America*. New York: Simon & Schuster Paperbacks.

Junkkaala, Eero. 2006. *Three Conquests of Canaan: A Comparative Study of Two Egyptian Military Campaigns and Joshua 10–12 in the Light of Recent Archaeological Evidence*. Åbo, Finland. Åbo Akademi University Press. https://bibbild.abo.fi/ediss/2006/JunkkaalaEero.pdf

Juster, Susan. 2011. "Heretics, Blasphemers, and Sabbath Breakers: The Prosecution of Religious Crime in Early America." In Beneke, Chris and Christopher S. Grenda, eds. *The First Prejudice: Religious Tolerance and Intolerance in Early America*, 123–42. Philadelphia: University of Pennsylvania Press.

Kamen, Henry. 2003. *Empire: How Spain Became a World Power 1492-1763*. New York: HarperCollins Publishers, Inc.

Karagiannis, Christos G. 2019. "The Time of the Establishment of Biblical Monotheism." In *International Journal of Orthodox Theology 10:2 (2019)*, 184–98. www.academia.edu/40933541/

Karl, Thomas R. and Pamela J. Young. 1987. "The 1986 Southeast Drought in Historical Perspective." In *Bulletin American Meteorological Society*, Vol. 68, No. 7, July 1987, 773–78. http://journals.ametsoc.org/doi/pdf/10.1175/1520-0477(1987)068%3C0773%3ATSDIHP%3E2.0.CO%3B2

Karr, Ronald Dale. 1998. "'Why Should You Be So Furious?': The Violence of the Pequot War." *The Journal of American History* 85, no. 3 (1998): 876–909. https://doi.org/10.2307/2567215

Kelley, Justin. 2009. "Toward a New Synthesis of the God of Edom and Yahweh." In *Antiguo Oriente* Vol 7 (2009), 255–80. www.academia.edu/211171/.

Kirsch, Jonathan. 2008. *The Grand Inquisitor's Manual: A History of Terror in the Name of God*. New York: HarperCollins.

Klein, George L. 1987. "An Introduction to Malachi" in Criswell Theological Review 2.1 (1987), pp 19–37. Dallas, TX: Criswell College. http://faculty.gordon.edu/hu/bi/ted_hildebrandt/otesources/39-malachi/text/articles/klein-malachiintro-ctr.pdf

Klein, Linda Kay. 2018. *Pure: Inside the Evangelical Movement That Shamed a Generation of Young Women and How I Broke Free*. New York: Touchstone.

Kloppenborg, John S. 2008. *Q, the Earliest Gospel: An Introduction to the Original Stories and Sayings of Jesus*. Louisville KY: Westminster John Knox Press. Accessed as http://www.baytagoodah.com/uploads/9/5/6/0/95600058/john-s-kloppenborg-q-the-earliest-gospel-christian-pdf.pdf

Knoppers, Gary N. 1997. "The Vanishing Solomon: The Disappearance of the United Monarchy from Recent Histories of Ancient Israel." In *Journal of Biblical Literature*, Vol. 116, No. 1 (Spring, 1997), 19–44. www.academia.edu/35620698/

———. 2001. "Rethinking the Relationship between Deuteronomy and the Deuteronomistic History: The Case of Kings." In *The Catholic Biblical Quarterly* 63 (2001), 393–415. www.academia.edu/download/39580157/

Knust, Jennifer Wright. 2012. *Unprotected Texts: The Bible's Surprising Contradictions About Sex and Desire*. New York: HarperOne.

Koester, Nancy. 1995. "The Future in Our Past: Post-millennialism in American Protestantism." In *Word & World*, Vol. XV, no. 2 (Spring 1995), 137-44.

http://wordandworld.luthersem.edu/content/pdfs/15-2_Revelation/15-2_N_Koester.pdf

Kugler, Gili. 2020. "Metaphysical Hatred and Sacred Genocide: The Questionable Role of Amalek in Biblical Literature." In *Journal of Genocide Research*, 2020, 1–16. www.academia.edu/44320122/

Kyle, Richard G. 2012. *Apocalyptic Fever: End-Time Prophecies in Modern America.* Eugene OR. Cascade Books.

Lacey, Robert and Danny Danziger. 2000. *The Year 1000: What Life Was Like at the Turn of the Millennium: An Englishman's World.* Boston: Little, Brown and Company.

Lambert, Malcolm. 2016. *God's Armies: Crusade and Jihad: Origins, History, Aftermath.* New York: Pegasus Books.

Landes, Richard. 1988. "Lest the Millennium be Fulfilled: Apocalyptic Expectations and the Pattern of Western Chronography, 100-800 CE." In *The Use and Abuse of Eschatology in the Middle Ages,* ed. W. Verbeke, D. Verhelst, and A. Welkenhuysen (Katholieke U., Leuven, 1988), 137-211. www.academia.edu/4773281/

———. 2002. "What Happens when Jesus Doesn't Come: Jewish and Christian Relations." In Apocalyptic Time, Terrorism and Political Violence, 14:1, 243-74. www.academia.edu/38438681/

———. 2005. "Patristic and Medieval Millennialism." In *Britannica,* "Millennialism." Last revised Feb 24, 2005. https://www.britannica.com/topic/millennialism/Patristic-and-medieval-millennialism

Lémonon, Jean–Pierre. 1981. *Pilate et le Gouvernement de la Judée: Textes et Monuments.* Paris: Librairie Lecaffre.

Levinson, Bernard M. 1992. "The human voice in divine revelation: The problem of authority in Biblical law." In Williams, Michael A., Collett Cox, and Martin S. Jaffee, editors. *Innovation in Religious Traditions,* 35–71. Berlin: Mouton de Gruyter.

———. 2001. "The Reconceptualization of Kingship in Deuteronomy and the Deuteronomistic History's Transformation of Torah." *Vetus Testamentum* 51 no. 4 (2001), 511-34. https://www.jstor.org/stable/1585679.

Lorein, G. W. 2001. "Some Aspects of the Life and Death of Antiochus IV Epiphanes: A New Presentation of Old Viewpoints." *Ancient Society* 31 (2001), 157-71. www.jstor.org/stable/44079823

Lucas, Ernest. 2002. *Daniel.* Apollos Old Testament Commentary 20. Leicester, UK: Apollos.

MacCarron, Maírín. 2012. "Bede, *Annus Domini* and the *Historia ecclesiastica gentis anglorum.*" In Rutherford, Janet E. and David Woods, editors. *The Mystery of Christ in the Fathers of Church,* 116-34. Dublin, Ireland: Four Courts Press, Ltd. www.academia.edu/1805062/

———. 2014. "Christology and the Future in Bede's Annus Domini," in Darby, P.

and F. Wallis, editors. *Bede and the Future*, 161-79. Farnham, UK: Ashgate Publishing. www.academia.edu/6611516/

MacCulloch, Diarmaid. 2005. *The Reformation: A History*. New York: Penguin Books.

Maclear, J. F. 1975. "New England and the Fifth Monarchy: The Quest for the Millennium in Early American Puritanism." *The William and Mary Quarterly* 32, no. 2 (1975): 223-60. https://doi.org/10.2307/1921563

Masters, William H. and Virginia E. Johnson. 1970. *Human Sexual Inadequacy*. Boston: Little, Brown and Company.

Matthews, Victor H. and Don C. Benjamin. 2006. *Old Testament Parallels: Laws and Stories from the Ancient Near East (3rd edition)*. New York: Paulist Press.

Mazzucchi, Roberto. 2009. "A Gymnasium in Jerusalem." In Xydopoulos I., A. Gémes, and F. Peyrou, editors. *Institutional Changes and Stability. Conflicts, Transitions, Social Values*, 19–34. Pisa Italy. www.academia.edu/14846879/

McGlynn, Sean. 2018. *Kill Them All: Cathars and Carnage in the Albigensian Crusade*. Stroud, Gloucestershire, UK: The History Press.

McGreevy, John T. 2022. *Catholicism: A Global History from the French Revolution to Pope Francis*. New York: W. W. Norton.

McLaren, James S. 2013. "Early Christian Polemic against Jews and the Persecution of Christians in Rome by Nero." In *Religious Conflict from Early Christianity to the Rise of Islam*. Wendy Mayer and Bronwen Neil, eds. Berlin: Walter de Gruyter GmbH.

Meacham, Jon. 2007. *American Gospel: God, The Founding Fathers, and The Making of a Nation*. New York: Random House Trade Paperbacks.

Meagher, Robert Emmet. 2014. *Killing From the Inside Out: Moral Injury and Just War*. Eugene OR: Cascade Books.

Metzger, B. M. 2015. "The Fourth Book of Ezra: A New Translation and Introduction." In *The Old Testament Pseudepigrapha, Vol. 1*, 517-24. Peabody MA: Hendrickson Publishers.

Miller, Robert J. 2016. *Helping Jesus Fulfill Prophecy*. Eugene OR: Wipf and Stock Publishers. Kindle.

Miner, Steven Merritt. 2003. *Stalin's Holy War: Religion, Nationalism, and Alliance Politics, 1941-1945*. Chapel Hill NC: The University of North Carolina Press.

Moore, Barrington, Jr. 2000. *Moral Purity and Persecution in History*. Princeton NJ: Princeton University Press.

Morris, Ellen Fowles. 2005. *The Architecture of Imperialism: Military Bases and the Evolution of Foreign Policy in Egypt's New Kingdom*. Leiden, Netherlands: Brill. www.academia.edu/239634/

Moss, Candida. 2014. *The Myth of Persecution: How Early Christians Invented a Story of Martyrdom*. New York: HarperCollins.

Na'aman, Nadav. 1994. "The 'Conquest of Canaan' in the Book of Joshua and in

History." In Finkelstein, Israel and Nadav Na'aman, eds. *From Nomadism to Monarchy*, 218–81. Jerusalem: Israel Exploration Society.

———. 2015. "Out of Egypt or Out of Canaan?" The Exodus Story between Memory and Historical Reality," in T.E. Levy, T. Schneider, and W.H.C. Propp, eds., *Israel's Exodus in Transdisciplinary Perspective: Text, Archaeology, Culture, and Geoscience*, pp 527–33. Cham, Switzerland: Springer International Publishing.

Neill, James. 2009. *The Origins and Role of Same-Sex Relations in Human Societies.* Jefferson, NC: McFarland & Company, Inc.

Niditch, Susan. 1997. *Ancient Israelite Religion.* New York: Oxford University Press.

Nirenberg, David. 2014. *Anti-Judaism: The Western Tradition.* New York: W. W. Norton and Company.

Nixey, Catherine. 2017. *The Darkening Age: The Christian Destruction of the Classical World.* Boston: Houghton Mifflin Harcourt.

NRSV(HC). *The New Revised Standard Version [of the Bible], HarperCollins Study Edition.* New York: HarperCollins Publishers, 1993.

Oberman, Heiko A. 2006. *Luther: Man Between God and the Devil.* New Haven CT: Yale University Press. Eileen Walliser-Schwartzbart, translator.

Olyan, Saul M. 2012. "Is Isaiah 40–55 Really Monotheistic?" In *Journal of Ancient Near Eastern Religions 12 (2012)*, 190–201. www.academia.edu/16369536

Otto, Eckart. 2013. "The History of the Legal-Religious Hermeneutics of the Book of Deuteronomy from the Assyrian to the Hellenistic Period." In Hagedorn, Anselm C. and Reinhard G. Krantz, editors. *Law and Religion in the Eastern Mediterranean: From Antiquity to Early Islam*, 211–50 Oxford, UK: OUP Oxford. www.academia.edu/9587713/

———. 2015. "Laws of Eshnunna." In Strawn, Brent A., editor in chief. *The Oxford Encyclopedia of Bible and Law*, 495–500. Oxford UK: Oxford University Press. www.academia.edu/89514929/

Palmer, James T. 2014. *The Apocalypse in the Early Middle Ages.* Cambridge, UK: Cambridge University Press.

Parsons, Timothy H. 2010. *The Rule of Empires: Those Who Built Them, Those Who Endured Them, and Why They Always Fall.* Oxford UK: Oxford University Press.

Pavlik, Steve. 1997. "Navajo Christianity: Historical Origins and Modern Trends." *Wicazo Sa Review* 12, no. 2 (1997): 43–58. https://doi.org/10.2307/1409206

Pearse, Meic. 2007. *The Gods of War: Is Religion the Primary Cause of Violent Conflict?* Nottingham, UK: Inter-Varsity Press.

Peris, Daniel. 1998. *Storming the Heavens: The Soviet League of the Militant Godless.* Ithaca NY: Cornell University Press.

Polk, Nicholas O. 2020. "Deuteronomy and Treaty Texts: A Critical Reexamination of Deuteronomy 13, 17, 27, and 28." PhD Diss., University of Chicago,

June   2020.   knowledge.uchicago.edu/record/2269/files/
Polk_uchicago_0330D_15212.pdf?register_download=0

Porter, Stanley E. and Brook W. R. Pearson. 2000. "Why the Split? Christians and Jews by the Fourth Century." In JGRChJ 1 (2000), 82–119.

Praet, Danny. 2014. "Violence against Christians and Violence by Christians in the First Three Centuries: Direct Violence, Cultural Violence and the Debate about Christian Exclusiveness." In Geljon, Albert C. and Riemer Roukema, eds. *Violence in Ancient Christianity: Victims and Perpetrators*, 31–55. Leiden, Netherlands: Brill.

Prucha, Francis Paul. 1988. "Two Roads to Conversion: Protestant and Catholic Missionaries in the Pacific Northwest." *The Pacific Northwest Quarterly* 79, no. 4 (1988): 130–37. http://www.jstor.org/stable/40490993

Redford, Donald B. 1992. *Egypt, Canaan, and Israel in Ancient Times*. Princeton, NJ: Princeton University Press.

Reston, James Jr. 1994. *Galileo: A Life*. New York: HarperCollins.

Riley-Smith, Jonathan. 1997. *The First Crusaders: 1095–1131*. Cambridge, UK: Cambridge University Pres.

Rollston, Chrisopher. 2003. "The Rise of Monotheism in Ancient Israel: Biblical and Epigraphic Evidence." In *Stone-Campbell Journal 6 (Spring 2003)*, 95–115. www.academia.edu/474501/

Römer, Thomas C. 2005. *The So-Called Deuteronomistic History: A Sociological, Historical, and Literary Introduction*. London: T & T Clark International.

———. 2013, "Yhwh, the Goddess and Evil: Is 'monotheism' an adequate concept to describe the Hebrew Bible's discourses about the God of Israel?" *Verbum et Ecclesia* 34(2), Art. #841, 5 pages. www.academia.edu/68415690/

———. 2015. *The Invention of God*. Cambridge MA: Harvard University Press. Raymond Geuss, transl.

———. 2017a. "Le Problème du Monothéisme Biblique." In *Revue Biblique* Vol1 124:1, 12–25. www.academia.edu/33110406/

———. 2017b. "The Rise and Fall of Josiah." In Lipschits, Oded, Yuval Gadot, and Matthew J. Adams, eds. *Rethinking Israel: Studies in the History and Archaeology of Ancient Israel in Honor of Israel Finkelstein*, 329–40. Winona Lake, IN: Eisenbrauns. www.academia.edu/41915207/

Rothwangl. Sepp. 2016. "The Scythian Dionysius Exiguus and His Invention of Anno Domini." https://www.researchgate.net/profile/Sepp-Rothwangl/publi cation/308654229_The_Scythian_Dionysius_Exiguus_and_His_Inven tion_of_Anno_Domini/links/57ea4dae08aeb34bc092b849/The-Scythian-Dionysius-Exiguus-and-His-Invention-of-Anno-Domini.pdf

Rowe, Paul. 2013. "Postponing Armageddon? Christian Zionist and Palestinian Christian Responses to the Problem of Peace." *Revue d'Histoire de l'Université de Balamand*, Numéro 28, 2013, 67-87. www.academia.edu/22665187/

Rowland, Ingrid D. 2009. *Giordano Bruno: Philosopher / Heretic*. Chicago: University of Chicago Press.

Rubenstein, Jay. 2011. *Armies of Heaven: The First Crusade and the Quest for Apocalypse*. New York: Basic Books.

Ryrie, Alec. 2017. *Protestants: The Faith That Made the Modern World*. New York: Viking.

Sacks, Jonathan. 2016. *Not in God's Name: Confronting Religious Violence*. London: Hodder & Stoughton, Ltd.

Sanders, Paul. 2007. "Argumenta ad Deum in the Plague Prayers of Mursili II and in the Book of Psalms." In: B.E.J.H. Becking, H.G.L. Peels (eds), *Psalms and Prayers: Papers Read at the Joint Meeting of the Society of Old Testament Study and Het Oudtestamentisch Werkgezelschap in Nederland en België*, 181–217. Apeldoorn, Netherlands: August 2006 (OTS 55; Leiden, 2007).

Satlow, Michael. 2014. *How The Bible Became Holy*. New Haven CT: Yale University Press.

Schenker, Adrian. 1997. "Nuntii Personarum Et Rerum [Le Monothéisme Israélite]." *Biblica* 78, no. 3 (1997): 436–50. http://www.jstor.org/stable/42614006.

Schmid, Konrad. 2016. "Divine Legislation in the Pentateuch in its Late Judean and Neo-Babylonian Context," in: Peter Dubovský, Dominik Markl, and Jean-Pierre Sonnet, editors, *The Fall of Jerusalem and the Rise of Torah*, 129–53. Tubingen, Germany: Mohr Siebeck. www.divlaw.uzh.ch/dam/jcr:0f155a9d-2f97-4807-baf5-1c98fd30b113/Divine%20Legislation%20FAT%20107.pdf

Schwab, Charlotte Rolnick. 2002. *Sex, Lies, and Rabbis: Breaking a Sacred Trust*. Bloomington, IN: 1stBooks.

Schwadel, Philip and Erik Johnson. 2017. "The Religious and Political Origins of Evangelical Protestants' Opposition to Environmental Spending." In *Journal for the Scientific Study of Religion* 56 (2017), 1-35. https://core.ac.uk/download/pdf/228383093.pdf

Sederholm, Carl. 2012. "The Trouble with Grace: Reading Jonathan Edwards's *Faithful Narrative*." *The New England Quarterly* 85 (2): 326–34. https://doi.org/10.1162/TNEQ_a_00188

Segal, Alan F. 2004. *Life After Death: A History of the Afterlife in Western Religion*. New York: Doubleday.

Segal, Charles M. and David C. Stineback. 1977. *Puritans, Indians, and Manifest Destiny*. New York: G. P. Putnam's Sons.

Setzer, Claudia. 1994. *Jewish Responses to Early Christians: History and Polemics, 30-150 C.E.* Minneapolis: Fortress Press.

Shaked, Shaul. 2016. "Eschatology in Zoroastrianism and Zoroastrian Afterlife." In Moazami, Mahnaz, ed., *Zoroastrianism: A Collection of Articles from the Encyclopedia Iranica, Volume Two*, 1522–34. New York: Encyclopedia Iranica Foundation. www.academia.edu/38781320/

Sider, Ronald. 2012. *The Early Church on Killing: A Comprehensive Source Book on War, Abortion, and Capital Punishment*. Grand Rapids MI: Baker Academic.

Sim, David. 2005. "How many Jews became Christians in the first century? The failure of the Christian mission to the Jews." *Hervormde Teologiese Studies* 61, 417–40. 10.4102/hts.v61i1/2.430.

Slezkine, Yuri. 2017. *The House of Government: A Saga of the Russian Revolution*. Princeton NJ: Princeton University Press.

Smith, Mark S. 2002. *The Early History of God: Yahweh and the Other Deities in Ancient Israel, 2nd ed*. Grand Rapids MI: William B. Eerdmans Publishing Company.

Smith, Rachel M., Dominic J. Parrot, Kevin M. Swartout, and Andra Teten Tharp. 2018. "Deconstructing Hegemonic Masculinity: The Roles of Antifemininity, Subordination to Women, and Sexual Dominance in Men's Perpetration of Sexual Aggression." Originally published as Psychol Men Masc. 2015 Apr; 16(2): 160–169; available in PMC 2018 Jun 25. www.ncbi.nlm.nih.gov/pmc/articles/PMC6016395/

Snuth, David L. 1990. "Divorce and Remarriage From the Early Church To John Wesley." *Trinity Journal* (Fall), 131–42. theologicalstudies.org.uk/article_divorce_snuth.html

Stahl, Michael J. 2020. "The Historical Origins of the Biblical God Yahweh." *Religion Compass 2020*. www.academia.edu/43756814/

Stanger-Hall, Kathrin F, and David W Hall. 2011. "Abstinence-only education and teen pregnancy rates: why we need comprehensive sex education in the U.S." *PloS one* vol. 6,10: e24658. doi:10.1371/journal.pone.0024658

Stark, Rodney. 1996. *The Rise of Christianity: A Sociologist Reconsiders History*. Princeton, NJ: Princeton University Press.

Stensvold, Anne. 2015. *A History of Pregnancy in Christianity: From Original Sin to Contemporary Abortion Debates*. New York: Routledge.

Sterling, Greg. 2001. "Mors Philosophi: The Death of Jesus in Luke." *The Harvard Theological Review* 94, no. 4: 383–402. www.jstor.org/stable/3657414

Stewart, David Tabb. 2020. "Categories of Sexuality Indigenous to Biblical Legal Materials." In Hilary Lipka and Bruce Wells, eds. *Sexuality and Law in the Torah*, 20–47. London: T&T Clark. Accessed as PDF graciously provided by the author.

Stone, Geoffrey R. 2017. *Sex and the Constitution: Sex, Religion, and Law from America's Origins to the Twenty-First Century*. New York: Liveright Publishing Corporation.

Straw, Carole. 1999. "*Timor Mortis* (Fear of Death)." In *Augustine Through the Ages: An Encyclopedia*, edited by Allan D. Fitzgerald, 838–42. Grand Rapids MI: William B. Eerdmans Publishing Company.

Sutton, Matthew Avery. 2017. *American Apocalypse: A History of Modern Evangelism*. Cambridge MA: The Belknap Press of Harvard University Press.

Swift, Louis J., "St. Ambrose on Violence and War." *Transactions and Proceedings of the American Philological Association* 101 (1970), 533–43 (https://doi.org/10. 2307/2936070).

Sykes, Adele. 1995. "'Vicars and Tarts': Medieval Prostitution and the Vicars Choral of York Minster, 1393-1485. York University (MA thesis), York, England. https://www.academia.edu/7051718/

Tanner, J. Paul. 1997. "The History of Interpretation of the Song of Songs." *Bibliotheca Sacra* 154: 613, 23–46. biblicalstudies.org.uk/article_song1_tanner. html#5.

Taylor, Alan. 2002. *American Colonies: The Settling of North America.* New York: Penguin Books.

Thayer, Bradley A., and Valerie M. Hudson. 2010. "Sex and the Shaheed: Insights from the Life Sciences on Islamic Suicide Terrorism." *International Security* 34, no. 4 (2010): 37–62. http://www.jstor.org/stable/40784561

Thelle, Ranfrid I. 2007. "The Biblical Conquest Account and Its Modern Hermeneutical Challenges." In *Studia Theologica* 61:1, 61–81. www.academia. edu/8529861/

Ulrich, Eugene. 2012. "The Jewish Scriptures: Texts, Versions, Canons." In Collins, John J. and Daniel C. Harlow, eds. *Early Judaism: A Comprehensive Overview*, 121–50. Grand Rapids MI: William B. Eerdmans Publishing Company.

Uusimäki, Elisa. 2018. "The Rise of the Sage in Greek and Jewish Antiquity." In *Journal for the Study of Judaism* 49/1, 1–29. www.academia.edu/33075492/

Van der Spek, R. J. 2014. "Cyrus the Great, Exiles, and Foreign Gods: A Comparison of Assyrian and Persian Policies on Subject Nations." In Kozuh, Michael, Wouter F. M. Henkelman, Charles E. Jones, and Christopher Woods, eds. *Extraction and Control: Studies in Honor of Matthew W. Stolper*, 233–64. Chicago: The Oriental Institute of the University of Chicago. www.academia.edu/3753890/

Veldman, Robin Globus. 2019. *The Gospel of Climate Skepticism: Why Evangelical Christians Oppose Action on Climate Change.* Oakland, CA: University of California Press.

Vermes, Géza. 2011a. Introduction, commentaries and notes, in *The Complete Dead Sea Scrolls in English*, fiftieth anniversary edition. London: Penguin Books.

———. 2011b. *Jesus in the Jewish World.* London: SCM Press.

———. 2013. "The Jewish Jesus Movement." In Shanks, Hershel, ed. *Partings: How Judaism and Christianity Became Two*," 1–25. Washington, DC: Biblical Archeological Society.

Warren, James A. 2018. *God, War, and Providence: The Epic Struggle of Roger Williams and the Narragansett Indians against the Puritans of New England.* New York: Scribner.

Wazana, Nili. 2016. "The Law of the King (Deut 17:14–20) in the Light of Empire and Destruction", in P. Dubovský, D. Markl, and J.-P. Sonnet, editors,

The Fall of Jerusalem and the Rise of the Torah, Forschungen zum Alten Testament (FAT), 169–94. Tübingen: Mohr Siebeck. www.academia.edu/29491159/

Weatherford, Jack. 2004. *Genghis Khan and the Making of the Modern World*. New York: Crown Publishers.

Weber, Max. [1920–21] 1976. *The Protestant Ethic and the Spirit of Capitalism*. Talcott Parsons, translator. New York: Charles Scribner's Sons.

Weinfeld, Moshe. 2004. *The Place of the Law in the Religion of Ancient Israel*. Leiden, Netherlands: Brill.

Weiss, John. 1996. *Ideology of Death: Why the Holocaust Happened in Germany*. Chicago: Ivan R. Dee.

Westbrook, Raymond. 1988. *Studies in Biblical and Cuneiform Law*. Paris: J. Gabalda et Cie.

Whealey, Alice. 2003. *Josephus on Jesus: The Testamonium Flavianum Controversy from Late Antiquity to Modern Times*. New York: Peter Lang.

White, L. Michael. 2005. *From Jesus to Christianity: How Four Generations of Visionaries & Storytellers Created the New Testament and Christian Faith*. New York: HarperCollins.

White, Lynn. 1967. "The Historical Roots of Our Ecological Crisis." In *Science* New Series, Vol. 155, No. 3767 (Mar. 10, 1967) , 1203-07. https://www.cmu.ca/faculty/gmatties/lynnwhiterootsofcrisis.pdf

Whitehead, Andrew L. and Samuel L. Perry. 2020. *Taking America Back for God: Christian Nationalism in the United States*. New York: Oxford University Press.

Whittock, Martyn. 2021. *The End Times, Again? 2000 Years of the Use and Misuse of Biblical Prophecy*. Eugene, OR: Cascade Books.

Wilken, Robert L. 1983. *John Chrysostom and the Jews: Rhetoric and Reality in the Late 4th Century*. Berkeley, CA: University of California Press.

———. 1984. *The Christians as the Romans Saw Them*. New Haven, CT: Yale University Press.

Willetts, Margaret M. 2016. Glory and Empire: The London Society for Promoting Christianity Amongst the Jews and the Road to the Balfour Declaration." [Master's Thesis for U. of Oklahoma]. https://shareok.org/bitstream/handle/11244/34660/2016_Willetts_Margaret_OU_Thesis.pdf?sequence=5

Wills, Gary. 2007. *Head and Heart: American Christianities*. New York: The Penguin Press.

Winship, Michael P. 1996. *Seers of God: Puritan Providentialism in the Restoration and Early Enlightenment*. Baltimore MD: The Johns Hopkins University Press.

Wrede, William. [1901] 1971. *The Messianic Secret*. Greenwood SC: The Attic Press. J. C. G. Greig, translator.

Wright, R. B. 2015. "Psalms of Solomon: A New Translation and Introduction." In *The Old Testament Pseudepigrapha, Vol. 2*, pp 640–50. Peabody. MA: Hendrickson Publishers.

Younger, K. Lawson Jr. 1990. *Ancient Conquest Accounts: A Study in Ancient Near Eastern and Biblical History Writing*. Sheffield UK: JSOT Press. b-ok.cc/book/871802/11e92e?dsource=recommend

Zevit, Ziony. 1990. "Three Ways to Look at the Ten Plagues," *Bible Review* 6.3 (Jun 1990): 16–23, 42. http://members.bib-arch.org/publication.asp?PubID=BSBR&Volume=6&Issue=3&ArticleID=13.

———. 2001. *The Religions of Ancient Israel: A Synthesis of Parallactic Approaches*. London: Continuum.

INDEX

Page numbers in bold refer to definitions.

Made in the USA
Columbia, SC
17 April 2023